Teacher Edition
Writer's Companion
Support and Practice for Writing
Grade 5

Harcourt School Publishers
www.harcourtschool.com

Printed in the United States of America

ISBN 10: 0-15-367082-7

ISBN 13: 978-0-15-367082-4

4 5 6 7 8 9 10   1409   17 16 15 14 13 12 11 10 09

Contents

Writer's Companion
Contents

Introduction

The *Writer's Companion* is designed to deepen students' understanding of the elements and traits of effective writing and to explicitly show students *how* to incorporate those elements and traits into their own writing. It is also designed to deliver carefully targeted instruction in the more difficult tasks that are associated with the writing process—in particular, *organizing, evaluating,* and *revising.*

The *Writer's Companion* includes the following features:

- short literature excerpts that serve as writing models for writer's skills
- student writing models as vehicles for teaching the crafts of evaluating and revising
- explicit instruction in writer's skills and the traits of good writing
- some grammar practice (sentence construction and common usage errors)
- practice using rubrics to evaluate writing
- practice with multiple-choice formats encountered in state writing assessment tests

There are 30 *Writer's Companion* lessons per grade. The lessons have different lengths and focuses, as follows:

LESSON	LENGTH	FOCUS
Lesson 1*	6 pages	Pages 1–3: Writer's craft focus, including a Literature Model Page 4: Example of a writing form (Student Model) Pages 5–6: Evaluating and revising (incorporates both the skill and the form)
Lesson 2	6 pages	Same as for Lesson 1
Lesson 3	6 pages	Same as for Lessons 1 and 2
Lesson 4	6 pages	Pages 1–3: Review of writer's skills from Lessons 1–3 Page 4: Example of a writing form (Student Model) Pages 5–6: Evaluating two Student Models using a rubric (incorporates both the skills and the form)
Lesson 5	6 pages	Pages 1–2: Extended Writing/Test Prep (self-selected topic) Pages 3–6: Test Prep (multiple-choice questions)

*Lesson 1 refers to the first lesson in a unit, Lesson 2 refers to the second lesson in the unit, and so on.

© Harcourt

A Closer Look at the Lessons

LESSONS 1–3 (6 pages each)

Pages 1–3 of each lesson use a Literature Model to teach a writer's skill.

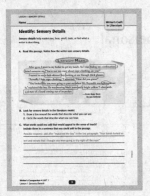 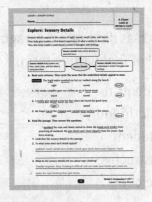 

Page 4 of each lesson teaches a writing form. It contains a Student Model that represents the form (personal narrative, character sketch, etc.) and incorporates the writer's skill. Students are prompted to identify examples of the writer's skill in the model, and to identify some of the organizational elements particular to the writing form.

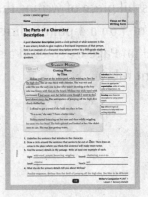

Page 5 of each lesson focuses on evaluating, using the Student Model on the previous page.

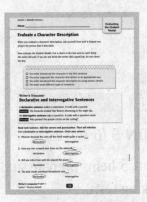

Page 6 of each lesson focuses on revising. Students are guided to revise portions of the Student Model, with a focus on writer's skill.

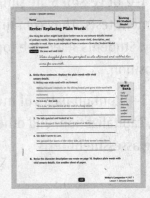

Writer's Companion
Introduction

A Closer Look at the Lessons

LESSON 4 (6 Pages)

Pages 1–3 of Lesson 4 review all of the writer's craft skills that were taught in Lessons 1–3.

Page 4 focuses on a writing form, such as descriptive paragraph or personal narrative. It contains a Student Model of that writing form.

Pages 5 and 6 of Lesson 4 allow students to evaluate a Student Model, using a child-friendly rubric. Each page contains a longer Student Model annotated with a teacher's constructive feedback. Page 5 provides an example of a successful piece of writing that achieved a score of 4 on a 4-point rubric. The Student Model on Page 6 achieved a score of 2 on a 4-point rubric.

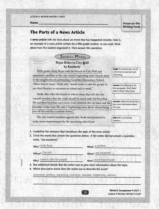
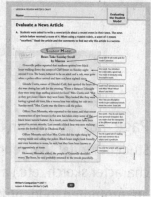

LESSON 5 (6 Pages)

Lesson 5 helps prepare students for long writing assignments and for taking tests.

Pages 1–2 of Lesson 5 are similar to tasks found on state writing assessment tests. They contain an open-ended, extended writing activity. Students select the topic and complete a full-length composition.

Pages 3–6 contain pages of multiple-choice questions that focus on usage, capitalization, and other skills typically encountered on state writing assessment tests.

© Harcourt

Introduction

Introduction

Writing is a way of sharing your ideas. Of course, you share ideas when you talk with others, too. When you write, however, you end up with a lasting record. Writing captures your thoughts just as a photograph captures your appearance.

This book will give you the skills, strategies, tips, and models you need to write easily and effectively. Let's start with an introduction to the writing process and some ongoing strategies.

The Writing Process

One big difference between writing and talking is the element of time. When you write, you have time to plan what you'll say, say it, and then make changes until it's just right. This is your writing process. Though there is no one correct way to write, many writers go through the following writing stages.

Prewriting

In this stage, you prepare to write. You plan what you will write by choosing a topic, identifying your audience, brainstorming and researching ideas, and organizing information.

Drafting

Next you follow your Prewriting plan to write a first draft. Don't expect your writing to be perfect—just let the sentences flow according to your plan.

Revising

Now you have the opportunity to improve your writing. As you edit, you will look for ways to make your writing clearer and stronger. You might edit by yourself or with a partner or group.

Proofreading

In this final stage of editing, you check for errors in grammar, spelling, capitalization, and punctuation. Then you make a clean, final copy.

Publishing

Finally, you decide how you will share your writing with your audience. You might create a newsletter, present a multimedia presentation, mail a letter, or assemble a class book.

Writer's Craft and Writing Traits

You've probably heard the phrase "arts and crafts" used to describe handmade items like quilts or pottery. Craftspeople make works of art that are both beautiful and useful. You can think of writing as a craft, too. Instead of using pieces of cloth to make a quilt, you use words to build a story, a letter, or a poem.

A key part of developing your craft is recognizing good writing. This web shows some of the traits you should look for in a piece of writing.

The Traits of Good Writing

Conventions
Correct punctuation, grammar, spelling

Word Choice
Exact nouns, vivid adjectives, strong verbs

Voice
Personal viewpoint and tone

Ideas
Interesting, focused content, supported by details and explanations. Related ideas are grouped and connected.

Sentence Fluency
Varied sentence structures, rhythm, flow

Organization
Clear structure, logical flow of ideas

Traits Checklist

Questions like these can help you improve your skills. Every time you answer "yes" to one of these questions, you recognize the strength of your writing.

☑ FOCUS/IDEAS	Is my writing clear and focused? Do I keep my purpose and audience in mind? Have I supported my ideas with interesting details and reasons?
☑ ORGANIZATION	Do my ideas have a logical flow? Is my beginning effective? What about my ending? Does each paragraph focus on one idea? Do I use transition words to tie ideas together?
☑ VOICE	Does the writing sound like I wrote it? Have I added personal touches? Have I shown that I care about what I am saying?
☑ WORD CHOICE	Do I use energetic words that create interest? Have I used strong verbs, precise nouns, and vivid adjectives?
☑ SENTENCE FLUENCY	Do I use different kinds of sentences? Do I use the best sentence structure for my ideas?
☑ CONVENTIONS	Are my spelling, grammar, and punctuation correct?

Identify: Sensory Details

OBJECTIVES

- To understand the term *sensory details*
- To identify *sensory details* in literature

Teach/Model   Read aloud the introduction. Tell students that writers use sensory words to tell readers *exactly* how something looks, sounds, smells, tastes, or feels. Point out that writers should try to appeal to all five senses, not just to the sense of sight (*how something looks*). If they describe the school cafeteria, for example, they should describe sounds, smells, and tastes, and even how it feels to carry a tray. Read aloud the Literature Model and have students listen for sensory details that help them picture they are with the narrator and his friend after gym.

Guided Practice   Point out that the writer used sensory details to describe how the the boy looks, for example, by decribing his "thick glasses." Guide students through Part B by asking them to find other sensory details that describe what they can see and hear.

Independent Writing Practice   Have students complete Part C independently.

Use a Literature Model

LESSON 1: SENSORY DETAILS

Name _____

Writer's Craft in Literature

Identify: Sensory Details

Sensory details help readers see, hear, smell, taste, or feel what a writer is describing.

A. Read this passage. Notice how the writer uses sensory details.

> ##### Literature Model
>
> After gym, I went to my locker to get my lunch. As I was dialing my combination, I heard someone say, "You're not too crazy about rope-climbing, are you?"
>
> I turned to see a dark-skinned boy looking at me through thick glasses.
>
> "Actually, I hate rope-climbing," I admitted. "How did you guess?"
>
> "You looked like you were going to pass out when Mr. Reynolds was talking about it," explained the boy. He was wearing black jeans and a bright yellow T-shirt with a picture of a lizard coming out of its pocket.
>
> —from *Rope Burn* by Jan Siebold

B. Look for sensory details in the literature model.
1. Draw a box around the words that describe what you can see.
2. Circle the words that describe what you can hear.

C. What words could you add that would appeal to the sense of touch? Include them in a sentence that you could add to the passage.

Possible response: add after "explained the boy" in the last paragraph: "You were as white as a

sheet, and your face was all wet and sweaty."

_____

_____

_____

Writer's Companion • UNIT 1
Lesson 1 *Sensory Details*   **8**

SHARING AND DISCUSSING

In small groups, have students read the sentences that they wrote and which used sensory details that appeal to the sense of touch. Ask students to identify the sensory details in each other's sentences. Invite them to discuss how the writer used sensory details to show that the narrator was afraid of climbing the rope. Have students make a list of other sensory details they could include to describe how the narrator feels about rope climbing.

Explore: Sensory Details

OBJECTIVES
- To reinforce students' understanding of sensory details
- To identify ways to use sensory details effectively

Standard: LA.5.3.1.1 generate ideas

Teach/Model Read aloud the diagram, using it to help students understand how writers can use sensory details to do more than just describe how something looks, sounds, smells, tastes, and feels. Explain that writers also use sensory details to add a personal voice to their writing. Sensory details can help make writing individual and unique. Also point out that writers can choose sensory details that will help readers know how the writer or characters feel about something.

Guided Practice Read aloud the directions for Part A and then read the example. Explain the meanings of the words *frigid* and *numbed* to show why they appeal to the sense of touch. Then guide students in completing Items 1–3. For Part B, guide students in completing Item 1.

Independent Writing Practice Have students independently complete Part B, Items 2–3.

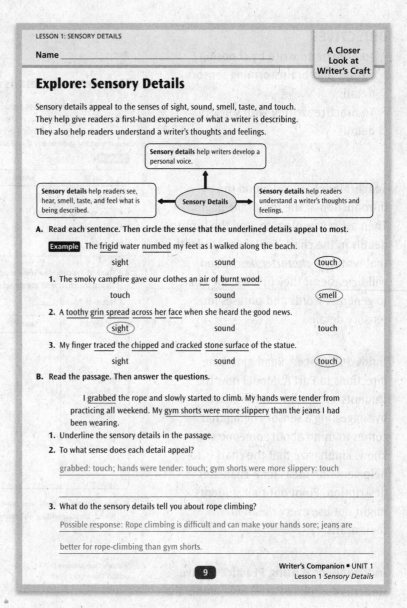

LESSON 1: SENSORY DETAILS

Name _____

A Closer Look at Writer's Craft

Explore: Sensory Details

Sensory details appeal to the senses of sight, sound, smell, taste, and touch. They help give readers a first-hand experience of what a writer is describing. They also help readers understand a writer's thoughts and feelings.

Sensory details help writers develop a personal voice.

Sensory details help readers see, hear, smell, taste, and feel what is being described.   ← Sensory Details →   **Sensory details** help readers understand a writer's thoughts and feelings.

A. Read each sentence. Then circle the sense that the underlined details appeal to most.

Example The frigid water numbed my feet as I walked along the beach.
   sight   sound   (touch)

1. The smoky campfire gave our clothes an air of burnt wood.
   touch   sound   (smell)

2. A toothy grin spread across her face when she heard the good news.
   (sight)   sound   touch

3. My finger traced the chipped and cracked stone surface of the statue.
   sight   sound   (touch)

B. Read the passage. Then answer the questions.

   I grabbed the rope and slowly started to climb. My hands were tender from practicing all weekend. My gym shorts were more slippery than the jeans I had been wearing.

1. Underline the sensory details in the passage.

2. To what sense does each detail appeal?

   grabbed: touch; hands were tender: touch; gym shorts were more slippery: touch

3. What do the sensory details tell you about rope climbing?

   Possible response: Rope climbing is difficult and can make your hands sore; jeans are

   better for rope-climbing than gym shorts.

9   **Writer's Companion** • UNIT 1
                     Lesson 1 *Sensory Details*

EXTENDING THE CONCEPT: SENSORY DETAILS

Explain to students that sensory details can help writers let readers know how they feel about a subject. Illustrate this by telling students that someone who loves to eat broccoli, for example, might use sensory details to describe broccoli this way: **The floral smell of the little green blossoms made my mouth water.** Someone who does not like broccoli might describe it this way: **I could barely stand to chew the mushy little green trees.** Point out that in neither example does the writer say she likes or dislikes broccoli. It is the sensory details that communicate the writer's feelings.

© Harcourt

Use: Sensory Details

OBJECTIVES
- To prepare to write by choosing a topic and brainstorming sensory details
- To practice writing with sensory details

Teach/Model   Read aloud the introduction at the top of the page. Then ask a volunteer to read the sensory details in the chart. Explain to students that writing a *character description* will be easier if they first use the chart to generate words and phrases for sensory details.

Guided Practice   Read aloud the directions to Part A. Model how the students should fill out the chart by suggesting a sensory detail that comes to mind about someone you know. Emphasize that the chart is to help generate ideas for a character description. Point out that students might not use every detail in their drafts.

Independent Writing Practice   Have students complete Part B independently.

LESSON 1: SENSORY DETAILS

Name _____

Use: Sensory Details

A **character description** gives a clear picture of what someone is like. Before you write a character description, make a chart of sensory details that come to mind when you think of that person. Here is how one student started to brainstorm about the time she met her friend Melissa.

Example

Sight	Sound	Smell	Touch	Taste
• wide-eyed • bouncing • wiggled • wildly	• "N–n–n–no" • quieted	• chlorine	• wet • cold • warm	

A. Think about someone you consider a good friend. Write his or her name on the line. Then fill out the chart with the sensory details that come to mind when you think of that person.

Name of Friend _____

Sight	Sound	Smell	Touch	Taste

B. Use information from your chart to write a draft of a character description about your friend. Do your writing on another sheet of paper.

Writer's Companion • UNIT 1
Lesson 1 *Sensory Details*

10

Reaching All Learners

BELOW LEVEL	ADVANCED	ENGLISH-LANGUAGE LEARNERS
Help students writing below grade level by asking them to focus on one sense at a time. Prompt them with guiding questions, such as: **What do your friends say when they are excited?**	Encourage students writing above grade level to generate sensory details that include *similes* that describe how something looks, sounds, smells, feels, or tastes.	Have less fluent English speakers generate a list in their first language. Then have them work with more fluent English speakers to write the sensory details in English.

The Parts of a Character Description

OBJECTIVES
- To understand the parts of a character description
- To analyze a Student Model

Teach/Model   Tell students that the Student Model is a character description. Explain that writers use character descriptions to show readers what a person looks like and how a person acts. Read aloud the introduction and then the call-outs to show how to organize a character description. Then read aloud the Student Model. As students listen, have them pay attention to how the writer organizes the details in the description.

Guided Practice   Point out the items below the Student Model. Then read aloud the first item. Guide students to find the sentence that introduces Melissa. Then guide students in completing Item 2. Explain that the sentence that begins "I had never seen her before…" should follow the first sentence because it helps explain why the narrator hadn't met her before.

Independent Writing Practice   Have students complete Items 3–4 independently. Invite volunteers to share their responses to Item 3 with the class.

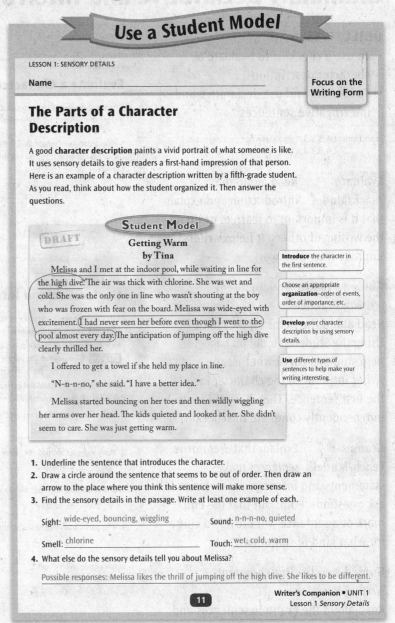

Use a Student Model

LESSON 1: SENSORY DETAILS

Name _____

Focus on the Writing Form

The Parts of a Character Description

A good **character description** paints a vivid portrait of what someone is like. It uses sensory details to give readers a first-hand impression of that person. Here is an example of a character description written by a fifth-grade student. As you read, think about how the student organized it. Then answer the questions.

Student Model

DRAFT

Getting Warm
by Tina

Melissa and I met at the indoor pool, while waiting in line for the high dive. The air was thick with chlorine. She was wet and cold. She was the only one in line who wasn't shouting at the boy who was frozen with fear on the board. Melissa was wide-eyed with excitement. I had never seen her before even though I went to the pool almost every day. The anticipation of jumping off the high dive clearly thrilled her.

I offered to get a towel if she held my place in line.

"N-n-n-no," she said. "I have a better idea."

Melissa started bouncing on her toes and then wildly wiggling her arms over her head. The kids quieted and looked at her. She didn't seem to care. She was just getting warm.

> **Introduce** the character in the first sentence.

> Choose an appropriate **organization**—order of events, order of importance, etc.

> **Develop** your character description by using sensory details.

> **Use** different types of sentences to help make your writing interesting.

1. Underline the sentence that introduces the character.
2. Draw a circle around the sentence that seems to be out of order. Then draw an arrow to the place where you think this sentence will make more sense.
3. Find the sensory details in the passage. Write at least one example of each.

Sight: _wide-eyed, bouncing, wiggling_   Sound: _n-n-n-no, quieted_

Smell: _chlorine_   Touch: _wet, cold, warm_

4. What else do the sensory details tell you about Melissa?

Possible responses: Melissa likes the thrill of jumping off the high dive. She likes to be different.

Writer's Companion • UNIT 1
Lesson 1 *Sensory Details*

11

EXTENDING THE CONCEPT: SENSORY DETAILS

Invite volunteers to read their responses to Item 4. Have students discuss how the writer uses sensory details to tell about Melissa's personality. Explain that writers can *show* how characters feel without actually *telling* readers.

To illustrate this idea, have students discuss how the writer could use sensory details to show that Melissa was nervous without actually telling readers, "Melissa was nervous."

© Harcourt

Evaluate a Character Description/ Grammar: Declarative and Interrogative Sentences

OBJECTIVES

- To use a checklist to evaluate a character description
- To identify and use declarative and interrogative sentences

Standards: LA.5.3.3.1 evaluate for writing traits;
        LA.5.3.4.3 use correct punctuation

Evaluate Teach/Model Read aloud the introduction and explain that it is important to learn to evaluate the writing of others. It helps writers improve their own work.

Guided Practice/Independent Writing Practice
Read aloud the items on the checklist. Using the Student Model on page 11, help students check whether the writer introduced the character in the first sentence. Then have students independently complete the checklist.

Grammar Teach/Model Explain that *declarative sentences* make statements and *interrogative sentences* ask questions. Point out that the end mark of a sentence will provide a clue for what kind of sentence it is.

Guided Practice/Independent Writing Practice
Read aloud the example sentences and guide students through Item 1. Have students complete Items 1–4 independently.

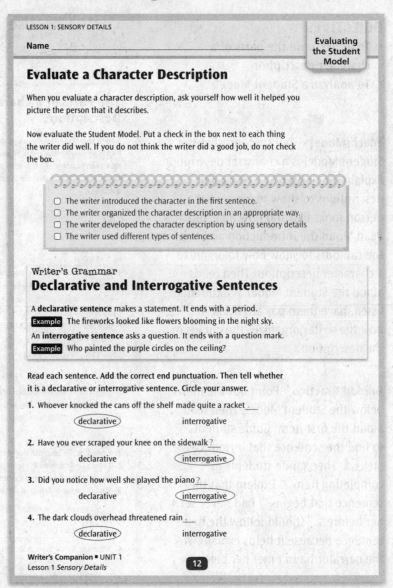

LESSON 1: SENSORY DETAILS

Name _____

Evaluating the Student Model

Evaluate a Character Description

When you evaluate a character description, ask yourself how well it helped you picture the person that it describes.

Now evaluate the Student Model. Put a check in the box next to each thing the writer did well. If you do not think the writer did a good job, do not check the box.

- ☐ The writer introduced the character in the first sentence.
- ☐ The writer organized the character description in an appropriate way.
- ☐ The writer developed the character description by using sensory details
- ☐ The writer used different types of sentences.

Writer's Grammar
Declarative and Interrogative Sentences

A **declarative sentence** makes a statement. It ends with a period.
Example The fireworks looked like flowers blooming in the night sky.

An **interrogative sentence** asks a question. It ends with a question mark.
Example Who painted the purple circles on the ceiling?

Read each sentence. Add the correct end punctuation. Then tell whether it is a declarative or interrogative sentence. Circle your answer.

1. Whoever knocked the cans off the shelf made quite a racket .
   (declarative)   interrogative

2. Have you ever scraped your knee on the sidewalk ?
   declarative   (interrogative)

3. Did you notice how well she played the piano ?
   declarative   (interrogative)

4. The dark clouds overhead threatened rain .
   (declarative)   interrogative

Writer's Companion ▪ UNIT 1
Lesson 1 *Sensory Details*   **12**

WRITER'S STRATEGY: EVALUATING YOUR OWN WRITING

Explain to students that sometimes it might be difficult for them to evaluate their own writing, especially immediately after completing a draft. Suggest that, if possible, students put aside their drafts for a period of time before they evaluate their writing. Explain that if they let some time pass they will be able to see their draft with "fresh eyes." Then they might find it easier to recognize how their writing could be improved.

© Harcourt

Revise: Replacing Plain Words

OBJECTIVES

- To understand the purpose of revising
- To revise by replacing plain words

Standard: LA.5.3.3.3 express ideas vividly

Teach/Model Tell students that *revising* is a process of improving a piece of writing by making changes to it. Explain that revising can mean making big changes, such as changing the main idea or organization. It can also mean making smaller changes, such as improving word choice or sentence fluency. Tell students that in this activity they will learn to revise by replacing plain words with words that give readers a better understanding of the topic.

Guided Practice Read aloud the introduction and example. Point out how the revised sentence replaces the plain word *wet* with vivid sensory details, "water drizzled from her ponytail." Explain that the writer is using sensory details to *show* readers that she is wet instead of simply saying, "She's wet." Guide students to complete Item 1 by asking how someone might act if he or she was excited. Then tell them to include this detail in their revision. Have students use the Word Bank, or their own words, to revise Items 2–4.

Independent Writing Practice Have students independently complete Part B.

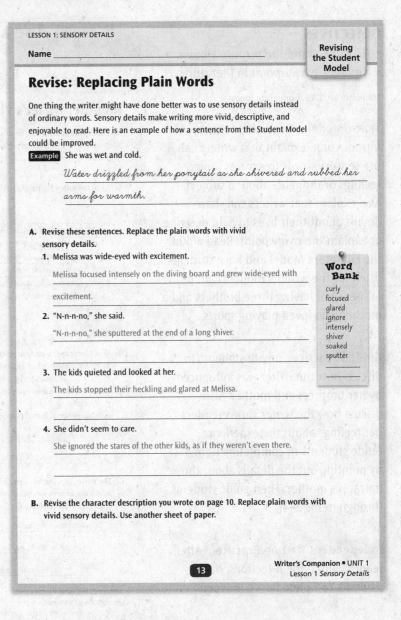

WRITER'S STRATEGY: BRAINSTORMING

Tell students that they can use a word web to help them brainstorm vivid sensory details that they can use to replace plain words. Have students work in small groups to identify the plain words in Part B, Items 1–4. Then have a volunteer draw a word web with a plain word in the center. As the others suggest vivid sensory details, the volunteer should add their words to the web. Then have students discuss which sensory details they like best and use them in their revisions.

© Harcourt

Identify: Writer's Viewpoint

OBJECTIVES
- To understand the term *viewpoint*
- To identify *viewpoint* in literature

Standard: LA.5.3.1.1 generate ideas

Teach/Model   Read aloud the introduction. Explain that writers can use sensory words to express their feelings or thoughts about a subject. Also explain that writers can share details about their lives to help describe or explain their viewpoint. Read aloud the Literature Model and have students listen for the writer's thoughts about the influence of having three brothers and a mother who loved playing sports.

Guided Practice   Invite students to discuss how the writer was influenced by her brothers and mother. Also discuss how the writer shows readers her feelings about the experience. Guide students in completing Item 1 by pointing out the details about the narrator's mother. Then guide students through Items 2–4.

Independent Writing Practice   After reading aloud the directions, have students complete Part C independently.

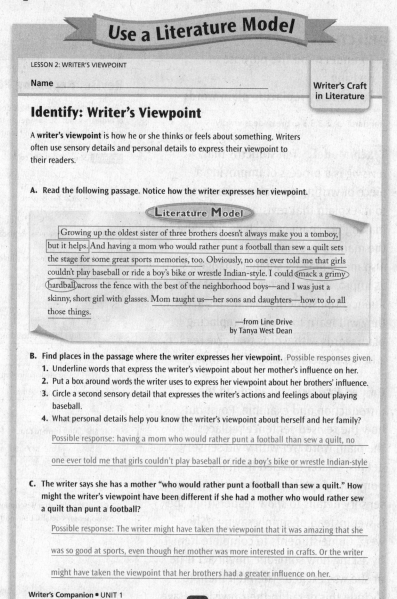

Use a Literature Model

LESSON 2: WRITER'S VIEWPOINT

Name _____

Writer's Craft in Literature

Identify: Writer's Viewpoint

A **writer's viewpoint** is how he or she thinks or feels about something. Writers often use sensory details and personal details to express their viewpoint to their readers.

A. Read the following passage. Notice how the writer expresses her viewpoint.

> **Literature Model**
>
> Growing up the oldest sister of three brothers doesn't always make you a tomboy, but it helps. And having a mom who would rather punt a football than sew a quilt sets the stage for some great sports memories, too. Obviously, no one ever told me that girls couldn't play baseball or ride a boy's bike or wrestle Indian-style. I could smack a grimy hardball across the fence with the best of the neighborhood boys—and I was just a skinny, short girl with glasses. Mom taught us—her sons and daughters—how to do all those things.
>
> —from *Line Drive*
> by Tanya West Dean

B. Find places in the passage where the writer expresses her viewpoint. Possible responses given.
1. Underline words that express the writer's viewpoint about her mother's influence on her.
2. Put a box around words the writer uses to express her viewpoint about her brothers' influence.
3. Circle a second sensory detail that expresses the writer's actions and feelings about playing baseball.
4. What personal details help you know the writer's viewpoint about herself and her family?

Possible response: having a mom who would rather punt a football than sew a quilt, no

one ever told me that girls couldn't play baseball or ride a boy's bike or wrestle Indian-style

C. The writer says she has a mother "who would rather punt a football than sew a quilt." How might the writer's viewpoint have been different if she had a mother who would rather sew a quilt than punt a football?

Possible response: The writer might have taken the viewpoint that it was amazing that she

was so good at sports, even though her mother was more interested in crafts. Or the writer

might have taken the viewpoint that her brothers had a greater influence on her.

Writer's Companion ▪ UNIT 1
Lesson 2 *Writer's Viewpoint*   **14**

EXTENDING THE CONCEPT: CHANGING VIEWPOINT

After students have completed Part C independently, invite volunteers to read aloud their responses. Then discuss with students how the writer might have chosen different sensory details and personal details if she had a mother who would rather sew a quilt than punt a football.

Ask students to think of words or personal details that would show the different viewpoint. Write their suggestions on the board. Then ask students to write a sentence using the words. Invite volunteers to read aloud their sentences.

Explore: Writer's Viewpoint

OBJECTIVES
- To reinforce students' understanding of viewpoint
- To identify how writers communicate viewpoint

Teach/Model   Use the diagram to explain that there is more than one way for writers to communicate their viewpoint. Point out that writers can communicate how they feel about a subject directly by telling readers exactly how they feel. Writers can also choose sensory details that make their viewpoint clear. For example, if a writer uses the word *slimy* to describe a liquid, readers will have a better idea of the writer's viewpoint than if the writer had used the word *wet*. Point out that writers can also use personal details to communicate their viewpoint by describing what they did or how they felt.

Guided Practice   Read aloud the directions and example in Part A. Model finding the words that express the writer's viewpoint. Guide students in completing Items 1–3.

Independent Writing Practice   Read aloud the directions for Part B. Have students complete Items 1–2 independently.

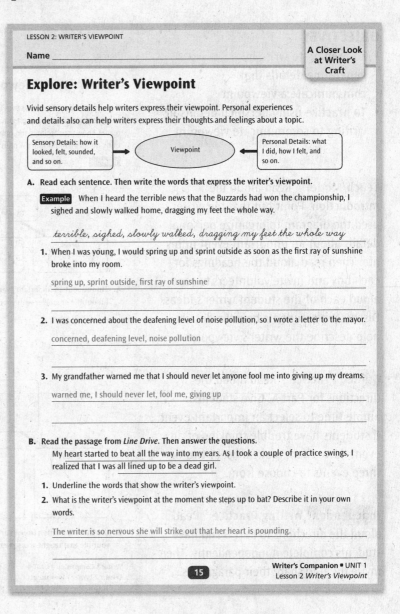

Reaching All Learners

BELOW LEVEL
Pair students writing below grade level with a partner or aide to work on Part B. Before responding to Item 2, have them discuss the details the writer uses to show how nervous she was.

ADVANCED
Challenge students writing above level to work independently or in pairs to write *similes* or *metaphors* that the writer could use to express her viewpoint.

ENGLISH-LANGUAGE LEARNERS
Point out the phrase "all lined up to be a dead girl." Explain that the writer uses this phrase to express her fear of going to bat. Explain that she is afraid that she might strike out or get hit by a pitch.

Use: Writer's Viewpoint

OBJECTIVES
- To prepare to write by generating details that communicate a viewpoint
- To practice using personal details in writing to communicate viewpoint

Teach/Model Read aloud the introduction. Point out that the writer used the diagram to organize personal details about an important event in his life. Then read aloud the headings for each box and invite volunteers to read aloud each of the student writer's ideas. Discuss with students how the details help describe the writer's viewpoint.

Guided Practice Read aloud the directions for Part A. Give students ample time to select an important event. If students have trouble thinking of an event, have them make a list of two or three events to choose from.

Independent Writing Practice Read aloud the directions to Part B and have students complete it independently. Then invite them to share their paragraphs.

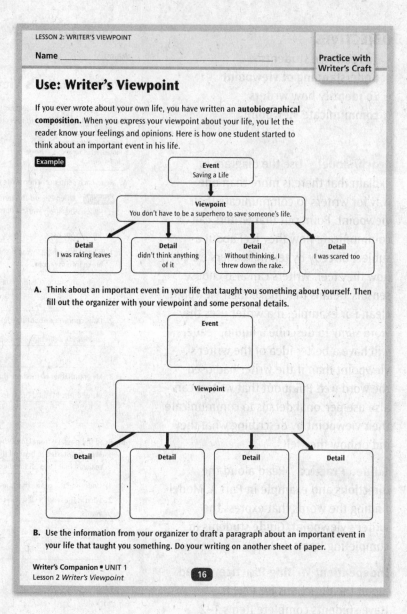

Reaching All Learners

BELOW LEVEL	ADVANCED	ENGLISH-LANGUAGE LEARNERS
For generating ideas for the viewpoint, prompt students by asking: **How did the event make you feel?** For generating ideas for details, ask: **What did you do? What did you see?** and so on.	Have students build on the organizer. Have them generate additional sensory words that will make each personal detail more descriptive. Tell them to use another sheet of paper, if necessary.	Pair less fluent English speakers with more fluent ones. Have students discuss the viewpoints and personal details. Then have them work together to find the appropriate words and phrases to include in the organizer.

© Harcourt

The Parts of an Autobiographical Composition

OBJECTIVES
- To understand the parts of an autobiographical composition
- To analyze a Student Model

Standard: LA.5.3.3.1 evaluate for writing traits

Teach/Model   Read aloud the introduction and explain that an *autobiographical composition* tells a true story about an event or events in a writer's life. Also explain that writers use personal details to communicate their viewpoint about the event they are describing. Read aloud the call-outs to show how an autobiographical composition is organized. Then read aloud the Student Model, asking students to listen for the personal details that the writer uses to develop his ideas.

Guided Practice   Read aloud Item 1 and guide students in finding where the writer explains how he feels about being a "superhero." For Item 2, guide students in finding the personal details the writer uses to support his viewpoint. Prompt students by asking: **What details show that the writer is just a normal person?**

Independent Writing Practice   Have students complete Item 3 independently.

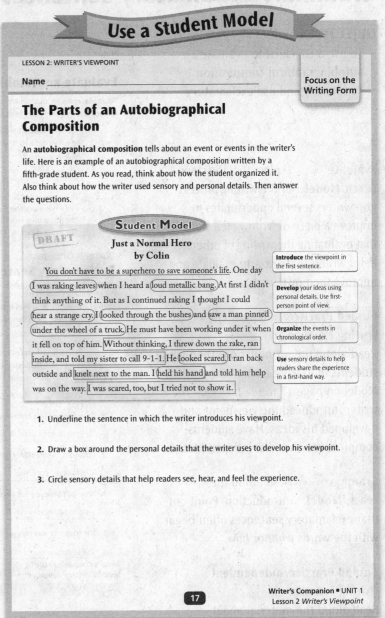

Use a Student Model

LESSON 2: WRITER'S VIEWPOINT

Name _____

Focus on the Writing Form

The Parts of an Autobiographical Composition

An **autobiographical composition** tells about an event or events in the writer's life. Here is an example of an autobiographical composition written by a fifth-grade student. As you read, think about how the student organized it. Also think about how the writer used sensory and personal details. Then answer the questions.

Student Model

DRAFT

Just a Normal Hero
by Colin

You don't have to be a superhero to save someone's life. One day I was raking leaves when I heard a loud metallic bang. At first I didn't think anything of it. But as I continued raking I thought I could hear a strange cry. I looked through the bushes and saw a man pinned under the wheel of a truck. He must have been working under it when it fell on top of him. Without thinking, I threw down the rake, ran inside, and told my sister to call 9-1-1. He looked scared. I ran back outside and knelt next to the man. I held his hand and told him help was on the way. I was scared, too, but I tried not to show it.

Introduce the viewpoint in the first sentence.

Develop your ideas using personal details. Use first-person point of view.

Organize the events in chronological order.

Use sensory details to help readers share the experience in a first-hand way.

1. Underline the sentence in which the writer introduces his viewpoint.

2. Draw a box around the personal details that the writer uses to develop his viewpoint.

3. Circle sensory details that help readers see, hear, and feel the experience.

17

Writer's Companion ▪ UNIT 1
Lesson 2 *Writer's Viewpoint*

EXTENDING THE CONCEPT: VIEWPOINT AND FIRST-PERSON POINT OF VIEW

Point out that the writer of the Student Model uses the first-person point of view to tell the story and express his viewpoint. Explain that in the first-person point of view, the writer can describe events as he or she experienced them, using words such as *I, me,* and *we*. Point out that the first-person point of view is appropriate for some writing forms, such as autobiographical compositions, but it is not appropriate for writing such as news stories, which should not include personal opinions.

Evaluate an Autobiographical Composition/ Grammar: Exclamatory Sentences

OBJECTIVES

- To use a checklist to evaluate an autobiographical composition
- To identify and use exclamatory sentences

Evaluate Teach/Model   Explain that the steps of the writing process give writers several opportunites to improve a piece of writing. Tell students that evaluating the writing of others helps writers learn how to evaluate and improve their own work.

Guided Practice/Independent Writing Practice

Read aloud the introduction. Then guide students in looking back at the Student Model on page 17 to see how well the writer introduced the viewpoint and developed his ideas. Have students complete the checklist independently.

Grammar Teach/Model   Read aloud the introduction. Point out that exclamatory sentences often begin with the words *what* or *how*.

Guided Practice/Independent Writing Practice

Read aloud the material about exclamations and guide students in completing Item 1. Have them complete Items 2–4 independently.

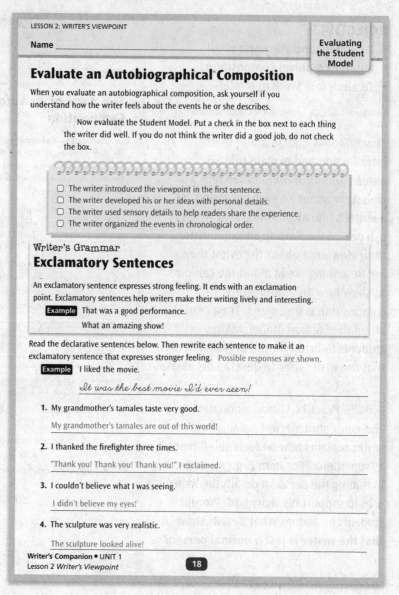

LESSON 2: WRITER'S VIEWPOINT

Name _____

Evaluating the Student Model

Evaluate an Autobiographical Composition

When you evaluate an autobiographical composition, ask yourself if you understand how the writer feels about the events he or she describes.

Now evaluate the Student Model. Put a check in the box next to each thing the writer did well. If you do not think the writer did a good job, do not check the box.

- ☐ The writer introduced the viewpoint in the first sentence.
- ☐ The writer developed his or her ideas with personal details.
- ☐ The writer used sensory details to help readers share the experience.
- ☐ The writer organized the events in chronological order.

Writer's Grammar
Exclamatory Sentences

An exclamatory sentence expresses strong feeling. It ends with an exclamation point. Exclamatory sentences help writers make their writing lively and interesting.

Example   That was a good performance.

                What an amazing show!

Read the declarative sentences below. Then rewrite each sentence to make it an exclamatory sentence that expresses stronger feeling.   Possible responses are shown.

Example   I liked the movie.

      It was the best movie I'd ever seen!

1. My grandmother's tamales taste very good.

    My grandmother's tamales are out of this world!

2. I thanked the firefighter three times.

    "Thank you! Thank you! Thank you!" I exclaimed.

3. I couldn't believe what I was seeing.

    I didn't believe my eyes!

4. The sculpture was very realistic.

    The sculpture looked alive!

Writer's Companion • UNIT 1
Lesson 2 *Writer's Viewpoint*   **18**

SHARING AND DISCUSSING

Invite volunteers to read aloud their exclamatory sentences from Items 1–4. Encourage students to read their sentences with enough expression to convey the appropriate emotion. Then have them compare and discuss the different ways that they rewrote the declarative sentences as exclamatory sentences. Remind students that, in general, they should not use too many exclamatory sentences in their writing. Explain that exclamatory sentences will lose their impact if they are used too often.

© Harcourt

Revise: Adding Personal Details

OBJECTIVES
- To understand the purpose of revising
- To revise by adding personal details

Standard: LA.5.3.3.3 express ideas vividly

Teach/Model   Tell students that even the best and most experienced writers improve their writing by revising. Explain that revising gives writers a chance to go back over their work. One thing writers can do when they revise is to make sure that their viewpoint is clear. Tell students that in this activity they will learn how to revise by adding personal details.

Guided Practice   Read aloud the introduction and the example. Point out how the writer added the personal detail "for my parents, like I do every Saturday morning in the fall." Explain that adding this personal detail helps the writer support the viewpoint of the Student Model, which was that even a normal boy can be a "superhero." Guide students in completing Item 1 by pointing out that they can use the Word Bank for possible personal details.

Independent Writing Practice   Have students complete Part A, Items 2–4, and Part B independently. Invite volunteers to read aloud their revisions.

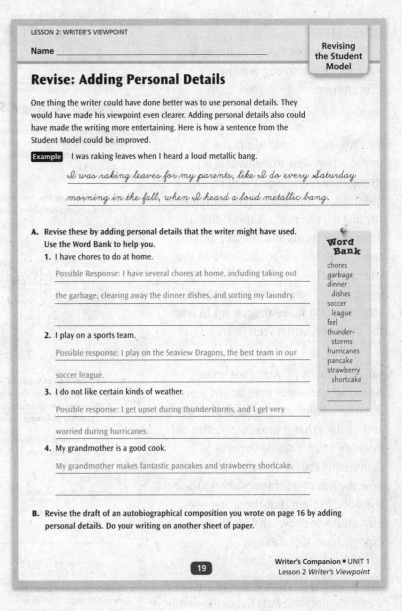

LESSON 2: WRITER'S VIEWPOINT

Name _____

Revising the Student Model

Revise: Adding Personal Details

One thing the writer could have done better was to use personal details. They would have made his viewpoint even clearer. Adding personal details also could have made the writing more entertaining. Here is how a sentence from the Student Model could be improved.

Example   I was raking leaves when I heard a loud metallic bang.

I was raking leaves for my parents, like I do every Saturday morning in the fall, when I heard a loud metallic bang.

A. Revise these by adding personal details that the writer might have used. Use the Word Bank to help you.

1. I have chores to do at home.

Possible Response: I have several chores at home, including taking out

the garbage, clearing away the dinner dishes, and sorting my laundry.

2. I play on a sports team.

Possible response: I play on the Seaview Dragons, the best team in our

soccer league.

3. I do not like certain kinds of weather.

Possible response: I get upset during thunderstorms, and I get very

worried during hurricanes.

4. My grandmother is a good cook.

My grandmother makes fantastic pancakes and strawberry shortcake.

B. Revise the draft of an autobiographical composition you wrote on page 16 by adding personal details. Do your writing on another sheet of paper.

Word Bank

chores
garbage
dinner
  dishes
soccer
  league
feel
thunder-
  storms
hurricanes
pancake
strawberry
  shortcake
_____

19

Writer's Companion • UNIT 1
Lesson 2 *Writer's Viewpoint*

WRITER'S STRATEGY: SENTENCE SURVEY

Before students revise the sentences in their autobiographical compositions, they should review their viewpoint by looking back at the organizer on page 16. Explain that they should only add personal details that support their viewpoint.

Suggest that students ask themselves the following questions as they reread each sentence of their paragraphs: **How does this sentence support the viewpoint? What personal details can I add to make my viewpoint clearer.**

© Harcourt

Identify: Writing A Strong Lead

OBJECTIVES
- To understand the term *strong lead*
- To identify a strong lead in literature

Standard: LA.5.3.1.1 generate ideas

Teach/Model Read aloud the introduction. Tell students that a strong lead often uses a statement, question, or quotation to make readers curious to read more. Explain that descriptive words and sensory details can strengthen a lead. Read aloud the Literature Model and tell students to listen for the words that catch their attention and make them want to read the interview with Evren Ozan.

Guided Practice Ask students to point out the words that caught their attention. Point out the word *prodigy* and explain that it means "an extremely talented child." Guide them in completing Part B. Have them discuss how the use of quotations sparks their curiosity. Explain that the writer uses quotations to show what opinions experts have about Evren.

Independent Writing Practice Have students complete Part C independently.

Use a Literature Model

LESSON 3: WRITING A STRONG LEAD

Name _____

Writer's Craft in Literature

Identify: Writing A Strong Lead

A **lead** is the first sentence or paragraph of a piece of writing. A **strong lead** sparks readers' attention and makes them want to continue reading. Descriptive words, sensory details, quotations, and interrogative sentences all can help make a strong lead.

A. Read this strong lead from an interview with ten-year-old musician Evren Ozan. Notice how the writer uses descriptive words to make the reader want to read further.

> **Literature Model**
>
> Although artists in the music circle tend to describe Evren as the "Native American Flute Prodigy," "An Old Soul Returned to the People," and the "Future of Native American Music," I found him to be an exceptional ten-year-old who is smart, talented, creative, resourceful, inspiring, and on the whole, awesome.
>
> —from *Evren Ozan, Musician*
> by Harsha Viswanathan

B. Find words that catch readers' interest. Possible responses are shown.
1. Underline the words the writer uses in the lead to catch the reader's attention.
2. The writer uses quotations to show the reader what others think about Evren. Put a box around the quotations that are used to spark readers' attention.

C. What other words would you choose to use to spark readers' interest in Evren Ozan? Write them on the lines below.

Possible responses: brilliant, astonishing, small-sized wonder, Can you picture a ten-year-old

who plays an instrument as well as full-grown professional?

_____

_____

SHARING AND DISCUSSING

After students have completed Part C independently, have them share their responses with a partner and discuss which words they think would be most effective for sparking the readers' interest in Evren. Then have partners brainstorm additional words, phrases, or sentences. Encourage students to use a thesaurus to generate ideas. When they have finished, invite volunteers to read aloud the new words, phrases, or sentences to the class.

Explore: Writing A Strong Lead

OBJECTIVES
- To reinforce students' understanding of strong leads
- To identify a strong lead

Teach/Model Read the introduction aloud and use the graphic organizer to help students understand the elements of a strong lead. Remind students that interrogative sentences ask a question and that writers often use questions in a lead. That is because questions are a good way to make readers think about the topic.

Guided Practice Read aloud the directions to Part A. Point out that the underlined sentence is a stronger lead because it asks a question that gets readers interested and involved. Tell students that the stronger lead might make them ask themselves, "How could a car possibly run on corn?" Emphasize that this might make readers want to keep reading to learn how. Guide students in completing Items 1–4.

Independent Writing Practice Have students complete Part B independently. Invite volunteers to read aloud their responses to the class.

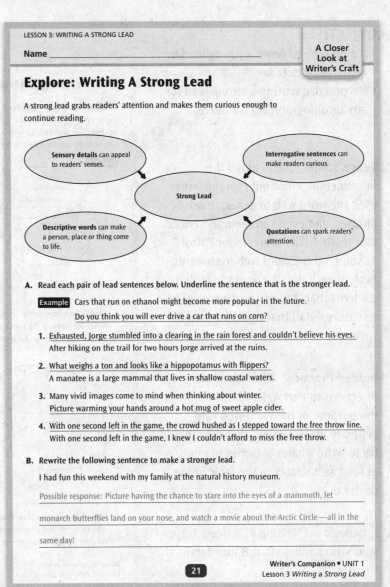

LESSON 3: WRITING A STRONG LEAD

Name _____

A Closer Look at Writer's Craft

Explore: Writing A Strong Lead

A strong lead grabs readers' attention and makes them curious enough to continue reading.

- Sensory details can appeal to readers' senses.
- Interrogative sentences can make readers curious.
- Strong Lead
- Descriptive words can make a person, place or thing come to life.
- Quotations can spark readers' attention.

A. Read each pair of lead sentences below. Underline the sentence that is the stronger lead.

Example Cars that run on ethanol might become more popular in the future.
Do you think you will ever drive a car that runs on corn?

1. Exhausted, Jorge stumbled into a clearing in the rain forest and couldn't believe his eyes.
   After hiking on the trail for two hours Jorge arrived at the ruins.

2. What weighs a ton and looks like a hippopotamus with flippers?
   A manatee is a large mammal that lives in shallow coastal waters.

3. Many vivid images come to mind when thinking about winter.
   Picture warming your hands around a hot mug of sweet apple cider.

4. With one second left in the game, the crowd hushed as I stepped toward the free throw line.
   With one second left in the game, I knew I couldn't afford to miss the free throw.

B. Rewrite the following sentence to make a stronger lead.
I had fun this weekend with my family at the natural history museum.

Possible response: Picture having the chance to stare into the eyes of a mammoth, let

monarch butterflies land on your nose, and watch a movie about the Arctic Circle—all in the

same day!

21

Writer's Companion • UNIT 1
Lesson 3 *Writing a Strong Lead*

EXTENDING THE CONCEPT: A STRONG LEAD

Explain to students that they can use quotations to make a strong lead. Have students look back to the Literature Model on page 20 to review how the writer used quotations to support her opinion about Evren Ozan. Tell students that in some forms of writing, such as character description paragraphs and autobiographical compositions, writers use dialogue to grab the readers' attention. For example, an autobiographical composition might begin with this lead: *"You'll never win," the coach told me.* Point out that this is a strong lead because it makes readers want to find out if the narrator will win the game.

© Harcourt

Use: Writing A Strong Lead

OBJECTIVES
- To prepare to write a strong lead by generating details
- To practice writing a strong lead for an autobiographical narrative

Teach/Model　Read aloud the introduction. Point out that the writer used the word web to generate words, phrases, and even complete sentences that relate to the topic "Litter Patrol." As you read the word web to students, explain each detail. For example, tell students that "bulging garbage bag" is a sensory detail that could be used to write a strong lead.

Guided Practice　Read aloud the directions to Part A. Emphasize that the purpose of the word web is to generate ideas. Explain that they should try to write whatever comes to mind, as long as it relates to the topic in the center oval.

Independent Writing Practice　Have students complete Part B independently.

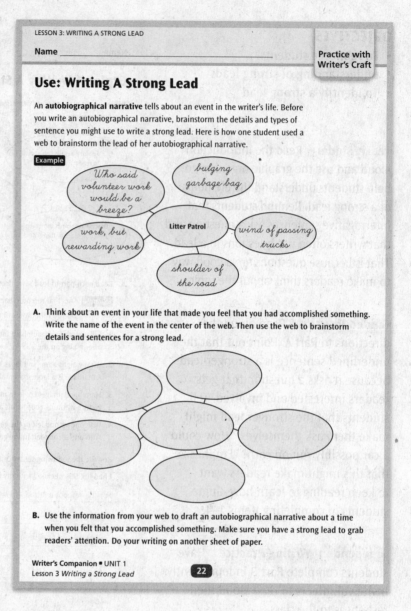

LESSON 3: WRITING A STRONG LEAD

Name _____

Practice with Writer's Craft

Use: Writing A Strong Lead

An **autobiographical narrative** tells about an event in the writer's life. Before you write an autobiographical narrative, brainstorm the details and types of sentence you might use to write a strong lead. Here is how one student used a web to brainstorm the lead of her autobiographical narrative.

Example

Who said volunteer work would be a breeze?

bulging garbage bag

Litter Patrol

work, but rewarding work

wind of passing trucks

shoulder of the road

A. Think about an event in your life that made you feel that you had accomplished something. Write the name of the event in the center of the web. Then use the web to brainstorm details and sentences for a strong lead.

B. Use the information from your web to draft an autobiographical narrative about a time when you felt that you accomplished something. Make sure you have a strong lead to grab readers' attention. Do your writing on another sheet of paper.

Writer's Companion • UNIT 1
Lesson 3 *Writing a Strong Lead*　　22

Reaching All Learners

BELOW LEVEL	ADVANCED	ENGLISH-LANGUAGE LEARNERS
Remind students that they should first focus on generating ideas and writing a draft. Explain that they can focus on conventions, such as spelling, later.	Challenge students to write three strong lead sentences for their narratives. Ask them to share each lead with a partner and then discuss which possibility is the strongest.	Encourage students to generate ideas for the word web in their first language. Then work with students to write the words, phrases, and sentences in English.

The Parts of an Autobiographical Narrative

OBJECTIVES

- To understand the parts of an autobiographical narrative
- To analyze a Student Model

Teach/Model   Explain to students that an autobiographical narrative tells a true story about an event in the writer's life. Read aloud the call-outs about how an autobiographical narrative is organized. Point out that the narrative should begin with a strong lead to make readers want to continue reading. Then read aloud the Student Model. Ask students to listen for the lead sentence and to notice the words that make it a strong lead.

Guided Practice   Read aloud Item 1 and guide students in discussing the details that make the lead sentence strong. Read aloud Item 2, telling students to circle words that show where the story takes place.

Independent Writing Practice   Have students complete Items 2–5 independently. Invite volunteers to share their responses to Item 5, explaining why the details were effective in capturing readers' attention.

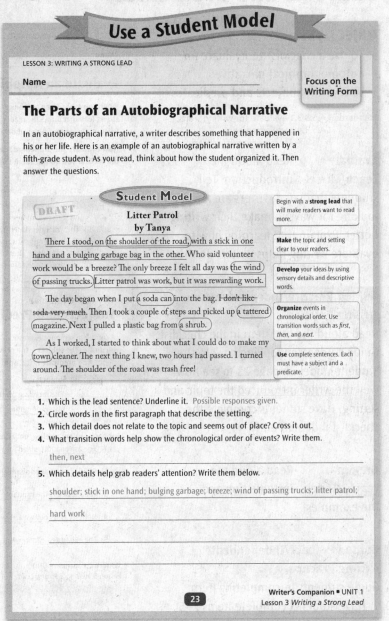

EXTENDING THE CONCEPT: A STRONG LEAD

Point out the lead sentence in the Student Model. Explain that it is a strong lead because it makes readers curious to find out why the writer was standing on the shoulder of the road. Also point out how the words *bulging* and *garbage* are used to make the image more interesting and clear. Explain that, if the writer hadn't included those details, readers might have pictured her holding a paper bag, shopping bag, or even a sandwich bag instead.

© Harcourt

Evaluate an Autobiographical Narrative/Grammar: Subjects and Predicates

OBJECTIVES
- To use a checklist to evaluate an autobiographical narrative
- To identify subjects and predicates

Standards: LA.5.3.3.1 evaluate for writing traits; LA.5.3.4.5 use agreement

Evaluate
Teach/Model Read aloud the introduction. Tell students that good writers are always looking for ways to make their writing better. Explain that learning how to evaluate writing helps writers do this.

Guided Practice/Independent Writing Practice
Read aloud the first item in the checklist. Guide students in looking back to the Student Model on page 23 to see how well the writer introduced the topic and setting. Have students complete the checklist independently.

Grammar
Teach/Model Read aloud the introduction and the examples.

Guided Practice/Independent Writing Practice
Guide students in completing Item 1. Have students complete Items 2–5 independently.

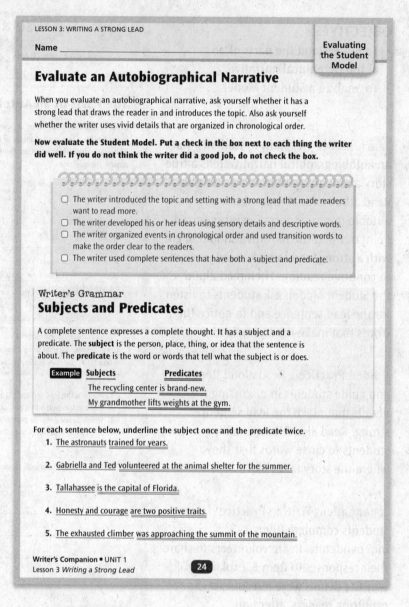

LESSON 3: WRITING A STRONG LEAD

Name _____

Evaluating the Student Model

Evaluate an Autobiographical Narrative

When you evaluate an autobiographical narrative, ask yourself whether it has a strong lead that draws the reader in and introduces the topic. Also ask yourself whether the writer uses vivid details that are organized in chronological order.

Now evaluate the Student Model. Put a check in the box next to each thing the writer did well. If you do not think the writer did a good job, do not check the box.

- ☐ The writer introduced the topic and setting with a strong lead that made readers want to read more.
- ☐ The writer developed his or her ideas using sensory details and descriptive words.
- ☐ The writer organized events in chronological order and used transition words to make the order clear to the readers.
- ☐ The writer used complete sentences that have both a subject and predicate.

Writer's Grammar
Subjects and Predicates

A complete sentence expresses a complete thought. It has a subject and a predicate. The **subject** is the person, place, thing, or idea that the sentence is about. The **predicate** is the word or words that tell what the subject is or does.

Example	Subjects	Predicates

The recycling center is brand-new.

My grandmother lifts weights at the gym.

For each sentence below, underline the subject once and the predicate twice.
1. The astronauts trained for years.
2. Gabriella and Ted volunteered at the animal shelter for the summer.
3. Tallahassee is the capital of Florida.
4. Honesty and courage are two positive traits.
5. The exhausted climber was approaching the summit of the mountain.

Writer's Companion • UNIT 1
Lesson 3 *Writing a Strong Lead*   24

WRITER'S STRATEGY: SENTENCE SURVEY

Tell students that checklists are useful for evaluating a piece of writing. Explain that checklists help focus readers' attention on one aspect of the writing at a time. Explain to students that they might find it helpful to read a draft from beginning to end for each item on the checklist. Point out that some items on a checklist might only require them to focus on one particular part, such as the lead sentence or the use of sensory details.

© Harcourt

Revise: Using Descriptive Words

OBJECTIVES
- To understand the purpose of revising
- To revise by using descriptive words

Standard: LA.5.3.1.1 generate ideas

Teach/Model Explain to students that revising allows writers to make their work more descriptive and detailed. Tell students that in this activity they will learn to revise by using descriptive words. Explain that using descriptive words will help readers have a more exact image of what is being described. Tell students that descriptive words also help readers understand a writer's feelings about a topic.

Guided Practice Read aloud the introduction and then the example. Point out how the writer replaced the word *wind* with the more descriptive words *gritty gusts*. Have students discuss how this revision gives readers a better idea of what it was like to stand on the shoulder of the road. Guide students in completing Part A, Item 1. Point out that they can use words from the Word Bank to better describe what the work was like.

Independent Writing Practice Have students complete Part A, Items 2–4 independently. Then guide students in looking back at the narrative they wrote on page 22. Have students complete Part B independently.

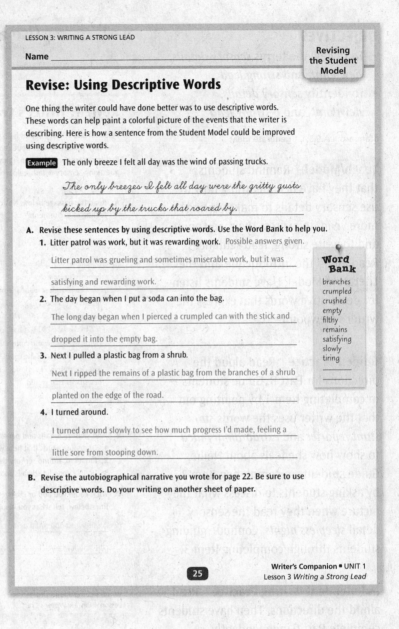

LESSON 3: WRITING A STRONG LEAD

Name _____

Revising the Student Model

Revise: Using Descriptive Words

One thing the writer could have done better was to use descriptive words. These words can help paint a colorful picture of the events that the writer is describing. Here is how a sentence from the Student Model could be improved using descriptive words.

Example The only breeze I felt all day was the wind of passing trucks.

The only breezes I felt all day were the gritty gusts kicked up by the trucks that roared by.

A. Revise these sentences by using descriptive words. Use the Word Bank to help you.
  1. Litter patrol was work, but it was rewarding work. Possible answers given.

  Litter patrol was grueling and sometimes miserable work, but it was

  satisfying and rewarding work.

  2. The day began when I put a soda can into the bag.

  The long day began when I pierced a crumpled can with the stick and

  dropped it into the empty bag.

  3. Next I pulled a plastic bag from a shrub.

  Next I ripped the remains of a plastic bag from the branches of a shrub

  planted on the edge of the road.

  4. I turned around.

  I turned around slowly to see how much progress I'd made, feeling a

  little sore from stooping down.

B. Revise the autobiographical narrative you wrote for page 22. Be sure to use descriptive words. Do your writing on another sheet of paper.

Word Bank
branches
crumpled
crushed
empty
filthy
remains
satisfying
slowly
tiring
_____

25

Writer's Companion • UNIT 1
Lesson 3 *Writing a Strong Lead*

SHARING AND DISCUSSING

After students have completed their revisions for Part B, have them select one sentence in which they added descriptive words. Ask students to read aloud the original sentence to a partner and then read aloud the revision. Tell partners to take notes as they listen, writing down the descriptive words that were added in the revision. Ask pairs to discuss the revisions each other made. Encourage pairs to work together to think of additional descriptive words for their sentences.

© Harcourt

Review Writer's Craft

OBJECTIVES
- To review the terms *sensory details, viewpoint,* and *strong lead*
- To identify *sensory details, viewpoint,* and *a strong lead*

Standard: LA.5.3.1.1 generate ideas

Teach/Model Remind students that they have been learning how to use sensory details to make writing more vivid, to express their viewpoint, and to write strong, lead sentences. Read aloud the introduction and the Literature Model. Have students listen for descriptive words that express the writer's viewpoint.

Guided Practice Read aloud the directions for Part B. Guide students in completing Item 1 by pointing out that the writer uses the words *star stunt reporter* and *extraordinary idea* to show how she feels about Nellie. Guide students in completing Item 2 by asking students to discuss what they picture when they read the sensory detail *sleepless nights.* Continue guiding students through completing Item 3.

Independent Writing Practice Read aloud the directions. Then have students complete Part C independently.

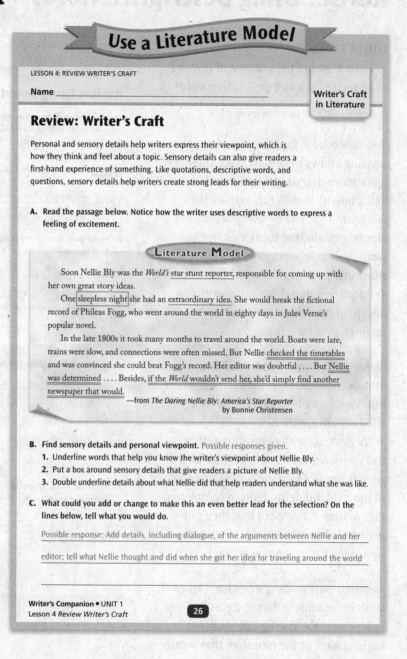

Use a Literature Model

LESSON 4: REVIEW WRITER'S CRAFT

Name _____

Writer's Craft in Literature

Review: Writer's Craft

Personal and sensory details help writers express their viewpoint, which is how they think and feel about a topic. Sensory details can also give readers a first-hand experience of something. Like quotations, descriptive words, and questions, sensory details help writers create strong leads for their writing.

A. Read the passage below. Notice how the writer uses descriptive words to express a feeling of excitement.

Literature Model

Soon Nellie Bly was the *World's* star stunt reporter, responsible for coming up with her own great story ideas.

One sleepless night she had an extraordinary idea. She would break the fictional record of Phileas Fogg, who went around the world in eighty days in Jules Verne's popular novel.

In the late 1800s it took many months to travel around the world. Boats were late, trains were slow, and connections were often missed. But Nellie checked the timetables and was convinced she could beat Fogg's record. Her editor was doubtful . . . . But Nellie was determined . . . . Besides, if the *World* wouldn't send her, she'd simply find another newspaper that would.

—from *The Daring Nellie Bly: America's Star Reporter*
by Bonnie Christensen

B. Find sensory details and personal viewpoint. Possible responses given.
1. Underline words that help you know the writer's viewpoint about Nellie Bly.
2. Put a box around sensory details that give readers a picture of Nellie Bly.
3. Double underline details about what Nellie did that help readers understand what she was like.

C. What could you add or change to make this an even better lead for the selection? On the lines below, tell what you would do.

Possible response: Add details, including dialogue, of the arguments between Nellie and her editor; tell what Nellie thought and did when she got her idea for traveling around the world

Writer's Companion • UNIT 1
Lesson 4 *Review Writer's Craft*   26

SHARING AND DISCUSSING

After students have completed Part C independently, have them share their responses in small groups. Then have them discuss what kinds of sensory and personal details they could use to write a better lead for the selection. Encourage students to brainstorm a short list of words and phrases that they could use to grab the readers' attention. Then invite a volunteer from each group to read aloud the list.

© Harcourt

Review Writer's Craft

OBJECTIVES
- To review the terms *sensory details,* and *strong lead*
- To identify sensory details and use them to write a strong lead

Teach/Model　Read aloud the introduction. Use the graphic organizer to point out how writers use personal voice to create sensory details and communicate a writer's viewpoint. Point out how word choice enables writers to create strong leads by using sensory details, quotations, and questions.

Guided Practice　Read aloud the directions and passage for Part A. Remind students to listen for sensory details and descriptive words that appeal to the senses of sight, sound, smell, touch, and taste. Guide students in completing Part A. Next read aloud the directions for Part B and the example. Point out the changes the writer made, explaining how these added details help spark the readers' interest.

Independent Writing Practice　Have students complete Part B, Items 1 and 2 independently.

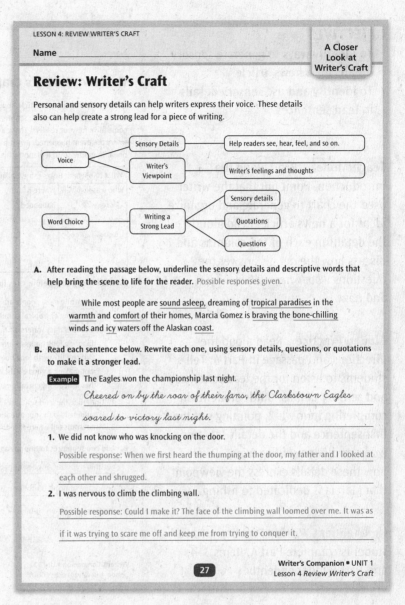

EXTENDING THE CONCEPT: A STRONG LEAD

Tell students that they can create a stong lead without using fancy vocabulary words and without stuffing a sentence full of sensory details. Explain that simple, everyday words can be just as effective for sparking the readers' interest. Tell students it is more important that the writer chooses words that communicate his or her thoughts clearly, in a way that will make the readers think about the subject in a new way and make them want to read more.

Review Writer's Craft

OBJECTIVES
- To identify ways to generate sensory details for a news article
- To identify and use sensory details in lead sentences

Teach/Model   Read aloud the introduction. Point out that the writer used the chart to generate and organize ideas for a news article. Read aloud the details in each of the columns and discuss how the details answer the questions *who, where, when, why,* and *how.*

Guided Practice   Read aloud the directions and passage in Part A. Tell students to listen for the lead sentence and sensory details. Guide students in completing Items 1–2, pointing out the first sentence and the details *safe and warm* and *bone-chilling winds.* Discuss how these details express the viewpoint that Marcia is dedicated to fishing.

Independent Writing Practice   Have students complete Part A, Items 3–4, and Part B independently.

LESSON 4: REVIEW WRITER'S CRAFT

Name _____

Practice with Writer's Craft

Review: Writer's Craft

Before you write a **news article** about something that happened in your community, think about the sensory details you could use to make the scene come alive for your readers. Those details should help readers know *when* and *where* the event happened, *why* it happened, and *how* it happened. Here is how one fifth grader started planning his news story.

What happened: Bears came walking into town one Sunday afternoon.				
Who was involved	Where it happened	When it happened	Why it happened	How it happened
Graceville police, Glenda Curtis, Officer Menasha	Graceville	Sunday night	Bears are losing their natural habitat	Bears walked down Cliff Street and then returned to woods

A. Read the passage below. Then follow the directions.

> While most people are (sound asleep, safe and warm) in their homes and (dreaming of tropical paradises,) Marcia Gomez is braving the (bone-chilling winds and icy waters) off the Alaskan coast. She works on a fishing boat, laboring long hours to bring in the fresh fish that graces our tables. It's a difficult life, with long hours, physical discomfort, and always the chance of not making a good catch. Why does she do it? "I love it," she says. "My family has fished for generations. It's in our blood."

1. Underline the lead sentence.
2. What details grab your attention in that sentence? Circle them.
3. What words tell where the story takes place? Box them.

B. Add two sentences to this passage. Use sensory details to make it come alive.

Possible response: She wakes each "morning" in the middle of the night, and she is at sea

before the sun comes up. She has to check her fishing lines, make sure her boat is running

properly, and fill up on fuel, all before she leaves the dock.

Reaching All Learners

BELOW LEVEL	ADVANCED	ENGLISH-LANGUAGE LEARNERS
Have students use a word web to generate sensory details. Then ask them to use one or two words to write a sentence about fishing.	Encourage students to incorporate quotations in their response for Part B. Suggest that they develop the viewpoint of the passage by picturing how Marcia would continue to describe why she loves fishing.	Pair less fluent English speakers with more fluent speakers and have them work together to complete Part A, Items 3 and 4. Encourage more fluent speakers to help explain sensory details such as *bone-chilling.*

© Harcourt

The Parts of a News Article

OBJECTIVES
- To understand the parts of a news article
- To analyze a Student Model

Standard: LA.5.4.2.2 record information

Teach/Model Read aloud the introduction. Explain that a news article tells the facts about an event by using details to answer the six questions *who, what, where, when, why,* and *how*. Read aloud the call-outs to show how a news article should be organized. Then read aloud the Student Model. Ask students to listen for how the writer answers the six questions in the first paragraph.

Guided Practice Point out the items below the Student Model. Read aloud Item 1 and guide students in finding the introductory sentence. Read aloud Item 2 and guide students by saying: Who is the article about? Where does the event take place?, and so on.

Independent Writing Practice Have students complete Items 3 and 4 independently. Invite volunteers to share their responses with the class.

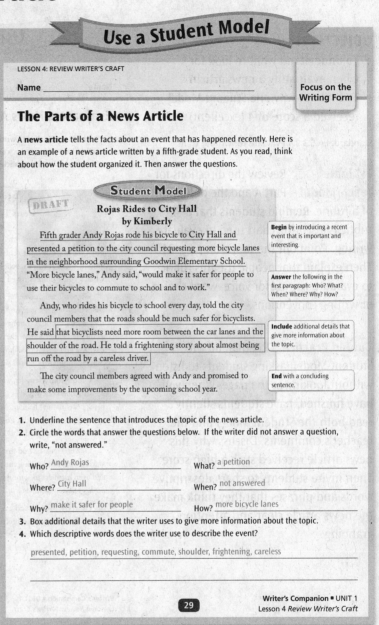

EXTENDING THE CONCEPT: VIEWPOINT

Remind students that the writer's viewpoint is how the writer feels or thinks about a subject. Explain that in some forms of writing, such as a news article, the writer should try not to express his or her viewpoint on the subject. Read aloud the Student Model and point out that the writer does a good job of reporting the facts without expressing her personal viewpoint about the subject. Also point out that the writer does a good job of describing the viewpoint of fifth grader Andy Rojas without expressing her own.

Evaluate a News Article

OBJECTIVES

- To understand what to look for when evaluating a news article
- To find out why one Student Model received a score of 4 (excellent)

Standard: LA.5.3.3.1 evaluate for writing traits

Evaluate Teach/Model Review the directions for Part A and the definition of a rubric. Remind students that a rubric is a scoring chart used to evaluate writing. Point out the rubric on page 31. Then explain that people use this rubric to evaluate writing for voice, word choice, or writing conventions.

Guided Practice Read aloud the Student Model, asking students to listen without looking at the page. When you have finished, have students silently read both the Student Model and the teacher's comments. Discuss why this news article received such a high score. Then invite students to share descriptive words and phrases that they think make the news article clear and attention grabbing.

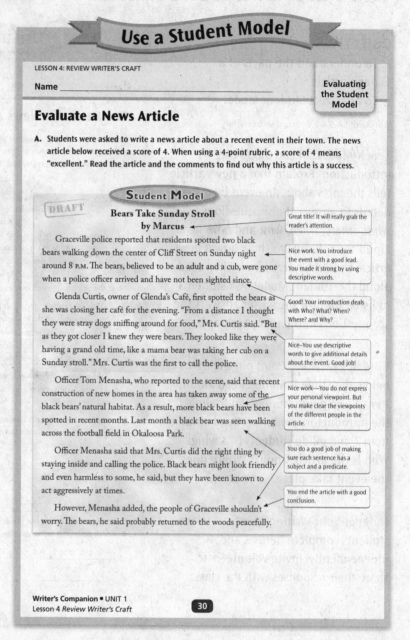

Use a Student Model

LESSON 4: REVIEW WRITER'S CRAFT

Name _____

Evaluating the Student Model

Evaluate a News Article

A. Students were asked to write a news article about a recent event in their town. The news article below received a score of 4. When using a 4-point rubric, a score of 4 means "excellent." Read the article and the comments to find out why this article is a success.

Student Model

DRAFT

Bears Take Sunday Stroll
by Marcus

Graceville police reported that residents spotted two black bears walking down the center of Cliff Street on Sunday night around 8 P.M. The bears, believed to be an adult and a cub, were gone when a police officer arrived and have not been sighted since.

Glenda Curtis, owner of Glenda's Café, first spotted the bears as she was closing her café for the evening. "From a distance I thought they were stray dogs sniffing around for food," Mrs. Curtis said. "But as they got closer I knew they were bears. They looked like they were having a grand old time, like a mama bear was taking her cub on a Sunday stroll." Mrs. Curtis was the first to call the police.

Officer Tom Menasha, who reported to the scene, said that recent construction of new homes in the area has taken away some of the black bears' natural habitat. As a result, more black bears have been spotted in recent months. Last month a black bear was seen walking across the football field in Okaloosa Park.

Officer Menasha said that Mrs. Curtis did the right thing by staying inside and calling the police. Black bears might look friendly and even harmless to some, he said, but they have been known to act aggressively at times.

However, Menasha added, the people of Graceville shouldn't worry. The bears, he said probably returned to the woods peacefully.

Great title! It will really grab the reader's attention.

Nice work. You introduce the event with a good lead. You made it strong by using descriptive words.

Good! Your introduction deals with Who? What? When? Where? and Why?

Nice–You use descriptive words to give additional details about the event. Good job!

Nice work—You do not express your personal viewpoint. But you make clear the viewpoints of the different people in the article.

You do a good job of making sure each sentence has a subject and a predicate.

You end the article with a good conclusion.

Writer's Companion • UNIT 1
Lesson 4 *Review Writer's Craft*   30

WRITER'S STRATEGY: WORD BANKS

Tell students that they should dedicate a section of their notebooks or journals to words or phrases that they think are interesting. Tell students that this will help them make their own personal Word Banks. Suggest that they can then use these Word Banks as a reference when they are looking for ideas for new writing assignments.

© Harcourt

Evaluate a News Article

OBJECTIVES

- To read a Student Model that received a score of 2 (needs improvement)
- To evaluate a news article using a rubric

Standard: LA.5.3.3.1 evaluate for writing traits

Teach/Model　Explain that the Student Model on this page received a score of 2 on a 4-point rubric. Read aloud the directions for Part B and the Student Model. Ask students to listen without reading along and try to identify parts that they think could be improved.

Guided Practice　Have students read the Student Model silently. Invite volunteers to identify and discuss which parts of the article they think were written well and which parts need improvement. Then read aloud the teacher's comments and discuss how they match or build upon what the students have already discussed. Have students summarize and discuss the steps the writer could take to improve the article.

Independent Writing Practice　Review how to use the 4-point rubric at the bottom of the page. Ask students to work independently to score the news article using the rubric.

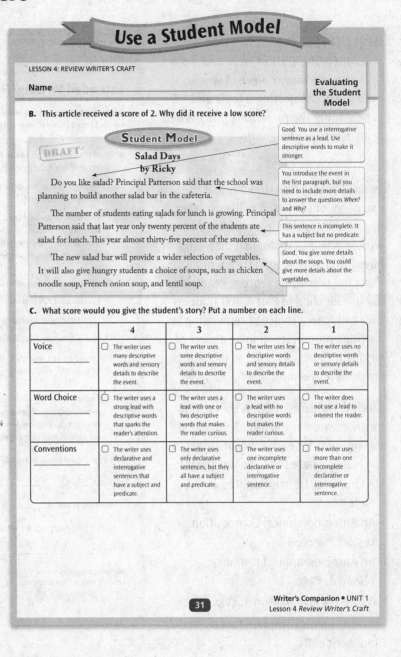

SHARING AND DISCUSSING

Explain to students that sometimes a rubric might not cover every aspect that they liked about a piece of writing. Tell students that when they evaluate a peer's writing, for example, they might first discuss the things they like about the writing, even if does not appear on the rubric. After students have completed evaluating the news article on the page, have them discuss in general terms what they liked about the article before sharing the results of their evaluations.

Writer's Companion • UNIT 1
Lesson 4 *Review Writer's Craft*

© Harcourt

Extended Writing/Test Prep

OBJECTIVES

- To apply the craft of *voice* and *word choice* in a longer piece of writing
- To practice selecting a topic and beginning the prewriting process in an assessment scenario

Teach/Model   Tell students that the first two pages of the lesson will provide an opportunity to choose a topic for a longer writing activity. Explain that they will have the chance to plan their writing by using the prewriting process. Read aloud the introduction to Part A. Tell students they will have a choice of responding to a writing prompt, continuing a piece of writing they began earlier in the unit, or choosing a new topic.

Guided Practice   Review the writing forms covered in the unit. Read aloud the call-outs for each Student Model in the lesson where the form was taught:

- A Character Description: Lesson 1, Page 11
- An Autobiographical Composition: Lesson 2, Page 17
- An Autobiographical Narrative: Lesson 3, Page 23
- A News Article: Lesson 4, Page 29

Have students complete Part B independently.

LESSON 5: WRITING TEST PRACTICE

Name _____

Extended Writing/Test Prep

Extended Writing/Test Prep

On the first two pages of this lesson, you will use what you have learned about voice and word choice to write a longer written work.

A. Read the three choices below. Put a star by the writing activity you would like to do.
   1. Respond to a Writing Prompt

   Writing Situation: We are all influenced by the people around us, especially by the members of our family.

   Directions for Writing: Think about a member of your family that has had a positive influence on your life. Now write an autobiographical narrative about a time that you have spent with this family member. Use descriptive words to describe the family member and to make your feelings and opinions clear to the reader.

   2. Choose one of the pieces of writing you started in this unit:
   - a character description paragraph (page 10)
   - an autobiographical composition (page 16)
   - an autobiographical narrative (page 22)

   Revise and expand your work into a complete piece of writing. Use what you have learned about voice and word choice.

   3. Choose a topic you would like to write about. You may write a character description, an autobiographical composition, an autobiographical narrative, or a news article. Use descriptive words to make your writing come alive and to make your viewpoint clear. Also, use a strong lead to draw your reader in.

B. Use the space below and on the next page to plan your writing.

TOPIC: _____

WRITING FORM: _____

HOW I WILL ORGANIZE MY WRITING: _____

_____

Writer's Companion • UNIT 1
Lesson 5 *Writing Test Practice*   **32**

Reaching All Learners

BELOW LEVEL

Have students restate the choices for the Extended Writing activity. Encourage students who have had difficulty choosing a topic in the past to work on a piece of writing from earlier in the unit.

ADVANCED

Encourage students who choose to work on an earlier piece of writing to push themselves to drastically revise the old material by adding descriptive words, sensory details, and personal details.

ENGLISH-LANGUAGE LEARNERS

Work individually with students, helping them reread Part A and discuss the choices for the writing activity. Encourage students to explain why they chose a writing activity.

© Harcourt

Extended Writing/Test Prep

OBJECTIVES
- To use a graphic organizer to plan a piece of writing
- To use the steps of the writing process to complete a longer piece of writing

Standard: LA.5.3.2.1 use a pre-writing plan

Teach/Model Read aloud the introduction to Part C, telling students to use a graphic organizer to generate and organize ideas. (They can use a new organizer or one from earlier lessons in the unit.) Have students review the web from Lesson 3, Page 22. Point out how the writer used the web to generate ideas. Invite a volunteer to share a topic for Part B and model how to use a web.

Guided Practice Once students have chosen an organizer, have them copy it into the space provided in Part C. Remind students that the prewriting process is where they should generate as many ideas as possible. They should not worry about conventions until the draft and revision steps.

Independent Writing

Draft, Revise, Publish Remind students to use their graphic organizers as they draft their piece of writing. Tell students to revise their work by adding descriptive words and personal details.

LESSON 5: WRITING TEST PRACTICE

Name _____

Extended Writing/Test Prep

C. In the space below, draw a graphic organizer that will help you plan your writing. Fill in the graphic organizer. Write additional notes on the lines below.

Notes

_____
_____
_____
_____
_____
_____
_____
_____

D. Do your writing on another sheet of paper.

33

Writer's Companion • UNIT 1
Lesson 5 *Writing Test Practice*

SHARING AND DISCUSSING

Once students have chosen a graphic organizer and copied it onto the student page for Part C, invite volunteers to share and discuss their choice with the class. Encourage volunteers to read any titles or labels they have written on the organizer and to discuss how they plan to complete it. Encourage a volunteer to draw his or her organizer on the board. To demonstrate how it might be used, have students offer suggestions for completing it. Encourage students to discuss other types of graphic organizers that might also be effective for generating and organizing ideas.

© Harcourt

Answering Multiple-Choice Questions

OBJECTIVES

- To become familiar with test items that require interpreting a writing plan
- To learn how to read the answer choices and identify the correct one

Teach/Model Read aloud the directions for Part A. Explain that the questions will help them learn how to interpret the information on a graphic organizer. Read aloud Manuel's Writing Plan. Model answering Item 1 by pointing out that the writer is using the plan to organize details that support his viewpoint. Model answering the question by eliminating A, explaining that a news article would not include the writer's viewpoint. Have students choose from the remaining options by choosing the form that would be best supported by the details.

Guided Practice Guide students in completing Item 2, asking them which detail does not relate to being a good student.

Independent Writing Practice Have students complete Item 3 independently.

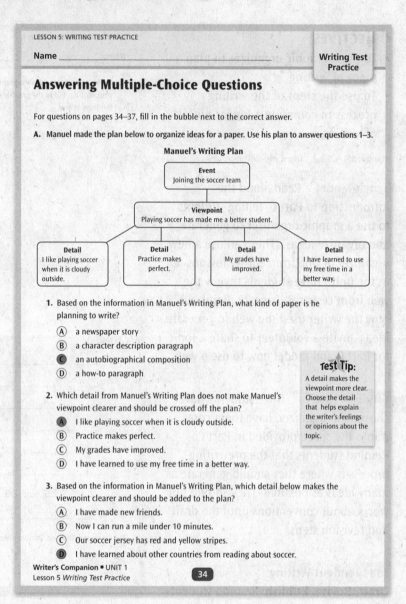

LESSON 5: WRITING TEST PRACTICE

Name _____

Writing Test Practice

Answering Multiple-Choice Questions

For questions on pages 34–37, fill in the bubble next to the correct answer.

A. Manuel made the plan below to organize ideas for a paper. Use his plan to answer questions 1–3.

Manuel's Writing Plan

Event
Joining the soccer team

Viewpoint
Playing soccer has made me a better student.

Detail
I like playing soccer when it is cloudy outside.

Detail
Practice makes perfect.

Detail
My grades have improved.

Detail
I have learned to use my free time in a better way.

1. Based on the information in Manuel's Writing Plan, what kind of paper is he planning to write?
   - (A) a newspaper story
   - (B) a character description paragraph
   - (C) an autobiographical composition
   - (D) a how-to paragraph

2. Which detail from Manuel's Writing Plan does not make Manuel's viewpoint clearer and should be crossed off the plan?
   - (A) I like playing soccer when it is cloudy outside.
   - (B) Practice makes perfect.
   - (C) My grades have improved.
   - (D) I have learned to use my free time in a better way.

3. Based on the information in Manuel's Writing Plan, which detail below makes the viewpoint clearer and should be added to the plan?
   - (A) I have made new friends.
   - (B) Now I can run a mile under 10 minutes.
   - (C) Our soccer jersey has red and yellow stripes.
   - (D) I have learned about other countries from reading about soccer.

Test Tip:
A detail makes the viewpoint more clear. Choose the detail that helps explain the writer's feelings or opinions about the topic.

Writer's Companion • UNIT 1
Lesson 5 *Writing Test Practice*

34

USING ACADEMIC LANGUAGE

Tell students that most tests contain what is known as academic language, which might be different from the language they are used to reading. Tell students that they might be accustomed to using graphic organizers, but they might not be accustomed to answering test questions about graphic organizers. Point out the term *writing plan* and explain that it is another term for graphic organizer. Also point out that the phrase "based on the information in Manuel's Writing Plan" is asking them to use the writing in the graphic organizer to answer the question.

Answering Multiple-Choice Questions (cont.)

OBJECTIVES

- To become familiar with a multiple-choice format that involves reading a passage
- To develop a strategy of choosing the word that best completes a sentence

Teach/Model Read aloud the directions to Part B. Explain that some multiple-choice tests will require them to read a passage before answering the questions. Read aloud the passage and then Item 1. Point out to students that each sentence of the passage is numbered to help them quickly find the sentences that the questions ask about. Model answering Item 1 by rereading sentence 1 and then reading choices A–D. Point out that students should choose B because it uses the most effective sensory details, such as *frog in my throat* and *trembling*.

Guided Practice Guide students in choosing the correct answer for Item 2 by reminding them that the lead sentence should spark the readers' interest. Point out that the best answer, A, uses a question that forces readers to think about the topic of the paragraph.

Independent Writing Practice Have students complete Item 3 independently.

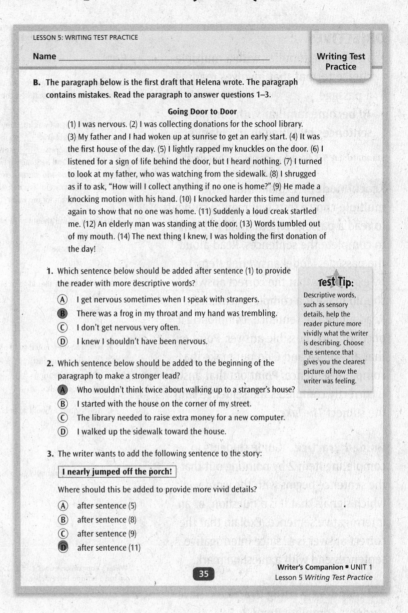

LESSON 5: WRITING TEST PRACTICE

Name _____

Writing Test Practice

B. The paragraph below is the first draft that Helena wrote. The paragraph contains mistakes. Read the paragraph to answer questions 1–3.

Going Door to Door

(1) I was nervous. (2) I was collecting donations for the school library. (3) My father and I had woken up at sunrise to get an early start. (4) It was the first house of the day. (5) I lightly rapped my knuckles on the door. (6) I listened for a sign of life behind the door, but I heard nothing. (7) I turned to look at my father, who was watching from the sidewalk. (8) I shrugged as if to ask, "How will I collect anything if no one is home?" (9) He made a knocking motion with his hand. (10) I knocked harder this time and turned again to show that no one was home. (11) Suddenly a loud creak startled me. (12) An elderly man was standing at the door. (13) Words tumbled out of my mouth. (14) The next thing I knew, I was holding the first donation of the day!

1. Which sentence below should be added after sentence (1) to provide the reader with more descriptive words?

 (A) I get nervous sometimes when I speak with strangers.
 (B) There was a frog in my throat and my hand was trembling.
 (C) I don't get nervous very often.
 (D) I knew I shouldn't have been nervous.

2. Which sentence below should be added to the beginning of the paragraph to make a stronger lead?

 (A) Who wouldn't think twice about walking up to a stranger's house?
 (B) I started with the house on the corner of my street.
 (C) The library needed to raise extra money for a new computer.
 (D) I walked up the sidewalk toward the house.

3. The writer wants to add the following sentence to the story:

 I nearly jumped off the porch!

 Where should this be added to provide more vivid details?

 (A) after sentence (5)
 (B) after sentence (8)
 (C) after sentence (9)
 (D) after sentence (11)

Test Tip:
Descriptive words, such as sensory details, help the reader picture more vividly what the writer is describing. Choose the sentence that gives you the clearest picture of how the writer was feeling.

35

Writer's Companion • UNIT 1
Lesson 5 *Writing Test Practice*

ASSESSING STUDENT RESPONSES

If students are consistently answering test items incorrectly, they might be misreading the directions. Ask the student to restate the directions to Part B and for Items 1–3. Make sure the student understands that the number in parentheses comes before the sentence, not after. For Item 1, have student identify sentence (1) in the passage and explain, or point to, where the new sentence should be added. For Item 2, make sure the student understands that the new sentence should come before Sentence (1).

© Harcourt

Answering Multiple-Choice Questions (cont.)

OBJECTIVES
- To become familiar with a multiple choice format that involves reading a passage
- To become familiar with completing sentences by filling in the blanks

Standard: LA.5.3.4.4 use parts of speech correctly

Teach/Model Explain that some multiple-choice tests will require students to read a passage and then fill in blanks to complete the sentences. Read aloud the passage. Model answering Item 1 by explaining that the correct answer should make it a complete sentence. Read aloud the sentence, completing it once for each possible answer. Point out that answers A and C do not make it a complete sentence. Point out that answer B correctly completes the sentence with the subject *The lake.*

Guided Practice Guide students in completing Item 2 by pointing out that the sentence begins with the word *why*, which signals that it is a question, or an interrogative sentence. Explain that the correct answer is A, since interrogative sentences end with a question mark.

Independent Writing Practice Have students complete Items 3–5 independently.

LESSON 5: WRITING TEST PRACTICE

Name _____

Writing Test Practice

C. Read the story "Meant for the Water." Choose the word, words, or punctuation mark that best completes questions 1–4.

Meant for the Water

When I was little, my brother Steven used to impress me by swimming across Star Lake and back. __(1)__ wasn't huge. It wasn't very deep either. Still, I was impressed. Why was I impressed __(2)__ Steven __(3)__ like an athlete. His arms and legs were long and skinny, and he slouched when he walked. In spite of his appearance, he used to make the round-trip journey effortlessly. On land he seemed awkward, but in the water he was as graceful as a dolphin. The difference was absolutely amazing __(4)__ I think Steven was meant for the water __(5)__

1. Which answer should go in blank (1)?
   - Ⓐ Really
   - Ⓑ The Lake
   - Ⓒ Actually

2. Which answer should go in blank (2)?
   - Ⓐ ?
   - Ⓑ !
   - Ⓒ .

3. Which answer should go in blank (3)?
   - Ⓐ swimming just
   - Ⓑ not appearing
   - Ⓒ didn't look

4. Which answer should go in blank (4)?
   - Ⓐ ?
   - Ⓑ !
   - Ⓒ ,

5. Which answer should go in blank (5)?
   - Ⓐ ?
   - Ⓑ ,
   - Ⓒ .

Test Tips:
Complete sentences have both a subject and a predicate. A subject names whom or what the sentence is about. The predicate tells what the subject is or does. Choose the word that makes the sentence complete.

Writer's Companion • UNIT 1
Lesson 5 *Writing Test Practice*

36

Reaching All Learners

BELOW LEVEL
If students are having difficulty with a test item, suggest that they rewrite the sentence from the passage next to the item. Students might find that the proximity enables them to better visualize the answer.

ADVANCED
Remind students writing above grade level to check their work in the event that they finish the test practice early. Point out that they might have filled in the wrong bubble, even though they knew the right answer.

ENGLISH-LANGUAGE LEARNERS
Extend the time allowed for the practice test for the less fluent English speakers. If time permits, you may give each student enough time to complete the test. Challenge students to decrease the test-taking time for each unit.

© Harcourt

Answering Multiple-Choice Questions (cont.)

OBJECTIVES
- To become familiar with a multiple-choice format that involves the type of correction needed
- To learn the strategy of identifying how to correct sentences

Standard: LA.5.3.4.3 use correct punctuation

Teach/Model   Tell students that some writing tests include multiple-choice questions that ask them to select which type of correction is needed in a sentence. Read aloud the directions to Part D and Item 1. Model answering Item 1 by reading aloud the sentence and then rereading the underlined portion. Ask what is wrong with those words. Elicit that *granfather* is spelled wrong. There is a spelling error, so the correct answer is C.

Guided Practice   Guide students in completing Item 2. Read aloud the Test Tip and the underlined portion of Item 2. Ask students to circle the mistakes. *(cant and Wow?)* Then tell students that they should pick the type of mistake they both are. *(Punctuation error)*

Independent Writing Practice   Have students complete Items 3–5 independently.

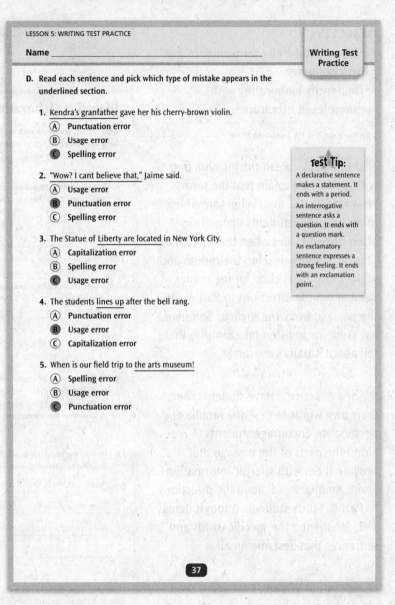

LESSON 5: WRITING TEST PRACTICE

Name _____

Writing Test Practice

D. Read each sentence and pick which type of mistake appears in the underlined section.

1. Kendra's granfather gave her his cherry-brown violin.
   - (A) Punctuation error
   - (B) Usage error
   - (C) Spelling error

2. "Wow? I cant believe that," Jaime said.
   - (A) Usage error
   - (B) Punctuation error
   - (C) Spelling error

3. The Statue of Liberty are located in New York City.
   - (A) Capitalization error
   - (B) Spelling error
   - (C) Usage error

4. The students lines up after the bell rang.
   - (A) Punctuation error
   - (B) Usage error
   - (C) Capitalization error

5. When is our field trip to the arts museum!
   - (A) Spelling error
   - (B) Usage error
   - (C) Punctuation error

Test Tip:
A declarative sentence makes a statement. It ends with a period.
An interrogative sentence asks a question. It ends with a question mark.
An exclamatory sentence expresses a strong feeling. It ends with an exclamation point.

37

SHARING AND DISCUSSING

Have students share their answers to the items in Parts A–D with a partner. If partners should have different answers, have them each explain why they chose their answers. Also encourage partners to discuss the test-taking strategies that they found to be most helpful.

© Harcourt

Identify: Elaborating with Examples

OBJECTIVES
- To understand the term *elaborating with examples*
- To identify elaborating with examples in literature

Standard: LA.5.3.1.1 generate ideas

Teach/Model   Read the introduction with students. Explain that the term *elaborate* means to develop something more fully. Tell students that writers often use examples when they elaborate. This helps them develop their ideas and make those ideas clear for the reader. Read aloud the directions to Part A and the passage from *The Night of San Juan*. Ask students to listen for examples that tell about Amalia's character.

Guided Practice   Have students use their own words to describe Amalia's personality. Encourage students to read aloud the parts of the passage that provide them with specific information about Amalia. Read aloud the directions to Part B. Guide students through Items 1–2, identifying the specific words and sentences that describe Amalia.

Independent Writing Practice   Read aloud the directions to Part C. Then have students complete Part C on their own.

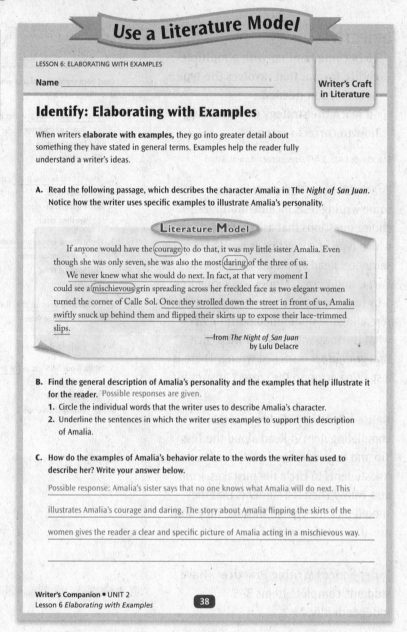

Use a Literature Model

LESSON 6: ELABORATING WITH EXAMPLES

Name _____

Writer's Craft in Literature

Identify: Elaborating with Examples

When writers **elaborate with examples,** they go into greater detail about something they have stated in general terms. Examples help the reader fully understand a writer's ideas.

A. Read the following passage, which describes the character Amalia in The *Night of San Juan*. Notice how the writer uses specific examples to illustrate Amalia's personality.

Literature Model

If anyone would have the courage to do that, it was my little sister Amalia. Even though she was only seven, she was also the most daring of the three of us.
    We never knew what she would do next. In fact, at that very moment I could see a mischievous grin spreading across her freckled face as two elegant women turned the corner of Calle Sol. Once they strolled down the street in front of us, Amalia swiftly snuck up behind them and flipped their skirts up to expose their lace-trimmed slips.

—from *The Night of San Juan*
by Lulu Delacre

B. Find the general description of Amalia's personality and the examples that help illustrate it for the reader. Possible responses are given.
1. Circle the individual words that the writer uses to describe Amalia's character.
2. Underline the sentences in which the writer uses examples to support this description of Amalia.

C. How do the examples of Amalia's behavior relate to the words the writer has used to describe her? Write your answer below.

Possible response: Amalia's sister says that no one knows what Amalia will do next. This

illustrates Amalia's courage and daring. The story about Amalia flipping the skirts of the

women gives the reader a clear and specific picture of Amalia acting in a mischievous way.

Writer's Companion • UNIT 2
Lesson 6 *Elaborating with Examples*

38

EXTENDING THE CONCEPT: ELABORATION

To prepare students to complete Part C independently, clarify that the question is asking them to describe the relationship between the specific words (*courage, daring, mischievous*) the writer uses and the examples the writer gives. Provide students with practice identifying this type of relationship. On the board write specific descriptive words, such as *shy, energetic,* or *unfriendly*. Then ask students to give examples of the type of action or behavior that illustrates each word.

© Harcourt

Explore: Elaborating with Examples

OBJECTIVES

- To understand the ways in which elaborating with examples strengthens writing
- To write sentences that elaborate with examples

Standard: LA.5.3.3.3 express ideas vividly

Teach/Model　Use the graphic organizer to review how elaborating with examples strengthens writing. You might wish to illustrate each concept. For example, you might provide students with a main idea and a list of supporting details and then discuss how each detail elaborates on the main idea.

Guided Practice　Read aloud the first example in Part A. Point out that the example (the boy uses words his father doesn't know) provides support for the idea that the boy has a good vocabulary. Read through each sentence with students, identifying the idea presented in each one. For additional help in completing Part A, see *Writer's Strategy*.

Independent Writing Practice　Read Part B aloud. Explain that students are asked to identify the reasons the children are afraid of the grandmother.

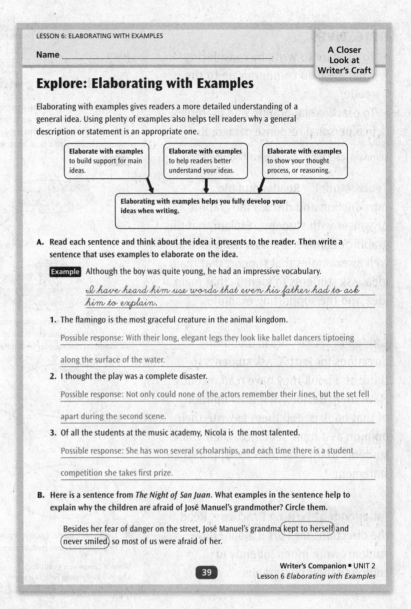

LESSON 6: ELABORATING WITH EXAMPLES

Name _____

A Closer Look at Writer's Craft

Explore: Elaborating with Examples

Elaborating with examples gives readers a more detailed understanding of a general idea. Using plenty of examples also helps tell readers why a general description or statement is an appropriate one.

| Elaborate with examples to build support for main ideas. | Elaborate with examples to help readers better understand your ideas. | Elaborate with examples to show your thought process, or reasoning. |

Elaborating with examples helps you fully develop your ideas when writing.

A. Read each sentence and think about the idea it presents to the reader. Then write a sentence that uses examples to elaborate on the idea.

Example　Although the boy was quite young, he had an impressive vocabulary.

I have heard him use words that even his father had to ask him to explain.

1. The flamingo is the most graceful creature in the animal kingdom.

Possible response: With their long, elegant legs they look like ballet dancers tiptoeing along the surface of the water.

2. I thought the play was a complete disaster.

Possible response: Not only could none of the actors remember their lines, but the set fell apart during the second scene.

3. Of all the students at the music academy, Nicola is the most talented.

Possible response: She has won several scholarships, and each time there is a student competition she takes first prize.

B. Here is a sentence from *The Night of San Juan*. What examples in the sentence help to explain why the children are afraid of José Manuel's grandmother? Circle them.

Besides her fear of danger on the street, José Manuel's grandma (kept to herself) and (never smiled) so most of us were afraid of her.

39

Writer's Companion ▪ UNIT 2
Lesson 6 *Elaborating with Examples*

WRITER'S STRATEGY: BRAINSTORMING

Tell students that *brainstorming* is a good way to begin thinking about ideas they can use in their writing. Explain that the point of brainstorming is to generate a lot of ideas without thinking too hard about whether the ideas will necessarily work. After a number of ideas are generated, students can look them over and determine which are most useful. As a class, brainstorm ideas for examples that will support the main idea in Sentence 1 of Part A. Then invite students to work individually to brainstorm ideas for Sentences 2 and 3. As they complete Part A, students should refer to their brainstorming lists for ideas.

© Harcourt

Use: Elaborating with Examples

OBJECTIVES
- To prepare to write by considering what ideas to communicate to the reader
- To practice elaborating with examples in a personal response paragraph

Standard: LA.5.3.2.1 use a pre-writing plan

Teach/Model   Read aloud the introduction and discuss the graphic organizer with students. Explain that this graphic organizer shows a main idea as well as examples that support that main idea. Ask students to identify that main idea and the supporting examples.

Guided Practice   Read aloud the directions for Part A. Ask students to think of a book they have read recently. Have them decide what their opinion of that book is. Tell them to write their opinion as a topic sentence. Then guide students to list examples to support their statement.

Independent Writing Practice   Read the directions for Part B aloud. Have students work independently to complete their paragraphs.

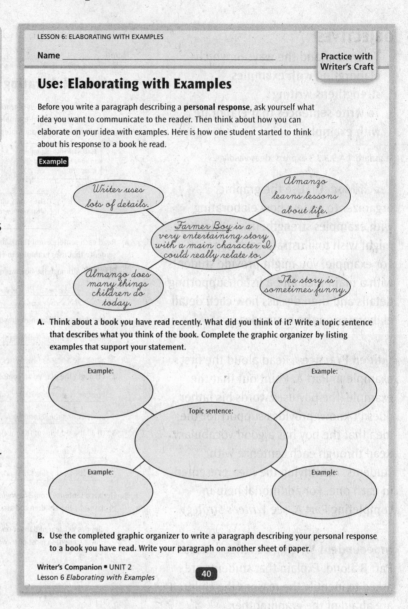

LESSON 6: ELABORATING WITH EXAMPLES

Name _____

Practice with Writer's Craft

Use: Elaborating with Examples

Before you write a paragraph describing a **personal response**, ask yourself what idea you want to communicate to the reader. Then think about how you can elaborate on your idea with examples. Here is how one student started to think about his response to a book he read.

Example

- Writer uses lots of details.
- Almanzo learns lessons about life.
- Farmer Boy is a very entertaining story with a main character I could really relate to.
- Almanzo does many things children do today.
- The story is sometimes funny.

A. Think about a book you have read recently. What did you think of it? Write a topic sentence that describes what you think of the book. Complete the graphic organizer by listing examples that support your statement.

Example: Example: Topic sentence: Example: Example:

B. Use the completed graphic organizer to write a paragraph describing your personal response to a book you have read. Write your paragraph on another sheet of paper.

Writer's Companion • UNIT 2
Lesson 6 *Elaborating with Examples*   40

SHARING AND DISCUSSING

Invite students to share their graphic organizers with a partner. Partners should read and discuss each other's topic sentences and examples. Have them identify the main idea expressed in the topic sentence and discuss how well each example elaborates on that main idea. Students should use this discussion as an opportunity to evaluate and refine their graphic organizers before they begin writing.

© Harcourt

The Parts of a Personal Response Paragraph

OBJECTIVES
- To understand the parts of a personal response paragraph
- To analyze a Student Model

Standard: LA.5.3.3.1 evaluate for writing traits

Teach/Model   Read aloud the introduction and discuss the definition of a *personal response paragraph*. Tell students they will read an example of a personal response paragraph written by a fifth grader. Read the model aloud, asking students to listen for the writer's opinion and how he supports it with examples. After you have read through the model once, read the text in each call-out box and ask students to identify where each organizational feature occurs in the paragraph.

Guided Practice   Call students' attention to the items below the model. Have students circle the topic sentence and underline the sentence that states the writer's opinion.

Independent Writing Practice   Have students answer items 3 and 4 on their own. Ask students to share and discuss their responses.

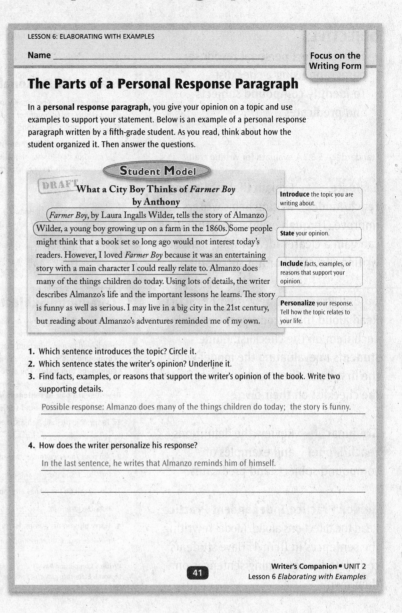

LESSON 6: ELABORATING WITH EXAMPLES

Name _____

Focus on the Writing Form

The Parts of a Personal Response Paragraph

In a **personal response paragraph,** you give your opinion on a topic and use examples to support your statement. Below is an example of a personal response paragraph written by a fifth-grade student. As you read, think about how the student organized it. Then answer the questions.

Student Model

DRAFT

What a City Boy Thinks of *Farmer Boy*
by Anthony

Farmer Boy, by Laura Ingalls Wilder, tells the story of Almanzo Wilder, a young boy growing up on a farm in the 1860s. Some people might think that a book set so long ago would not interest today's readers. However, I loved *Farmer Boy* because it was an entertaining story with a main character I could really relate to. Almanzo does many of the things children do today. Using lots of details, the writer describes Almanzo's life and the important lessons he learns. The story is funny as well as serious. I may live in a big city in the 21st century, but reading about Almanzo's adventures reminded me of my own.

Introduce the topic you are writing about.

State your opinion.

Include facts, examples, or reasons that support your opinion.

Personalize your response. Tell how the topic relates to your life.

1. Which sentence introduces the topic? Circle it.
2. Which sentence states the writer's opinion? Underline it.
3. Find facts, examples, or reasons that support the writer's opinion of the book. Write two supporting details.

   Possible response: Almanzo does many of the things children do today; the story is funny.

4. How does the writer personalize his response?

   In the last sentence, he writes that Almanzo reminds him of himself.

41

Writer's Companion • UNIT 2
Lesson 6 *Elaborating with Examples*

EXTENDING THE CONCEPT: PERSONAL RESPONSE AND WRITER'S VOICE

Encourage students to discuss what it means to "personalize" something. Invite students to think of everyday examples of personalizing things, such as personalizing a notebook with stickers. Guide students to relate these examples to the idea of writing. Explain that in successful writing, the writer uses his or her personal voice to give readers a sense of the person behind the words. Read passages from different types of writing and ask students to describe the voice they hear. Then ask students to discuss how they can bring their own voice to their personal response paragraphs.

Evaluate a Personal Response Paragraph/Grammar

OBJECTIVES
- To evaluate a personal response paragraph using a checklist
- To identify compound subjects and predicates

Standard: LA.5.3.3.1 evaluate for writing traits

Evaluate Teach/Model Explain that evaluating writing helps writers improve. Through evaluation, students can gain a clearer idea of what makes writing successful or not successful.

Guided Practice/Independent Practice
Read aloud the introductory text and each item on the checklist. Guide students in evaluating the model with the first item. Then have students finish the checklist on their own.

Grammar Teach/Model Review the definitions and examples of compound subjects and predicates.

Guided Practice/Independent Practice
Read the directions aloud. Model rewriting the sentences in Item 1. Have students complete the remaining sentences on their own.

LESSON 6: ELABORATING WITH EXAMPLES

Name _____

Evaluating the Student Model

Evaluate a Personal Response Paragraph

When you evaluate a personal response paragraph, ask yourself whether the writer clearly stated his or her opinion and supported that opinion with plenty of facts, examples, or reasons.

Now use the checklist to evaluate the Student Model. Put a check in the box next to each thing the writer did well. If you do not think the writer did a good job, do not check the box.

- ☐ The topic is introduced.
- ☐ The writer's opinion is clearly stated.
- ☐ There are many specific examples to support the writer's opinion.
- ☐ The writer connects the topic to his or her life.
- ☐ The paragraph is organized in a logical way.

Writer's Grammar
Compound Subjects and Predicates

A compound subject is two or more subjects, joined by a conjunction, that have the same verb. Likewise, a compound predicate has two or more verbs, also joined by a conjunction, that have the same subject.
Compound Subject Joshua and his friend Amina are studying for tomorrow's quiz.
Compound Predicate The performers will sing, dance, or play an instrument.

Rewrite each pair of sentences with a compound subject or compound predicate. Draw a line under each compound subject. Circle each compound predicate.

1. Tanja stole the ball. Tanja kicked the ball. Tanja scored a goal. Sentences may vary.
   Possible response: Tanja stole the ball, kicked the ball, and scored a goal.

2. Xin read *The Friends* over the summer. Xin's sister read *The Friends* over the summer.
   Possible response: Xin and her sister read *The Friends* over the summer.

3. Carlos will do the dishes after supper. Peter will do the dishes after supper.
   Possible response: Carlos or Peter will do the dishes after supper.

4. Harry puts on his glasses. Harry looks closely at the mysterious note.
   Possible response: Harry puts on his glasses and looks closely at the mysterious note.

Writer's Companion • UNIT 2
Lesson 6 *Elaborating with Examples*   42

Reaching All Learners

BELOW LEVEL	ADVANCED	ENGLISH-LANGUAGE LEARNERS
Have partners take turns reading their grammar sentences aloud. Have students discuss whether the new sentences will require a compound subject or predicate before writing the final sentences.	Have students write two versions of the new grammar sentences, combining them a different way each time. Ask students to share their sentences, having students identify which version works best and why.	Suggest that students develop ideas for combining sentences orally before they work to combine them in writing.

© Harcourt

Revise: Adding Examples

OBJECTIVES
- To revise by adding examples
- To revise their own writing by adding examples

Teach/Model Discuss why revising is an important part of the writing process. Emphasize that revising helps writers improve their work. Tell students that one way to improve writing is to add examples. Discuss the importance of adding ideas that are relevant to the topic and that support the ideas expressed in the writing.

Guided Practice Read aloud the introduction and the example. Ask students to compare the sentence before and after revision. Then talk with them about why the revised sentence is an improvement. Afterwards, read the directions to Part A and model how to revise it. Read through the words in the Word Bank and invite students to add their own words to the list. Remind them that the Word Bank is a resource they can use for ideas as they revise the sentences.

Independent Writing Practice Have students revise the sentences in Part A. Then read the directions to Part B and ask them to complete their writing independently.

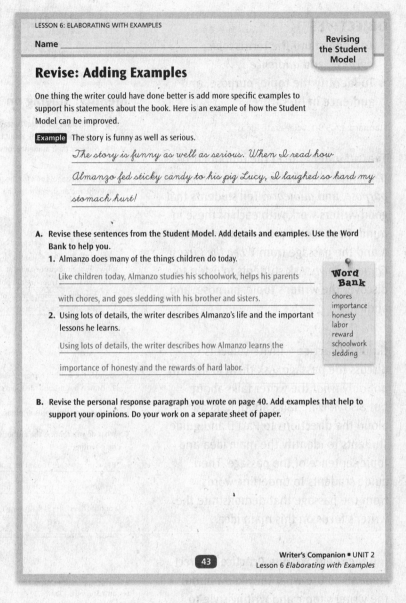

WRITER'S STRATEGY: SENTENCES

Tell students that when they add examples to sentences, they may also wish to revise the types of sentence they have written. Point out that the sentence in Item 1 of Part A is a simple sentence; it has neither a compound subject nor compound predicate. Show students how the sentence was revised with what Almanzo does. Explain that the new sentence may be rewritten with a compound predicate. Review other sentence variations, discussing how each type may help them improve their work.

Identify: Staying on Topic

OBJECTIVES

- To understand the terms *topic*, *purpose*, and *audience*
- To identify the topic, purpose, and audience in literature

Standard: LA.5.3.1.1 generate ideas

Teach/Model Read the introductory paragraph and discuss the terms *topic*, *purpose,* and *audience*. Tell students that good writers work with each of these in mind. Read aloud the directions to Part A and the passage from *When the Circus Came to Town*. Ask students to listen to discover the writer's topic, purpose, and audience.

Guided Practice Invite students to discuss the passage. Ask them to identify not only *what* the writer talks about but also *how* he talks about it. Read aloud the directions to Part B and guide students to identify the main idea and topic sentence of the passage. Then guide students to underline words from the passage that demonstrate the writer's focus on this main idea.

Independent Writing Practice Direct students to use what they know about the writer's topic and writing style to help them determine his purpose and audience.

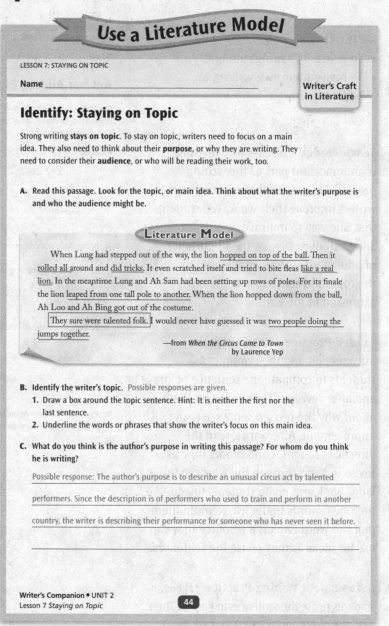

Use a Literature Model

Name _____

Writer's Craft in Literature

Identify: Staying on Topic

Strong writing **stays on topic**. To stay on topic, writers need to focus on a main idea. They also need to think about their **purpose**, or why they are writing. They need to consider their **audience**, or who will be reading their work, too.

A. Read this passage. Look for the topic, or main idea. Think about what the writer's purpose is and who the audience might be.

Literature Model

When Lung had stepped out of the way, the lion hopped on top of the ball. Then it rolled all around and did tricks. It even scratched itself and tried to bite fleas like a real lion. In the meantime Lung and Ah Sam had been setting up rows of poles. For its finale the lion leaped from one tall pole to another. When the lion hopped down from the ball, Ah Loo and Ah Bing got out of the costume.

They sure were talented folk. I would never have guessed it was two people doing the jumps together.

—from *When the Circus Came to Town* by Laurence Yep

B. Identify the writer's topic. Possible responses are given.
1. Draw a box around the topic sentence. Hint: It is neither the first nor the last sentence.
2. Underline the words or phrases that show the writer's focus on this main idea.

C. What do you think is the author's purpose in writing this passage? For whom do you think he is writing?

Possible response: The author's purpose is to describe an unusual circus act by talented

performers. Since the description is of performers who used to train and perform in another

country, the writer is describing their performance for someone who has never seen it before.

_____

EXTENDING THE CONCEPT: PURPOSE AND AUDIENCE

Explain that in order for writers to establish a focus, they need to be very clear about the purpose and audience for their writing. Ask students to discuss how they think audience and purpose affects how a writer approaches a topic. Divide students into small groups and assign each group a purpose and audience, for example, to inform the readers of a newspaper. Ask students to revise a sentence from the passage to reflect this purpose and audience. Have groups share and discuss their sentences.

© Harcourt

Explore: Staying on Topic

OBJECTIVES

- To understand how topic, audience, and purpose contribute to focused writing
- To identify writer's purpose for sample sentences

Standard: LA.5.3.1.2 determine purpose/audience

Teach/Model Using the graphic organizer, talk with students about how writing with the topic, audience, and purpose in mind helps make writing more effective. Guide students to recognize the importance of considering precisely *what, for whom,* and *why* they are writing.

Guided Practice Read the directions to Part A and discuss the example with the class. Ask students how they know that the purpose of the sentence isn't to entertain or persuade or some other purpose. Guide students through Items 1–3 of Part A.

Independent Writing Practice Read Part B aloud. Have students read the paragraph silently, telling them to think about the main idea of the paragraph. Then invite students to write a topic sentence that expresses this main idea.

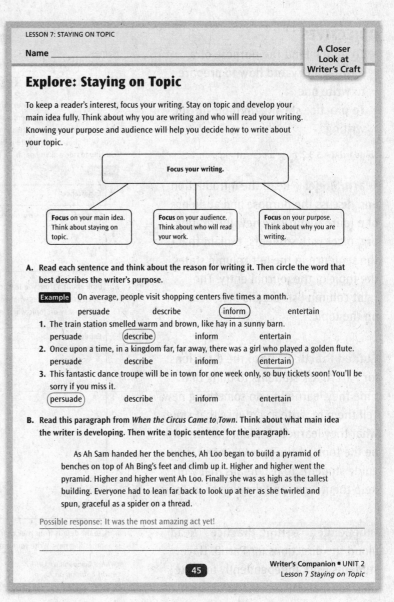

LESSON 7: STAYING ON TOPIC

Name _____

A Closer Look at Writer's Craft

Explore: Staying on Topic

To keep a reader's interest, focus your writing. Stay on topic and develop your main idea fully. Think about why you are writing and who will read your writing. Knowing your purpose and audience will help you decide how to write about your topic.

Focus your writing.

Focus on your main idea. Think about staying on topic.

Focus on your audience. Think about who will read your work.

Focus on your purpose. Think about why you are writing.

A. Read each sentence and think about the reason for writing it. Then circle the word that best describes the writer's purpose.

Example   On average, people visit shopping centers five times a month.

persuade   describe   (inform)   entertain

1. The train station smelled warm and brown, like hay in a sunny barn.
   persuade   (describe)   inform   entertain

2. Once upon a time, in a kingdom far, far away, there was a girl who played a golden flute.
   persuade   describe   inform   (entertain)

3. This fantastic dance troupe will be in town for one week only, so buy tickets soon! You'll be sorry if you miss it.
   (persuade)   describe   inform   entertain

B. Read this paragraph from *When the Circus Came to Town*. Think about what main idea the writer is developing. Then write a topic sentence for the paragraph.

As Ah Sam handed her the benches, Ah Loo began to build a pyramid of benches on top of Ah Bing's feet and climb up it. Higher and higher went the pyramid. Higher and higher went Ah Loo. Finally she was as high as the tallest building. Everyone had to lean far back to look up at her as she twirled and spun, graceful as a spider on a thread.

Possible response: It was the most amazing act yet!

_____

45   **Writer's Companion •** UNIT 2
Lesson 7 *Staying on Topic*

SHARING AND DISCUSSING

Invite students to read aloud their responses to Part B. Ask them to explain how their sentences express the main idea and how they chose their words to fit the audience and purpose of the paragraph. Record some students' sentences on the board. Encourage students to discuss the similarities and differences among the sentences. Point out that similar ideas can be expressed in many different ways.

Use: Staying on Topic

OBJECTIVES
- To understand the purpose of a journal entry and how to prepare to write one
- To practice staying on topic during writing

Standard: LA.5.3.2.1 use a pre-writing plan

Teach/Model Read the introduction and discuss the purpose and audience of a journal entry. Review the graphic organizer with students. Explain that the sentence in the left column states the topic of the journal entry. The right column lists details that focus on the topic.

Guided Practice Read the directions for Part A. Ask students to think of a time they learned to do something new. Tell them to write a sentence that states what they learned. Explain that this will be the topic of the journal entry. Then guide students to list details that will help them focus and develop their topic.

Independent Writing Practice Read aloud the directions for Part B. Have students work independently to write their journal entries.

LESSON 7: STAYING ON TOPIC

Name _____

Practice with Writer's Craft

Use: Staying on Topic

One purpose for writing a **journal entry** is to remember an experience or event. The audience for a journal entry is yourself, although you may share the entry with others. Before you write a journal entry, list details that you will use to focus your chosen topic. Here is how one student started to record details about learning to ride a skateboard.

Example

Experience	Details
I learned to ride a skateboard.	• purple board with red and black flames • birthday wish • I was nervous but determined.

A. Think about a time you learned to do something new. In the left column, write a sentence that states what you learned. In the right column, list details that will help you stay on topic when you write.

Experience	Details

B. Use the details from your chart to write a journal entry describing a time you learned to do something new. Write your entry on another sheet of paper.

Writer's Companion • UNIT 2
Lesson 7 *Staying on Topic*

46

Reaching All Learners

BELOW LEVEL
Once students have chosen a topic, have them brainstorm details they might include. Help students review their brainstorming list. Have them circle details that are on topic and cross out ones that are not.

ADVANCED
Ask students to include sensory details, specific word choices, or ideas for similes and metaphors in their graphic organizers.

ENGLISH-LANGUAGE LEARNERS
A journal entry is a very personal piece of writing. With this in mind, encourage students to think of words, phrases, or sayings from their first language that would be appropriate to include in their journal entry.

© Harcourt

The Parts of a Journal Entry

USE A STUDENT MODEL
- To understand the parts of a journal entry
- To analyze a Student Model

Teach/Model   Read aloud the introduction and discuss the description of a journal entry. Tell students that the Student Model is a draft of a journal entry written by a fifth grader. Read the model aloud, asking students to pay attention to the writer's topic, purpose, and audience. Then read the text in each call-out box, reviewing how a journal entry is organized. Talk with students about how a journal entry is like and unlike other types of writing.

Guided Practice   Ask students to answer the items that follow the model. Read Item 1 aloud and guide students to find the sentences that introduce the topic. Then have students circle them. Go on to Item 2 and ask students to identify the sentence that is off topic and explain how they recognized it.

Independent Writing Practice   Direct students to answer items 3 and 4 on their own. Ask students to share and discuss their responses.

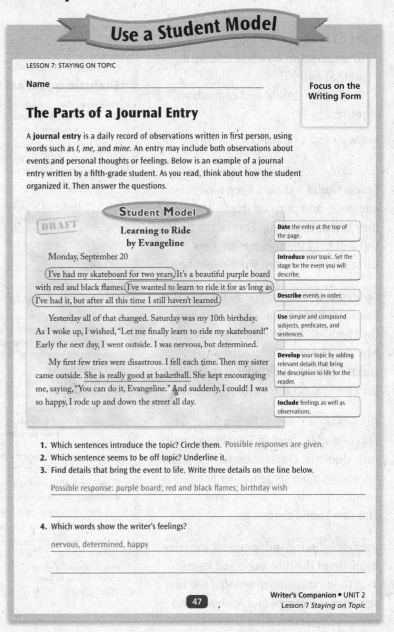

Use a Student Model

LESSON 7: STAYING ON TOPIC

Name _____

Focus on the Writing Form

The Parts of a Journal Entry

A **journal entry** is a daily record of observations written in first person, using words such as *I*, *me*, and *mine*. An entry may include both observations about events and personal thoughts or feelings. Below is an example of a journal entry written by a fifth-grade student. As you read, think about how the student organized it. Then answer the questions.

DRAFT

Student Model

Learning to Ride
by Evangeline

Monday, September 20

I've had my skateboard for two years. It's a beautiful purple board with red and black flames. I've wanted to learn to ride it for as long as I've had it, but after all this time I still haven't learned.

Yesterday all of that changed. Saturday was my 10th birthday. As I woke up, I wished, "Let me finally learn to ride my skateboard!" Early the next day, I went outside. I was nervous, but determined.

My first few tries were disastrous. I fell each time. Then my sister came outside. She is really good at basketball. She kept encouraging me, saying, "You can do it, Evangeline." And suddenly, I could! I was so happy, I rode up and down the street all day.

Date the entry at the top of the page.

Introduce your topic. Set the stage for the event you will describe.

Describe events in order.

Use simple and compound subjects, predicates, and sentences.

Develop your topic by adding relevant details that bring the description to life for the reader.

Include feelings as well as observations.

1. Which sentences introduce the topic? Circle them. Possible responses are given.
2. Which sentence seems to be off topic? Underline it.
3. Find details that bring the event to life. Write three details on the line below.

   Possible response: purple board; red and black flames; birthday wish

4. Which words show the writer's feelings?

   nervous, determined, happy

47   Writer's Companion • UNIT 2
Lesson 7 *Staying on Topic*

WRITER'S STRATEGY: FORMAL AND INFORMAL LANGUAGE

Ask students to reread the Student Model, thinking about the topic, audience, and purpose. Then ask students to discuss the writer's tone. Explain that the writer chose to use an informal tone in the journal entry. Ask students to discuss whether they think an informal tone works for this type of writing and why.

Then ask students to work with a partner to write a list of three or four topics they might write about. Have students consider the audience and purpose for each topic on their list. Ask: **Would you choose formal or informal language to write about the topic? Why?**

Evaluate a Journal Entry/Grammar

OBJECTIVES

- To understand how to evaluate a journal entry
- To identify simple and compound sentences

Standard: LA.5.3.3.1 evaluate for writing traits

Evaluate Teach/Model Discuss why writers should keep topic, audience, and purpose in mind when they evaluate writing. Emphasize that this will help them judge just how successful the written work might be.

Guided Practice/Independent Practice

Read aloud the introductory text and the checklist. Guide students to evaluate whether the entry is focused on a specific topic. Have students complete the checklist on their own.

Grammar Teach/Model Read the introduction and review the examples with students. Emphasize the distinction between simple sentences with compound subjects and/or predicates and compound sentences.

Guided Practice/Independent Practice

Read aloud the directions and Items 1–2. Guide students to see that the first sentence is a compound sentence and the second sentence is a simple sentence with a compound predicate. Have students complete the rest of the items.

LESSON 7: STAYING ON TOPIC

Name _____

Evaluating the Student Model

Evaluate a Journal Entry

When you evaluate a journal entry, ask yourself whether the writer stays focused on a specific topic. You should also consider whether the writing clearly shows the writer's purpose and intended audience.

Now use the checklist to evaluate the Student Model. Put a check in the box next to each thing the writer did well. If you do not think the writer did a good job, do not check the box.

- ☐ The entry is focused on a specific topic.
- ☐ The entry is written in first person and shows the writer's feelings.
- ☐ Events are described in order.
- ☐ The writer uses specific and relevant details to develop the topic.
- ☐ The writer uses simple and compound subjects, predicates, and sentences.

Writer's Grammar
Simple and Compound Sentences

A **simple sentence** is a group of words that together express one complete thought. It includes a simple or compound subject and a simple or compound predicate. A **compound sentence** is made up of two or more simples sentences joined by conjunctions, such as *and, but,* or *or.*

Simple Sentences
Danita and her friends go to the park after school.
The performers jumped and twirled around the stage.

Compound Sentences
You can go to the movies, or you can go swimming.
Sometimes I make pancakes for breakfast, but today I made waffles.

Label each sentence *simple* or *compound.*
1. I like to ride my bike, and my sister likes to go hiking. _compound_
2. The crowd shouted and applauded as the home team took the lead. _simple_
3. My cousin Tal and I went to the market to buy apples and carrots. _simple_
5. Father put his glasses on the table, or he left them in the car. _compound_
6. Insects have three basic body parts: the head, thorax, and abdomen. _simple_
7. Some people say that nuclear power is a cheap source of energy, but others are concerned about its danger. _compound_

Writer's Companion ▪ UNIT 2
Lesson 7 *Staying on Topic*   **48**

SHARING AND DISCUSSING

Have partners review their evaluations of the Student Model. Ask students to discuss how they evaluated each item on the checklist and why they evaluated it in that way. Encourage partners to justify their responses with examples from the Student Model. Have pairs summarize their discussion and report it to the class.

© Harcourt

Revise: Adding Relevant Details

OBJECTIVES
- To revise by adding relevant details
- To revise students' own writing and focus it by adding relevant details

Standard: LA.5.3.3.3 express ideas vividly

Teach/Model Discuss how revision can make writing stronger and clearer. Explain that one way to make writing stronger is to replace details that are not relevant to the topic with ones that are. Ask students to suppose that you are writing about a trip to the zoo. Have them suggest details that would and would not be relevant.

Guided Practice Read the introduction and example aloud. Discuss what details were added to the sentence and how they add interest to the writing. Then read the directions to Part A and guide students through the revision of the sentence in Item 1. Call students' attention to the Word Bank and suggest that they use it as a resource for ideas as they revise each sentence.

Independent Writing Practice Have students revise the sentences in Items 2 and 3 in Part A. Then read the directions to Part B and ask students to complete it independently. Invite students to share their revised journal entries, if they wish.

LESSON 7: STAYING ON TOPIC

Name _____

Revising the Student Model

Revise: Adding Relevant Details

One thing the writer could have done better is to add specific and relevant details to make her journal entry really come alive. Here is an example of how the Student Model can be improved.

Example I've wanted to learn to ride it for as long as I've had it, but after all this time I still haven't learned.

I've wanted to learn to ride it for as long as I've had it, but after all this time the only skill I have is in getting bruises.

A. Revise these sentences. Add relevant details. Use the Word Bank to help you.
1. Early the next day I went outside.

Early the next day I strapped on my helmet, pulled on my elbow and knee pads, and bravely went outside

2. I fell each time.

I smashed into the pavement, again and again.

3. She is really good at basketball.

She is supportive, and she makes me feel like a champion.

Word Bank
bravely
champion
elbow pads
helmet
pavement
smashed
supportive

B. Revise the journal entry you wrote on page 46. Focus your writing by adding relevant details and removing details that stray from your topic. Do your work on a separate sheet of paper.

_____

_____

_____

49

Writer's Companion • UNIT 2
Lesson 7 *Staying on Topic*

EXTENDING THE CONCEPT: WORD CHOICE

Explain that when they revise, students should reread each sentence. They should make sure each sentence is clear and that it says precisely what they want it to say. Tell students that careful word choice often means the difference between writing that is simply okay and writing that is great.

Ask students to examine their writing and ask themselves: *Is this the most effective word I can use? Would choosing another word make my meaning clearer?* Tell students that their goal should be to use words effectively in every single sentence they write.

© Harcourt

Identify: Time-Order Words

OBJECTIVES
- To understand the term *time-order words*
- To identify time-order words in literature

Teach/Model Read the introduction aloud. Ask a volunteer to define the term *time-order words* and call students' attention to the three examples of time-order words in the introduction. Record these on the board and invite students to add other time-order words to the list. Then read aloud the directions to Part A as well as the passage from *When Washington Crossed the Delaware*. Ask students to listen for time-order words in the passage.

Guided Practice Have students discuss the order of events in the passage, asking them to identify which event comes first, which comes second, and so on. Read aloud the directions to Part B and guide students to identify the words that indicate the sequence of events.

Independent Writing Practice Read aloud the directions to Part C. Then have students complete the exercise independently.

Use a Literature Model

LESSON 8: TIME-ORDER WORDS

Name _____

Writer's Craft in Literature

Identify: Time-Order Words

Time-order words include words and phrases such as *finally, at that time,* and *next*. These transition words help readers understand the sequence in which events happen.

A. Read the following passage from *When Washington Crossed the Delaware*. Look for words that indicate the sequence of events.

Literature Model

About one o'clock in the morning on January 3, Washington and the main body of his army moved out. Cannon wheels were muffled with rags. Officers whispered orders. The Americans did everything they could to be quiet, and their plan worked. It was dawn before Cornwallis realized they were gone.

The morning was clear and cold as Washington and his men neared Princeton. In farmland outside the town a part of the American army encountered British troops. During the fight that followed, many of the Americans fell. The dazed survivors retreated.

—from *When Washington Crossed the Delaware* by Lynne Cheney

B. Identify the words that tell the sequence of events in the passage. Possible responses are given.
1. Underline the phrase that tells you the time of the event in the first sentence.
2. Circle the words that tell you when Cornwallis realized the army was gone.
3. Draw a box around the words that tell you when Washington and his men arrived in Princeton.
4. Write the phrase that tells you what happened after the American army encountered the British. Double underline the two time-order words in that phrase.

During the fight that followed

C. About how much time passes from the beginning of the passage to the end? How do you know?

Possible response: The passage covers less than a day. It begins very early in the morning on one day, describes events that take place throughout the morning, and mentions that a fight follows those events.

Writer's Companion • UNIT 2
Lesson 8 *Time-Order Words*
50

EXTENDING THE CONCEPT: SEQUENCE OF EVENTS

Help students think about how time-order words are used in everyday life. Begin by asking them to write a paragraph that describes a sequence of events. Suggest that students write a paragraph that answers a question, such as, *What did you do after school yesterday?* Invite students to share their finished paragraphs with the class. Ask the class to identify the different time-order or transition words each student uses.

© Harcourt

Explore: Time-Order Words

OBJECTIVES

- To deepen students' understanding of time-order words
- To understand how time-order words help readers transition from one event or idea to the next

Standard: LA.5.3.1.1 generate ideas

Teach/Model Use the graphic organizer to help students understand writing about a sequence of events. Read and discuss each step of the organizer with students.

Guided Practice Read aloud the directions to Part A and model how to identify the sequence word in the example. Remind students that there are many different words and phrases that indicate time order. Guide students in completing Items 1–3 in Part A.

Independent Writing Practice Direct students to complete Part B. Suggest that they read the paragraph to themselves before filling in the blanks. Then suggest that they reread it when they are finished to make sure the sequence of events makes sense. Read the directions for Part C. Before students begin writing, have them list possible transition words they can use. Then ask students to rewrite the paragraph using new words to show the sequence of events.

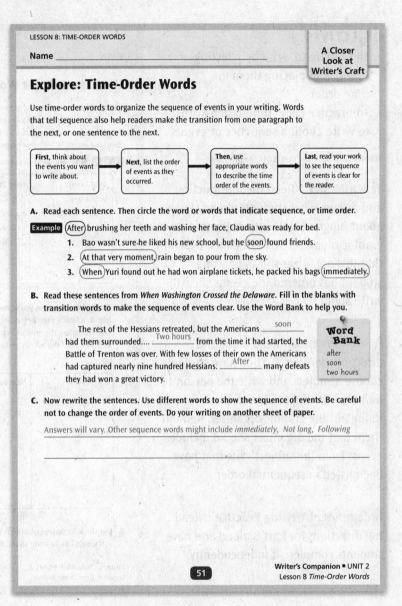

LESSON 8: TIME-ORDER WORDS

Name _____

A Closer Look at Writer's Craft

Explore: Time-Order Words

Use time-order words to organize the sequence of events in your writing. Words that tell sequence also help readers make the transition from one paragraph to the next, or one sentence to the next.

| **First**, think about the events you want to write about. | → | **Next**, list the order of events as they occurred. | → | **Then**, use appropriate words to describe the time order of the events. | → | **Last**, read your work to see the sequence of events is clear for the reader. |

A. Read each sentence. Then circle the word or words that indicate sequence, or time order.

Example (After) brushing her teeth and washing her face, Claudia was ready for bed.

1. Bao wasn't sure he liked his new school, but he (soon) found friends.
2. (At that very moment,) rain began to pour from the sky.
3. (When) Yuri found out he had won airplane tickets, he packed his bags (immediately.)

B. Read these sentences from *When Washington Crossed the Delaware*. Fill in the blanks with transition words to make the sequence of events clear. Use the Word Bank to help you.

The rest of the Hessians retreated, but the Americans ___soon___ had them surrounded.... ___Two hours___ from the time it had started, the Battle of Trenton was over. With few losses of their own the Americans had captured nearly nine hundred Hessians. ___After___ many defeats they had won a great victory.

Word Bank
after
soon
two hours

C. Now rewrite the sentences. Use different words to show the sequence of events. Be careful not to change the order of events. Do your writing on another sheet of paper.

Answers will vary. Other sequence words might include *immediately, Not long, Following*

51

Writer's Companion • UNIT 2
Lesson 8 *Time-Order Words*

Reaching All Learners

BELOW LEVEL

For Part C, students can work with partners to first brainstorm a list of possible transition words. Have them discuss which word suits or does not suit each sentence.

ADVANCED

Invite students to use a thesaurus to find other time-order words to use for Part C. Encourage them to be creative, but caution them against using words or phrases that make the paragraph read awkwardly.

ENGLISH-LANGUAGE LEARNERS

Suggest that English-Language Learners list transition words in their first language. They then can translate the words into English equivalents and use them to complete the paragraph.

© Harcourt

Use: Time-Order Words

OBJECTIVES

- To prepare to write by selecting events and placing them in time order
- To practice using time-order words to write about a sequence of events

Standard: LA.5.3.2.1 use a pre-writing plan

Teach/Model Read the introduction and discuss what students already know about biographical writing. Review the graphic organizer with students. Explain that this organizer shows how one student has ordered the events she will write about.

Guided Practice Read aloud the directions for Part A. Then have students choose a subject and write the person's name on the line. Guide students in filling out the graphic organizer. Remind them that the organizer should include events from the subject's life that have been listed in sequential order.

Independent Writing Practice Read the directions for Part B aloud and have students complete it independently.

Name _____   Practice with Writer's Craft

Use: Time-Order Words

A **biography** is an account of someone's life. Before you write a biography, list some of the important events in that person's life. One way to order the events is in chronological, or time, order. Here is how one student started to plan to write about the events in her great-grandmother's life.

Example Who: My Great-Grandmother

First Event:	Next Event:	Next Event:	Last Event:
Ishvani Kumar was born in 1915.	left India at age 16 and moved to Paris, France	moved to New York City in 1941 to study art	met Hamilton Sanders at artist's studio and they began working together

A. Think about a person you know who would make a good subject for a biography. It can be a friend, a family member, or someone you know about. Write that person's name on the line. Then complete the graphic organizer with the most important events in that person's life. Be sure to put the events in chronological order.

Who:

First Event:	Next Event:	Next Event:	Last Event:

B. Use the information from your graphic organizer to draft a biographical sketch of a person you would like to write about. Write your biography on another sheet of paper.

WRITER'S STRATEGY: PREPARING TO WRITE

Before students complete Parts A and B, have them write general notes about their subject's life. They might wish to list details about particular life events or write descriptive words about their subject. Alternatively, they may simply record relevant dates and places. Tell students that freewriting in this way helps them explore their topic and generate ideas for writing. Suggest that students choose the ideas that are of the most interest and then arrange those ideas in chronological order. Have students use their notes for reference as they complete Parts A and B.

The Parts of a Biography

OBJECTIVES
• To understand the parts of a biography
• To analyze a Student Model

Teach/Model Read aloud the introduction. Tell students that the Student Model is a draft of a biographical sketch written by a fifth grader. Read the model aloud. As students listen, have them pay careful attention to how the sequence of the paragraph is organized. Then read the call-out boxes, reviewing the organization and features of a biography.

Guided Practice Point out the items below the Student Model. Read the first item aloud. Guide students to find the sentence that introduces the subject of the biography and have them underline it. Then go on to Item 2, asking students to identify the transition and time-order words that guide the reader through the sequence of events.

Independent Writing Practice Direct students to answer Items 3–4 on their own. When they have finished, have students explain their answers and how they found them.

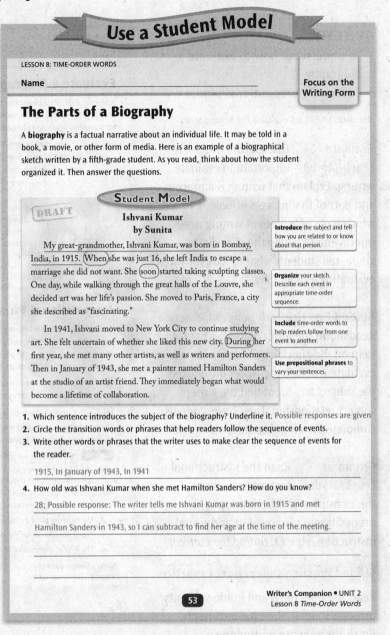

Use a Student Model

LESSON 8: TIME-ORDER WORDS

Name _____

Focus on the Writing Form

The Parts of a Biography

A **biography** is a factual narrative about an individual life. It may be told in a book, a movie, or other form of media. Here is an example of a biographical sketch written by a fifth-grade student. As you read, think about how the student organized it. Then answer the questions.

Student Model

DRAFT

Ishvani Kumar
by Sunita

My great-grandmother, Ishvani Kumar, was born in Bombay, India, in 1915. When she was just 16, she left India to escape a marriage she did not want. She soon started taking sculpting classes. One day, while walking through the great halls of the Louvre, she decided art was her life's passion. She moved to Paris, France, a city she described as "fascinating."

In 1941, Ishvani moved to New York City to continue studying art. She felt uncertain of whether she liked this new city. During her first year, she met many other artists, as well as writers and performers. Then in January of 1943, she met a painter named Hamilton Sanders at the studio of an artist friend. They immediately began what would become a lifetime of collaboration.

Introduce the subject and tell how you are related to or know about that person.

Organize your sketch. Describe each event in appropriate time-order sequence.

Include time-order words to help readers follow from one event to another.

Use prepositional phrases to vary your sentences.

1. Which sentence introduces the subject of the biography? Underline it. Possible responses are given
2. Circle the transition words or phrases that help readers follow the sequence of events.
3. Write other words or phrases that the writer uses to make clear the sequence of events for the reader.

   1915, In January of 1943, In 1941

4. How old was Ishvani Kumar when she met Hamilton Sanders? How do you know?

   28; Possible response: The writer tells me Ishvani Kumar was born in 1915 and met

   Hamilton Sanders in 1943, so I can subtract to find her age at the time of the meeting.

   _____

   _____

53   **Writer's Companion • UNIT 2**
      Lesson 8 *Time-Order Words*

EXTENDING THE CONCEPT: BIOGRAPHY

Have students work in small groups to compare and contrast biographical narratives with other types of narratives. Begin by inviting students to name biographical books or movies they have seen or heard about. Ask students to use what they know about these biographical narratives to discuss the following questions: *How are biographical narratives similar to other types of narratives? How are they different? Are time-order and other transition words especially important in biographical stories? Why or why not?* Ask each group to summarize its conclusions for the class.

Evaluate a Biography/Grammar

OBJECTIVES
- To understand how to evaluate a biography
- To identify prepositional phrases

Standard: LA.5.3.3.1 evaluate for writing traits

Evaluate Teach/Model . Discuss why it is important to evaluate writing. Explain that writing is a process and part of that process is looking to see which parts of a piece of writing need improvement. Using the checklist as a guide, tell students what to look for when evaluating a biography.

Guided Practice/Independent Practice
Read aloud the introductory text and each item on the checklist. Guide students to evaluate whether the writer introduced the subject and identified the writer-subject relationship. Then have students complete the checklist independently.

Grammar Teach/Model Read the instructional text and review the examples of different types of prepositional phrases. For additional instruction, stee *Extending the Concept.*

Guided Practice/Independent Practice
Read the directions and guide students through Item 1. Then have students finish the exercise on their own.

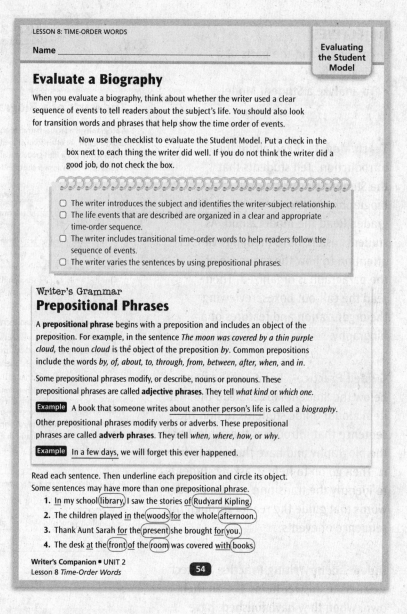

EXTENDING THE CONCEPT: ADJECTIVES AND ADVERBS

Remind students that adjectives describe nouns and pronouns and adverbs describe adjectives, verbs, and other adverbs. Point out that these definitions are helpful in describing prepositional phrases, as well. A prepositional phrase that describes a noun functions like an adjective.

A prepositional phrase that describes a verb functions like an adverb. Provide students with sample phrases and challenge them to identify its object and whether it functions as an adjective or adverb.

© Harcourt

Revise: Putting Events in Time Order

OBJECTIVES
- To revise by putting events in time order
- To revise students' own writing by putting events in time order

Teach/Model   Explain to students that when they revise they can correct mistakes and strengthen their word choice and organization. Tell students that in this activity they will work on revising their organization by putting events in time order.

Guided Practice   Read the introduction and example paragraphs aloud. Ask students how the order of the sentences was changed and how this affects the overall organization of the original paragraph. Then read aloud the directions for Part A and ask students how they could revise the paragraph to make the order of events clearer. Elicit students' responses and use their suggestions to begin revising the paragraph. Then point out the Word Bank and suggest students use it as a resource as they continue the revision.

Independent Writing Practice   Have students complete the revision of the paragraph in Part A. Then read the directions to Part B and ask students to work independently to complete the revision of the biography they wrote.

© Harcourt

LESSON 8: TIME-ORDER WORDS

Name _____

Revising the Student Model

Revise: Putting Events in Time Order

One thing the writer of the biographical sketch could have done better is to organize events in clear chronological order. Here is how the first paragraph of the sketch could be improved.

Example   My great-grandmother, Ishvani Kumar, was born in Bombay, India, in 1915. When she was just 16, she left India to escape a marriage she did not want. She soon started taking sculpting classes. One day, while walking through the great halls of the Louvre, she decided that art was her life's passion. She moved to Paris, France, a city she described as "fascinating."

My great-grandmother, Ishvani Kumar, was born in Bombay, India in 1915. When she was just 16, she left India to escape a marriage she did not want. She moved to Paris, France, a city she described as "fascinating." One day, while walking through the great halls of the Louvre, she decided that art was her life's passion. She started taking sculpting classes soon after.

A. Revise this paragraph. Put events in appropriate time order. Use transition words from the Word Bank to help you.

Word Bank
after
immediately
then

1.   She pays the cashier for her new brushes, colored paints, and canvas. She sprints into the art store and goes to the painting section. Her mom parks the car. Josephine jumps out of the car in a flash.

After her mom parks the car, Josephine jumps out in a flash. She immediately sprints into the art store and goes to the painting section. Then she pays the cashier for her new brushes, colored paints, and canvas.

B. Revise the biography you wrote on page 52. Check that all events are in time order and that there are transition words to help the reader follow the sequence of events. Write your revision on another sheet of paper.

55

Writer's Companion • UNIT 2
Lesson 8 *Time-Order Words*

SHARING AND DISCUSSING

Discuss the importance of evaluating and revising writing. Then invite students to read aloud the original and revised versions of their biographies.

Suggest that they share why they made the changes they made.

Review Writer's Craft

OBJECTIVES
- To review characteristics of focused writing
- To identify the topic sentence, supporting details, and transition words in a Literature Model

Teach/Model　Read aloud the introduction. Explain that in this lesson students will review what they have learned about ideas and organization. Read the directions for Part A aloud. Then read the paragraph from *Leonardo's Horse* and ask students to listen carefully for traits of effective writing.

Guided Practice　Ask students to discuss how ideas are organized in the passage. Direct students to find the topic sentence and time-order words. Help students see how some transition words connect ideas and others help put the events in sequence. Guide students through Items 1–3 of Part B.

Independent Writing Practice　Read aloud the directions to Part C. Remind students that a writer's purpose is the reason why he or she writes about a particular topic or idea. Then have students complete the exercise on their own.

Use a Literature Model

LESSON 9: REVIEW WRITER'S CRAFT

Name _____

Writer's Craft in Literature

Review Writer's Craft

Effective writers produce focused writing. Writing that is focused stays on topic and elaborates with plenty of examples. Good writers also use time-order words to help readers make the transition from one idea, or action, to the next.

A. Read the passage below. Notice how the writer stays on topic and uses examples to elaborate on the ideas. Also notice how the writer uses transition words to help readers follow the sequence of events.

Literature Model

The horse would always be Charlie's dream, but as soon as Nina went to work, he had to become her horse, too. She had studied in Italy for eleven years. Her favorite Renaissance artist was Verrochio, Leonardo's teacher. It was lucky that she was there to carry on with Charlie's dream.

First Nina made an eight-foot clay horse. From it a second eight-foot horse was made of plaster. Using the plaster model as a guide, a twenty-four-foot horse was made in clay.

Everyone went to work to get the horse exactly right. Finally he was ready to be cast in bronze.

—from *Leonardo's Horse* by Jean Fritz

B. Review why the writing in this passage is effective.
1. Underline the topic sentence. Look for the sentence that establishes the writer's main idea.
2. Draw a box around the words that show time order.
3. The writer believes it was lucky that Nina was there to help realize Charlie's dream. List the examples that she gives to support this idea.

Like Charlie, Nina has spent time in Italy. Because she admires Verrochio, she has a connection to Leonardo, as well.

C. What do you think is the purpose of describing Nina's work process?

Possible response: This description helps to illustrate the writer's statement that Nina is excited about the horse sculpture just as Charlie was.

Writer's Companion • UNIT 2
Lesson 9 *Review Writer's Craft*　　56

EXTENDING THE CONCEPT: EXPOSITORY WRITING

Before students complete Part C, discuss the phrase *expository writing*. Explain that the phrase is used to describe writing that gives information. Ask students to consider how careful use of ideas and organization help make expository writing successful. Tell students that writers give information to readers for specific reasons. Guide students to see that the detailed discussion of Nina's work helps illustrate her devotion to completing Charlie's sculpture of the horse.

© Harcourt

Review Writer's Craft

OBJECTIVES
- To deepen students' understanding of effective writing traits
- To review the importance of staying on topic, elaborating with examples, and using time-order words

Standard: LA.5.3.1.1 generate ideas

Teach/Model Use the graphic organizer to review the traits of focused, effective writing. Remind students that good writers establish a topic and keep their audience and purpose in mind as they write. Explain that good writers use examples to support their ideas and that they include transition words to connect the events.

Guided Practice Read aloud the directions and passage for Part A. Then read aloud the directions for Part B and model matching the example sentence to the kind of effective writing it represents. Guide students in completing the rest of Part B.

Independent Writing Practice Read aloud the directions for Part C. For additional instruction, see *Sharing and Discussing*. Direct students to complete Part C independently.

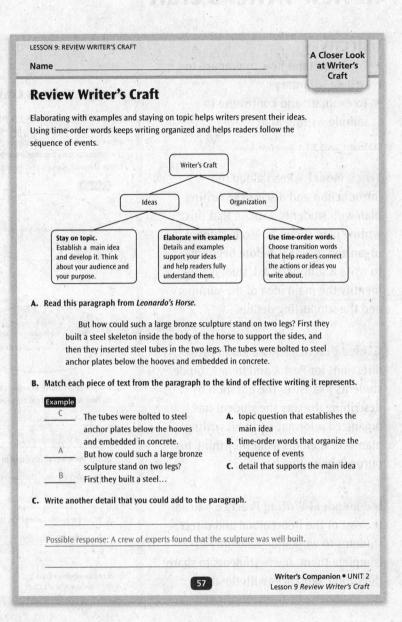

SHARING AND DISCUSSING

Before students complete Part C, have them partner with another student to identify the main idea of the paragraph. Also have them discuss what sort of details would work to support this main idea. Ask partners to share ideas with the class. After students complete Part C, invite them to share their sentences with the class. Invite students to read the entire paragraph from Part A, incorporating their sentence as they read. Lead a discussion comparing the different details students provide.

© Harcourt

Review Writer's Craft

OBJECTIVES

- To understand how to prepare to write a summary
- To evaluate and contribute to a sample writing plan

Standard: LA.5.3.1.1 generate ideas

Teach/Model Read aloud the introduction and discuss the writing plan with students. Explain that this writing plan shows how one student has organized his ideas before beginning to write a summary. Ask students to identify the main idea of the summary and the supporting details.

Guided Practice Read aloud the directions for Part A and Item 1. Guide students to answer the question by describing the way the student has organized information in his writing plan. Ask students what they think his purpose in writing is.

Independent Writing Practice Read the rest of the items aloud and direct students to work independently to complete them. Invite students to share their topic sentences with the class.

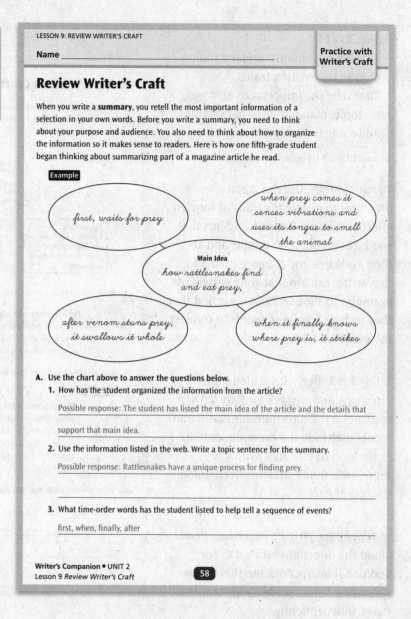

LESSON 9: REVIEW WRITER'S CRAFT

Name _____

Practice with Writer's Craft

Review Writer's Craft

When you write a **summary**, you retell the most important information of a selection in your own words. Before you write a summary, you need to think about your purpose and audience. You also need to think about how to organize the information so it makes sense to readers. Here is how one fifth-grade student began thinking about summarizing part of a magazine article he read.

Example

- first, waits for prey
- when prey comes it senses vibrations and uses its tongue to smell the animal
- **Main Idea** how rattlesnakes find and eat prey,
- after venom stuns prey, it swallows it whole
- when it finally knows where prey is, it strikes

A. Use the chart above to answer the questions below.

1. How has the student organized the information from the article?

   Possible response: The student has listed the main idea of the article and the details that

   support that main idea.

2. Use the information listed in the web. Write a topic sentence for the summary.

   Possible response: Rattlesnakes have a unique process for finding prey.

3. What time-order words has the student listed to help tell a sequence of events?

   first, when, finally, after

Writer's Companion • UNIT 2
Lesson 9 *Review Writer's Craft*

58

WRITER'S STRATEGY: STRONG TOPIC SENTENCES

Remind students that a *topic sentence* is a general statement that expresses the main idea of a paragraph. Explain that a topic sentence often, but not always, is at the beginning of a paragraph. Point out that a paragraph with a strong opening sentence catches readers' interest. Explain that a strong opening sentence is both interesting and clear. Strategies for making sentences clear and interesting include using specific words and phrases and checking for mistakes in spelling and grammar. Have students review the topic sentence they wrote for the summary, having them revise it to make it clearer. Invite students to share their revised sentences and discuss the revisions they made.

© Harcourt

The Parts of a Summary

OBJECTIVES
- To understand how elements of a summary are organized
- To analyze a Student Model

Standards: LA.5.3.3.1 evaluate for writing traits

Teach/Model Explain that the Student Model on this page is a draft of a summary paragraph written by a fifth grader. Read aloud the introduction and the steps for how to organize a summary. Then read the model aloud and ask students to listen for each of the elements you have mentioned.

Guided Practice Point out the questions below the Student Model. Read the first question aloud. Guide students to understand that the writer's purpose is to share the main points of a longer article about how rattlesnakes find prey.

Independent Writing Practice Direct students to answer Questions 2–4 on their own. Then discuss why the sentences in Question 4 should be left out. Have students explain what makes a sentence an opinion rather than a fact. Ask them why this opinion and the sentence about lizards should not be part of the student's summary.

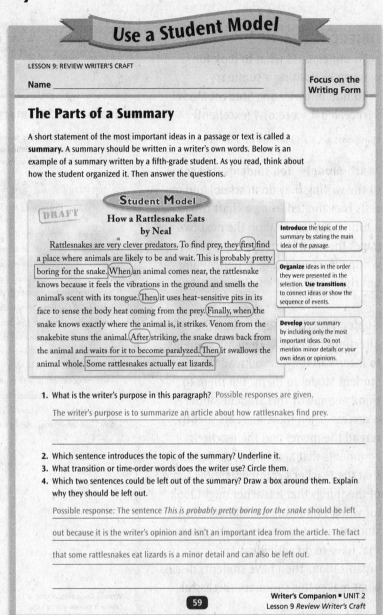

Use a Student Model

LESSON 9: REVIEW WRITER'S CRAFT

Name _____

Focus on the Writing Form

The Parts of a Summary

A short statement of the most important ideas in a passage or text is called a **summary**. A summary should be written in a writer's own words. Below is an example of a summary written by a fifth-grade student. As you read, think about how the student organized it. Then answer the questions.

Student Model

DRAFT

How a Rattlesnake Eats
by Neal

Rattlesnakes are very clever predators. To find prey, they first find a place where animals are likely to be and wait. This is probably pretty boring for the snake. When an animal comes near, the rattlesnake knows because it feels the vibrations in the ground and smells the animal's scent with its tongue. Then it uses heat-sensitive pits in its face to sense the body heat coming from the prey. Finally, when the snake knows exactly where the animal is, it strikes. Venom from the snakebite stuns the animal. After striking, the snake draws back from the animal and waits for it to become paralyzed. Then it swallows the animal whole. Some rattlesnakes actually eat lizards.

Introduce the topic of the summary by stating the main idea of the passage.

Organize ideas in the order they were presented in the selection. **Use transitions** to connect ideas or show the sequence of events.

Develop your summary by including only the most important ideas. Do not mention minor details or your own ideas or opinions.

1. What is the writer's purpose in this paragraph? Possible responses are given.

   The writer's purpose is to summarize an article about how rattlesnakes find prey.

2. Which sentence introduces the topic of the summary? Underline it.
3. What transition or time-order words does the writer use? Circle them.
4. Which two sentences could be left out of the summary? Draw a box around them. Explain why they should be left out.

   Possible response: The sentence *This is probably pretty boring for the snake* should be left out because it is the writer's opinion and isn't an important idea from the article. The fact that some rattlesnakes eat lizards is a minor detail and can also be left out.

59

Writer's Companion • UNIT 2
Lesson 9 *Review Writer's Craft*

WRITER'S STRATEGY: PRACTICE WITH SUMMARIES

Explain to students that the purpose of a summary is to restate the most important ideas of the original piece of writing. Tell students that they can prepare for writing summaries by practicing restating main ideas from things they read. Remind students that restating the ideas means telling the ideas in their own words. Have students select an article from a newspaper or magazine. Suggest that they underline topic sentences and key words. Then have them write a summary of the main ideas.

© Harcourt

Evaluate a Summary

OBJECTIVES
- To understand what to look for when evaluating a summary
- To find out why one Student Model received a score of 4 (excellent)

Standard: LA.5.3.3.1 evaluate for writing traits

Teach/Model Tell students that some of the writing they do in school and on tests is evaluated using a chart called a rubric. Explain that on the next two pages they will learn more about how writing is scored using a rubric. Point out the rubric on the following page.

Guided Practice Read aloud the directions for Part A. Then ask students to listen carefully as you read the Student Model to them. Tell them to think about why this Student Model is a success. Then have students silently reread the model and the teacher's comments that accompany it. Explain that the teacher's comments show some of the things that a teacher might look for when evaluating a summary. Have students identify the teacher's comments that have to do with ideas and organization. Then have students discuss what makes this summary successful.

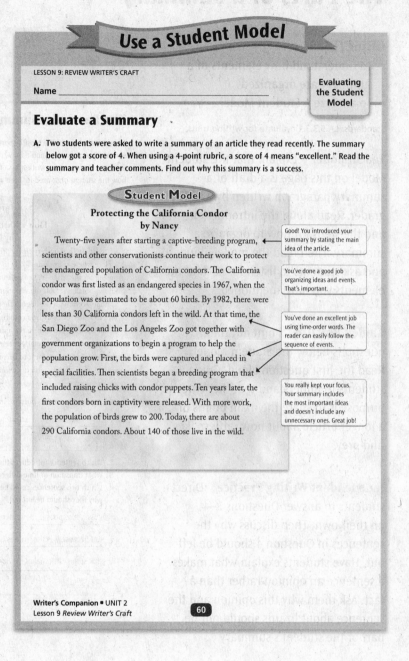

Use a Student Model

LESSON 9: REVIEW WRITER'S CRAFT

Name _____

Evaluating the Student Model

Evaluate a Summary

A. Two students were asked to write a summary of an article they read recently. The summary below got a score of 4. When using a 4-point rubric, a score of 4 means "excellent." Read the summary and teacher comments. Find out why this summary is a success.

Student Model

Protecting the California Condor
by Nancy

Twenty-five years after starting a captive-breeding program, scientists and other conservationists continue their work to protect the endangered population of California condors. The California condor was first listed as an endangered species in 1967, when the population was estimated to be about 60 birds. By 1982, there were less than 30 California condors left in the wild. At that time, the San Diego Zoo and the Los Angeles Zoo got together with government organizations to begin a program to help the population grow. First, the birds were captured and placed in special facilities. Then scientists began a breeding program that included raising chicks with condor puppets. Ten years later, the first condors born in captivity were released. With more work, the population of birds grew to 200. Today, there are about 290 California condors. About 140 of those live in the wild.

Good! You introduced your summary by stating the main idea of the article.

You've done a good job organizing ideas and events. That's important.

You've done an excellent job using time-order words. The reader can easily follow the sequence of events.

You really kept your focus. Your summary includes the most important ideas and doesn't include any unnecessary ones. Great job!

Writer's Companion • UNIT 2
Lesson 9 *Review Writer's Craft*

60

SHARING AND DISCUSSING

Ask students to work in small groups to discuss the Student Models on this page and the following page. Write the following questions on the board:
- Does the summary give you a clear understanding of the article that was read by the student?
- Does it include main ideas and details?
- Is it organized clearly?

Have students discuss the questions as a group.

© Harcourt

Evaluate a Summary

OBJECTIVES

- To read a Student Model that received a score of 2 (needs improvement)
- To evaluate a summary using a rubric

Standard: LA.5.3.3.1 evaluate for writing traits

Teach/Model Tell students that they will read a summary that received a score of 2 on a 4-point rubric scale. Read the Student Model aloud. Ask students to listen (without looking at the summary) and think about why the summary needs improvement.

Guided Practice Ask students to comment on any strengths or weaknesses they noticed in the summary. Then have them silently read the Student Model and the teacher's comments. Ask students to explain why the summary needs improvement.

Independent Writing Practice Explain how to use the rubric at the bottom of the page. Ask students to complete reviewing the summary with the rubric and to decide what score they would give the summary.

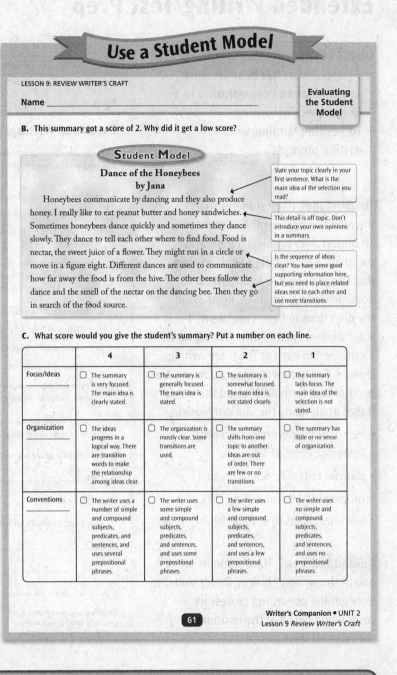

LESSON 9: REVIEW WRITER'S CRAFT

Name _____

Evaluating the Student Model

B. This summary got a score of 2. Why did it get a low score?

Student Model

Dance of the Honeybees
by Jana

Honeybees communicate by dancing and they also produce honey. I really like to eat peanut butter and honey sandwiches. Sometimes honeybees dance quickly and sometimes they dance slowly. They dance to tell each other where to find food. Food is nectar, the sweet juice of a flower. They might run in a circle or move in a figure eight. Different dances are used to communicate how far away the food is from the hive. The other bees follow the dance and the smell of the nectar on the dancing bee. Then they go in search of the food source.

> State your topic clearly in your first sentence. What is the main idea of the selection you read?

> This detail is off topic. Don't introduce your own opinions in a summary.

> Is the sequence of ideas clear? You have some good supporting information here, but you need to place related ideas next to each other and use more transitions.

C. What score would you give the student's summary? Put a number on each line.

	4	3	2	1
Focus/Ideas ____	☐ The summary is very focused. The main idea is clearly stated.	☐ The summary is generally focused. The main idea is stated.	☐ The summary is somewhat focused. The main idea is not stated clearly.	☐ The summary lacks focus. The main idea of the selection is not stated.
Organization ____	☐ The ideas progress in a logical way. There are transition words to make the relationship among ideas clear.	☐ The organization is mostly clear. Some transitions are used.	☐ The summary shifts from one topic to another. Ideas are out of order. There are few or no transitions.	☐ The summary has little or no sense of organization.
Conventions ____	☐ The writer uses a number of simple and compound subjects, predicates, and sentences, and uses several prepositional phrases.	☐ The writer uses some simple and compound subjects, predicates, and sentences, and uses some prepositional phrases.	☐ The writer uses a few simple and compound subjects, predicates, and sentences, and uses a few prepositional phrases.	☐ The writer uses no simple and compound subjects, predicates, and sentences, and uses no prepositional phrases.

61

Writer's Companion • UNIT 2
Lesson 9 *Review Writer's Craft*

Reaching All Learners

BELOW LEVEL

Suggest that students work through the rubric one section at a time. Have them read the text in each row and ask themselves, *Does this describe the writing?* When the answer is *yes*, they should record that number.

ADVANCED

Encourage students to write "teacher's comments" of their own. Suggest that they write one comment for each of the rubric categories. Each comment should justify the score given on the rubric.

ENGLISH-LANGUAGE LEARNERS

Pair less fluent English speakers with more fluent English speakers. Have partners discuss the Student Model and rubric. Have them work together to complete the rubric and score the summary.

© Harcourt

Extended Writing/Test Prep

OBJECTIVES

- To apply what has been learned about ideas and organization to a longer piece of writing
- To become familiar with writing prompts

Teach/Model Tell students that the next two pages will give them an opportunity to select a topic and complete a long written work. Explain that they can choose from several possible writing activities. Read aloud the directions in Part A and Items 1–3. Have students identify the writing forms mentioned in each of the three writing choices. For each writing form, review the parts of that form and reread the tips for it that accompany the Student Model.

- Personal Response Paragraph: Lesson 6, Page 41
- Journal Entry: Lesson 7, Page 47
- Biography: Lesson 8, Page 53
- Summary: Lesson 9, Page 59

Guided Practice Have students select one of the writing choices. Direct students to begin the prewriting process by completing Part B at the bottom of the page on their own.

Use a Literature Model

LESSON 10: WRITING TEST PRACTICE

Name _____

Extended Writing/Test Prep

Extended Writing/Test Prep

On the first two pages of this lesson, you will use what you have learned about ideas and organization to write a longer written work.

A. Read the three choices below. Put a star by the writing activity you would like to do.

1. Respond to a Writing Prompt

   Writing Situation: Think about a time something exciting happened. Why do you remember this event?

   Directions for Writing: Think about what details are relevant to your retelling of an exciting event. Now, write a journal entry retelling what you saw, thought, and felt. Use time-order words to help retell the events.

2. Choose one of the pieces of writing you started in this unit:

   - a personal response paragraph (page 40)

   - a journal entry (page 46)

   - a biography (page 52)

   Revise and expand your work into a complete piece of writing. Use what you have learned about ideas and organization.

3. Choose a topic you would like to write about. Read an article written about this topic, then write a summary of the article. Include the most important ideas in your summary.

B. Use the space below and on the next page to plan your writing.

TOPIC: _____

WRITING FORM: _____

HOW I WILL ORGANIZE MY WRITING: _____

_____

_____

_____

Writer's Companion ▪ UNIT 2
Lesson 10 *Writing Test Practice*   62

SHARING AND DISCUSSING

Have partners discuss their topic choices. Ask students to explain what they will write about and what writing form they will use. Instruct partners to ask each other questions about how the writing form will be organized and what they will do to make the writing clear and interesting to read.

© Harcourt

Extended Writing/Test Prep

OBJECTIVES
- To use the writing process to complete a long written work
- To use a graphic organizer to plan a piece of writing

Teach/Model   Explain to students that in Part C they will select a graphic organizer and use it to plan their writing. Tell students they can pick a new organizer or reuse one from one of the previous lessons. Model how to complete one of the graphic organizers. Emphasize the usefulness of the organizer in developing a writing plan.

Guided Practice   Have students complete their organizers. Answer questions and provide guidance as needed.

Independent Writing

Draft, Revise, and Publish Briefly review the steps of the writing process. Have students draft their writing pieces on separate sheets of paper. After students have finished their drafts, direct them to revise their work. Remind them to focus on adding examples, adding details, and placing events in time order. Ask students what form they would like to use to publish their work.

LESSON 10: WRITING TEST PRACTICE

Name _____

Extended Writing/Test Prep

C.   In the space below, draw a graphic organizer that will help you plan your writing. Fill in the graphic organizer. Write additional notes on the lines below.

Notes

_____

_____

_____

_____

_____

_____

_____

D.   Do your writing on another sheet of paper.

63

Writer's Companion • UNIT 2
Lesson 10 *Writing Test Practice*

Reaching All Learners

BELOW LEVEL	ADVANCED	ENGLISH-LANGUAGE LEARNERS
Encourage students to select an appropriate organizer from a previous lesson and use it as a model. Tell them to follow that organizer but use their own topic and ideas.	Suggest that students use other writing tools in their prewriting process. They might brainstorm specific words to use in a journal entry or create a word web to plan a summary.	Work with students individually or in a small group. Help them identify ideas for their topics and order those ideas with an appropriate graphic organizer.

© Harcourt

Answering Multiple-Choice Questions

OBJECTIVES

- To answer questions that involve reading and evaluating a writing plan
- To develop the strategy of reading all parts of a writing plan before answering questions about it

Standard: LA.5.3.1.1 generate ideas

Teach/Model   Tell students that this page requires them to read and evaluate a writing plan. Explain that they will answer multiple-choice questions about that plan. Read aloud the directions and the Test Tip. Model how to answer the first test item. Read each part of the writing plan carefully. Then discuss how each example does or does not relate to the topic sentence. Identify the one that does not. Finish by saying: **This is the example that should be taken off the plan. The answer is choice C.**

Guided Practice   Read Question 2 aloud and ask students to read the answer choices silently. Remind students to consider the information from the writing plan when selecting their answer. Have students mark the correct answer.

Independent Writing Practice   Ask students to complete the last test question independently.

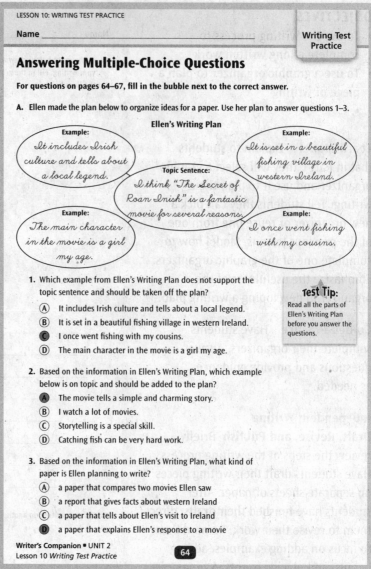

LESSON 10: WRITING TEST PRACTICE

Name _____

Writing Test Practice

Answering Multiple-Choice Questions

For questions on pages 64–67, fill in the bubble next to the correct answer.

A. Ellen made the plan below to organize ideas for a paper. Use her plan to answer questions 1–3.

Ellen's Writing Plan

Example: It includes Irish culture and tells about a local legend.

Example: It is set in a beautiful fishing village in western Ireland.

Topic Sentence: I think "The Secret of Roan Inish" is a fantastic movie for several reasons.

Example: The main character in the movie is a girl my age.

Example: I once went fishing with my cousins.

1. Which example from Ellen's Writing Plan does not support the topic sentence and should be taken off the plan?
   - (A) It includes Irish culture and tells about a local legend.
   - (B) It is set in a beautiful fishing village in western Ireland.
   - (C) I once went fishing with my cousins.
   - (D) The main character in the movie is a girl my age.

   Test Tip: Read all the parts of Ellen's Writing Plan before you answer the questions.

2. Based on the information in Ellen's Writing Plan, which example below is on topic and should be added to the plan?
   - (A) The movie tells a simple and charming story.
   - (B) I watch a lot of movies.
   - (C) Storytelling is a special skill.
   - (D) Catching fish can be very hard work.

3. Based on the information in Ellen's Writing Plan, what kind of paper is Ellen planning to write?
   - (A) a paper that compares two movies Ellen saw
   - (B) a report that gives facts about western Ireland
   - (C) a paper that tells about Ellen's visit to Ireland
   - (D) a paper that explains Ellen's response to a movie

Writer's Companion • UNIT 2
Lesson 10 *Writing Test Practice*   64

USING ACADEMIC LANGUAGE

Tell students that most tests contain academic language that includes words they may not see in their regular reading. Before students complete the test items on this page, review words and phrases such as *organize, writing plan, topic sentence, based on the information,* and *on topic.* Remind students to read each question and its answer choices carefully before marking their answer.

© Harcourt

Answering Multiple-Choice Questions (cont.)

OBJECTIVES
- To answer questions that involve reading a passage
- To learn how to identify a sentence that is off topic

Standard: LA.5.3.3.2 clarify by deleting/organizing

Teach/Model Explain to students that some multiple-choice question formats will ask them to read a passage and then answer questions about it. Read aloud the directions for Part B and read the boxed Test Tip. Then have students read the passage silently to themselves. Read aloud the first test question. Model how to read each sentence to determine whether it is on topic or not. Model marking the correct answer choice.

Guided Practice Direct students to use the same process to answer Question 2. Emphasize the importance of rereading the passage to determine which answer choice supports the ideas of the second paragraph. Guide students to see that answer choice A best supports the ideas in the paragraph.

Independent Writing Practice Direct students to answer Question 3 on their own.

LESSON 10: WRITING TEST PRACTICE

Name _____

Writing Test Practice

B. Max wrote the following journal entry. The entry contains mistakes. Read the journal entry to answer questions 1–3.

Saturday, October 5

(1) I got my dog Lolly about six months ago. (2) She now weighs 15 pounds and is golden brown with a snowy white streak on her forehead. (3) Her eyes are brown, and they are always smiling. (4) My cat Lucy has green eyes.

(5) My brother and I have been trying to teach Lolly tricks for the past three months. (6) But after hours and hours of training, she still did not understand any of our commands.

(7) Today was different. (8) Lolly followed every single command we gave her. (9) I can't believe it! (10) Now I'm thinking about entering her in the local dog show.

1. Which sentence is off topic and should be taken out of the entry?
   Ⓐ sentence (1)
   Ⓑ sentence (4)
   Ⓒ sentence (6)
   Ⓓ sentence (10)

2. Which sentence below should be added after sentence (6) to support the ideas in the second paragraph?
   Ⓐ She would sit when we asked her to lie down and lie down when we asked her to fetch.
   Ⓑ I feed Lolly twice a day, and I walk her three times a day.
   Ⓒ My brother can get her to sit up and beg, if he offers her a treat.
   Ⓓ Lolly was adopted from the animal shelter on Smith Street.

3. The writer wants to add the following sentence to the story:

   | Now she sits, lies down, rolls over, and fetches. |

   Where would this detail be added to correctly organize the ideas?
   Ⓐ after sentence (2)
   Ⓑ after sentence (5)
   Ⓒ after sentence (8)
   Ⓓ after sentence (10)

Test Tip: Staying on topic means focusing on a main idea. It also means thinking about the purpose and audience.

65

Writer's Companion • UNIT 2
Lesson 10 Writing Test Practice

Reaching All Learners

BELOW LEVEL	ADVANCED	ENGLISH-LANGUAGE LEARNERS
Help students read and restate what each question asks them to do. For example: **This question asks me to figure out which sentence listed would best fit with the ideas in the second paragraph.**	Encourage students to write alternative sentences that could be added to the story. Have students share them with a partner and discuss where the sentence could be added to keep the ideas correctly organized.	Work with students in a small group. Discuss the answer choices and talk about which ones should be eliminated as possible correct answers and why.

© Harcourt

Answering Multiple-Choice Questions (cont.)

OBJECTIVES

- To practice answering multiple-choice questions that involve reading a passage
- To use knowledge of prepositions to correctly complete sentences

Standard: LA.5.3.4.4 use parts of speech correctly

Teach/Model   Explain that all of the test questions on this page ask students to choose the word or words that correctly complete sentences from a passage. Read aloud the directions for Part C. Have students read the passage silently. Point out that the missing words will make reading the passage somewhat difficult. Still, students should read to gain a sense of the topic of the passage and to identify what kinds of words are missing from the sentences. Then read the Test Tip and model using it to answer Question 1. Read the sentence with blank (1) three times, replacing the blank with each word choice. Explain that the word *on* tells where the ship encountered ice. Model marking the correct answer choice.

Guided Practice   Guide students to answer Question 2. Remind them to consider all of the answer choices before making their selection.

Independent Writing Practice   Have students complete Questions 3–5 independently.

LESSON 10: WRITING TEST PRACTICE

Name _____

Writing Test Practice

C. Read the paragraph, "Into the Ice." Choose the word or words that correctly completes questions 1–5.

Into the Ice

In December of 1914, Ernest Shackleton and a crew of about twenty-five men left England for Antarctica. __(1)__ its way, the ship entered a pack of ice in the ocean. Shackleton patiently waited for an opening in the ice. __(2)__ several days passed, Shackleton __(3)__ his crew realized they were stuck. __(4)__, the men continued to use the ship as a shelter from the wind and bitter cold. Finally, the pressure of the ice threatened to snap the ship into pieces. The ship was completely destroyed, __(5)__ the crew unloaded all of the food, equipment, and supplies. They would make camp on the ice.

1. Which answer should go in blank (1)?
   - Ⓐ After
   - Ⓑ On
   - Ⓒ By

2. Which answer should go in blank (2)?
   - Ⓐ After
   - Ⓑ Immediately
   - Ⓒ Meanwhile

3. Which answer should go in blank (3)?
   - Ⓐ but
   - Ⓑ or
   - Ⓒ and

4. Which answer should go in blank (4)?
   - Ⓐ For months
   - Ⓑ Over the mountain
   - Ⓒ Because

5. Which answer should go in blank (5)?
   - Ⓐ because
   - Ⓑ so
   - Ⓒ or

Test Tip:
Prepositional phrases tell *what kind, which one, when, where, how,* or *why.*

Writer's Companion ▪ UNIT 2
Lesson 10 *Writing Test Practice*   66

ASSESSING STUDENT RESPONSES

If students are consistently answering questions incorrectly, explore where their understanding is lacking. Students may be neglecting to reread passages as they work through test items. Ask students to explain the process by which they chose their answers. If they do not describe rereading the passage to help them make their choice, emphasize the importance of doing so. Then read each answer choice with students. Model eliminating incorrect answers and choosing the correct one.

© Harcourt

Answering Multiple-Choice Questions (cont.)

OBJECTIVES
- To answer questions that require choosing a correctly written sentence
- To use knowledge of sentence structure to answer test questions

Teach/Model   Tell students that some multiple-choice tests require them to read several sentences and decide which is correctly written. Read the Test Tip to students, pointing out that the tip provides information that can help them determine which sentences are written correctly. Read Question 1 and each of the answer choices. Model using the information from the boxed tip to choose the correct answer. Discuss that the boxed sentences in Question 1 each have a different subject completing different actions. Help students see that the compound sentence is the correct way to combine these two sentences. Mark the correct answer.

Guided Practice   Ask a volunteer to read Question 2 and have students silently read the three answer choices. Ask them to find the sentence that combines all three sentences with a compound predicate. Have students mark the correct answer.

Independent Writing Practice   Have students complete Question 3 on their own.

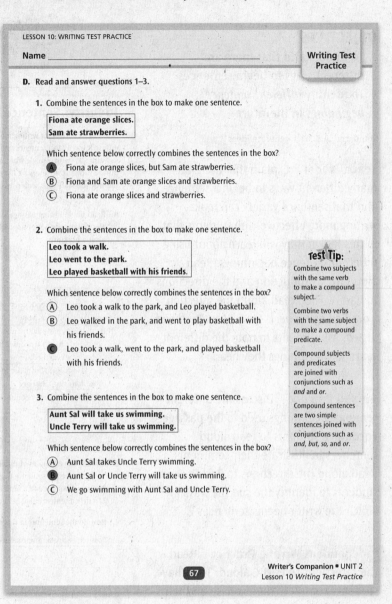

LESSON 10: WRITING TEST PRACTICE

Name _____

Writing Test Practice

D. Read and answer questions 1–3.

1. Combine the sentences in the box to make one sentence.

> Fiona ate orange slices.
> Sam ate strawberries.

Which sentence below correctly combines the sentences in the box?
- (A) Fiona ate orange slices, but Sam ate strawberries.
- (B) Fiona and Sam ate orange slices and strawberries.
- (C) Fiona ate orange slices and strawberries.

2. Combine the sentences in the box to make one sentence.

> Leo took a walk.
> Leo went to the park.
> Leo played basketball with his friends.

Which sentence below correctly combines the sentences in the box?
- (A) Leo took a walk to the park, and Leo played basketball.
- (B) Leo walked in the park, and went to play basketball with his friends.
- (C) Leo took a walk, went to the park, and played basketball with his friends.

3. Combine the sentences in the box to make one sentence.

> Aunt Sal will take us swimming.
> Uncle Terry will take us swimming.

Which sentence below correctly combines the sentences in the box?
- (A) Aunt Sal takes Uncle Terry swimming.
- (B) Aunt Sal or Uncle Terry will take us swimming.
- (C) We go swimming with Aunt Sal and Uncle Terry.

Test Tip:
Combine two subjects with the same verb to make a compound subject.

Combine two verbs with the same subject to make a compound predicate.

Compound subjects and predicates are joined with conjunctions such as *and* and *or*.

Compound sentences are two simple sentences joined with conjunctions such as *and*, *but*, *so*, and *or*.

67

Writer's Companion ▪ UNIT 2
Lesson 10 *Writing Test Practice*

SHARING AND DISCUSSING

Have students work in small groups to discuss simple and compound sentences. Ask them to identify the differences between simple sentences with compound subjects or compound predicates and compound sentences. Ask them to work as a group to write examples of each type of sentence. Have groups share their work with the class.

© Harcourt

Identify: Sentence Beginnings

OBJECTIVES

- To understand that there are different ways to begin sentences
- To identify *different sentence beginnings* in literature

Standard: LA.5.3.1.1 generate ideas

Teach/Model   Explain that there are many different ways to begin a sentence, and that sentence variety can make writing more effective. Tell students that in this lesson they will learn about using different sentence beginnings. Read aloud the introduction and the directions to Part A. Then read aloud the selection from *Sailing Home: A Story of a Childhood at Sea*. Ask students to note the different sentence beginnings they hear.

Guided Practice   Discuss the different sentence beginnings used in the passage. Encourage students to read aloud sentences to illustrate their comments. Read aloud the directions to Part B. Guide students to identify the specific ways in which the writer begins sentences.

Independent Writing Practice   Read the directions to Part C aloud. Then have students complete the exercise on their own. Invite volunteers to share their responses.

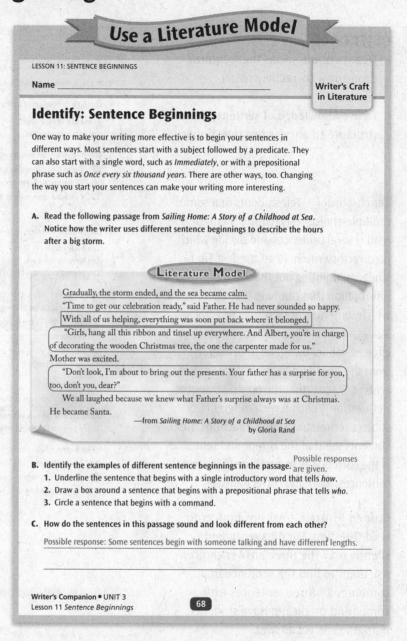

Use a Literature Model

LESSON 11: SENTENCE BEGINNINGS

Name _____

Writer's Craft in Literature

Identify: Sentence Beginnings

One way to make your writing more effective is to begin your sentences in different ways. Most sentences start with a subject followed by a predicate. They can also start with a single word, such as *Immediately*, or with a prepositional phrase such as *Once every six thousand years*. There are other ways, too. Changing the way you start your sentences can make your writing more interesting.

A. Read the following passage from *Sailing Home: A Story of a Childhood at Sea*. Notice how the writer uses different sentence beginnings to describe the hours after a big storm.

Literature Model

Gradually, the storm ended, and the sea became calm.
"Time to get our celebration ready," said Father. He had never sounded so happy.
With all of us helping, everything was soon put back where it belonged.
"Girls, hang all this ribbon and tinsel up everywhere. And Albert, you're in charge of decorating the wooden Christmas tree, the one the carpenter made for us."
Mother was excited.
"Don't look, I'm about to bring out the presents. Your father has a surprise for you, too, don't you, dear?"
We all laughed because we knew what Father's surprise always was at Christmas. He became Santa.

—from *Sailing Home: A Story of a Childhood at Sea* by Gloria Rand

B. Identify the examples of different sentence beginnings in the passage. Possible responses are given.
1. Underline the sentence that begins with a single introductory word that tells *how*.
2. Draw a box around a sentence that begins with a prepositional phrase that tells *who*.
3. Circle a sentence that begins with a command.

C. How do the sentences in this passage sound and look different from each other?

Possible response: Some sentences begin with someone talking and have different lengths.
_____

Writer's Companion • UNIT 3
Lesson 11 *Sentence Beginnings*   68

WRITER'S STRATEGY: INCORPORATING VARIETY

Explain that variety is a key ingredient in good writing. Tell students that repetitive writing can become boring for readers. Suggest that students think of writing as having a rhythm. They should vary this rhythm to keep the writing lively and interesting. Encourage students to jot down a few sentences about a holiday party or other festive event. Then have them review their sentences to see if they all begin in the same way. Have students change one or two of the sentences to create variety.

Explore: Sentence Beginnings

OBJECTIVES
- To identify different ways to begin sentences
- To practice changing sentence beginnings

Standard: LA.5.3.3.2 create clarity using sentence structures

Teach/Model Use the text and the graphic organizer at the top of the page to help students understand the various ways they can begin sentences. Read the examples in each section of the organizer and ask students to volunteer additional examples.

Guided Practice Explain that when students change sentence beginnings they may need to delete words, rearrange words, or introduce new words. Read the directions for Part A and review the example. Point out that the words from the original sentence have been rearranged to make the new sentence. Emphasize that the new sentence still has the same meaning, even though the beginning has been changed. Guide students in completing Items 1 and 2.

Independent Writing Practice After reading Parts B and C aloud, ask students to work independently to complete the page.

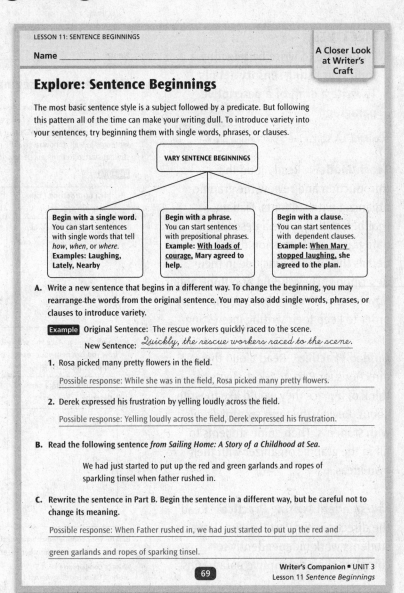

LESSON 11: SENTENCE BEGINNINGS

Name _____

A Closer Look at Writer's Craft

Explore: Sentence Beginnings

The most basic sentence style is a subject followed by a predicate. But following this pattern all of the time can make your writing dull. To introduce variety into your sentences, try beginning them with single words, phrases, or clauses.

VARY SENTENCE BEGINNINGS

Begin with a single word. You can start sentences with single words that tell *how*, *when*, or *where*. **Examples: Laughing, Lately, Nearby**

Begin with a phrase. You can start sentences with prepositional phrases. **Example: With loads of courage,** Mary agreed to help.

Begin with a clause. You can start sentences with dependent clauses. **Example: When Mary stopped laughing,** she agreed to the plan.

A. Write a new sentence that begins in a different way. To change the beginning, you may rearrange the words from the original sentence. You may also add single words, phrases, or clauses to introduce variety.

Example Original Sentence: The rescue workers quickly raced to the scene.
New Sentence: *Quickly, the rescue workers raced to the scene.*

1. Rosa picked many pretty flowers in the field.

   Possible response: While she was in the field, Rosa picked many pretty flowers.

2. Derek expressed his frustration by yelling loudly across the field.

   Possible response: Yelling loudly across the field, Derek expressed his frustration.

B. Read the following sentence *from Sailing Home: A Story of a Childhood at Sea.*

   We had just started to put up the red and green garlands and ropes of sparkling tinsel when father rushed in.

C. Rewrite the sentence in Part B. Begin the sentence in a different way, but be careful not to change its meaning.

   Possible response: When Father rushed in, we had just started to put up the red and

   green garlands and ropes of sparking tinsel.

69

Writer's Companion ▪ UNIT 3
Lesson 11 *Sentence Beginnings*

SHARING AND DISCUSSING

Invite students to share the sentences they wrote for Parts A and C on page 69. Have students discuss the different ways the class approached writing the sentences. Challenge students to identify how the original sentence was changed. Say: **Are there new words or phrases? Are the words arranged in a new order? Have any words been deleted?**

© Harcourt

Use: Sentence Beginnings

OBJECTIVES

- To prepare to write by selecting a topic and listing sensory details
- To write a draft of a descriptive paragraph

Standard: LA.5.3.2.1 use a pre-writing plan

Teach/Model   Read aloud the introduction and review the graphic organizer with students. Explain that before they write a descriptive paragraph, students should plan what details they want to include in their description. They should also think about how to vary their sentence beginnings in order to keep their writing interesting.

Guided Practice   Read aloud the directions for Part A. Ask students to think of a place they would like to write about. Review the term *sensory details* with students. Then guide students to fill in the graphic organizer with their own ideas.

Independent Writing Practice   Read the directions for Part B aloud. Have students work independently to complete their descriptive paragraphs.

LESSON 11: SENTENCE BEGINNINGS

Name _____

Practice with Writer's Craft

Use: Sentence Beginnings

A good **descriptive paragraph** allows a reader to see, hear, smell, touch, and sometimes even taste what is being described. Before you write a paragraph that describes a setting, think about how you can vary the beginnings of your sentences as well as how to give the reader a sense of the place. Here is how one student started to think about describing an empty lot near her school.

Example

Idea for a setting I can describe	Sensory details I can use in my description	What I can do to vary my sentence beginnings
the empty lot I see on the way to school each day	• silver color of the chain fence • whirring of machinery in lot next door • smell of trash and flowers	• start with prepositional phrases • start with a single word that tells when or how

A. Think about a place you see every day. What is unique about this setting? Think about how you can help your readers understand the place's atmosphere, or mood. Then complete the chart.

Idea for a setting I can describe	Sensory details I can use in my description	What I can do to vary my sentence beginnings

B. Use your completed chart to draft a paragraph describing a place you see every day. Write your paragraph on another sheet of paper.

Writer's Companion ▪ UNIT 3
Lesson 11 *Sentence Beginnings*   70

Reaching All Learners

BELOW LEVEL

Prompt students by asking them questions such as: **What is a place you go to every day? What is this place like?** Then encourage students to follow the graphic organizer model but complete it with their own details.

ADVANCED

Encourage students to think about their chosen location as they record sensory details. Have them ask themselves what words and sentence rhythms will best show this atmosphere to readers.

ENGLISH-LANGUAGE LEARNERS

Work with less fluent English speakers in small groups. Have students discuss their chosen settings and help each other identify appropriate English words and phrases to include in their descriptions.

© Harcourt

The Parts of a Descriptive Paragraph

OBJECTIVES
- To understand the parts of a descriptive paragraph
- To analyze a Student Model

Standards: LA.5.3.3.1 evaluate for writing traits

Teach/Model Read aloud the introduction and discuss what makes a descriptive paragraph effective. Explain that the writing sample is a draft of a descriptive paragraph written by a fifth grader. Read the boxed call-outs aloud to give students a sense of how the paragraph is organized. Then read the model aloud, asking students to listen for details that appeal to their senses. After you have read the model, invite students to comment on the atmosphere, or mood, of the setting described in the paragraph.

Guided Practice Call students' attention to the questions below the model. Direct students to Item 1 and help them find the sentence that introduces the setting. Then read Item 2 aloud and guide students to see that "I am late for school" is off topic and does not belong in the paragraph.

Independent Writing Practice Have students complete Item 3 on their own. Invite students to share their answers. For Item 4, see *Extending the Concept.*

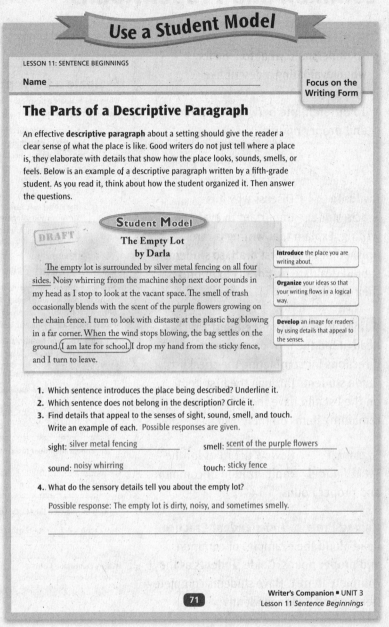

EXTENDING THE CONCEPT: SENSORY DETAILS

Before students complete Item 4, have them picture the scene portrayed in the Student Model. Ask students to identify words or phrases that give them a clear mental picture of the setting. Have students break into groups to discuss the mental pictures they saw and the words and phrases that suggested those pictures. Ask groups to share their responses as you record them on the board. Encourage students to discuss what these tell them about the lot and about how the writer feels about it.

© Harcourt

Evaluate a Descriptive Paragraph/Grammar: Common and Proper Nouns

OBJECTIVES

- To understand what to look for when evaluating a descriptive paragraph
- To differentiate between common and proper nouns

Evaluate Teach/Model Discuss why it is important to evaluate writing. Explain that writing is rarely finished after the first draft, so students should evaluate first drafts to improve their writing.

Guided Practice/Independent Practice

Read aloud the introduction and directions for completing the checklist. Guide students through the first item on the list and have them finish the remaining items on their own.

Grammar Teach/Model Review the rules for the capitalization of common and proper nouns.

Guided Practice/Independent Practice

Read aloud the examples of common and proper nouns. Guide students as they complete Item 1. Have students complete Items 2 and 3 independently.

LESSON 11: SENTENCE BEGINNINGS

Name _____

Evaluating the Student Model

Evaluate a Descriptive Paragraph

When you evaluate a descriptive paragraph of a setting, ask yourself how well you were able to picture the place the writer described.

Now use the checklist to evaluate the Student Model. Put a check in the box next to each thing the writer did well. If you do not think the writer did a good job, do not check the box.

- ☐ The writer introduced the place being described.
- ☐ The ideas flow clearly in an order that makes sense.
- ☐ There are many details that appeal to the senses.
- ☐ The writer used different sentence beginnings.

Writer's Grammar
Common and Proper Nouns

A *common noun* is a general name for a person, place, or thing. Common nouns are not capitalized unless they begin a sentence, are part of a title, or begin a quotation. A *proper noun* names a particular person, place, or thing. Proper nouns are capitalized. Here are some examples:

Example **Common Nouns:** architect, holiday, building, state
Proper Nouns: Maya Lin, Memorial Day, Chrysler Building, Hawaii

Rewrite each sentence. Correct any errors in capitalization.

1. I know uncle Steve lives in California, but he is originally from mexico.

   I know Uncle Steve lives in California, but he is originally from Mexico.

2. Antonia and I went to a Los Angeles Lakers Game last saturday.

   Antonia and I went to a Los Angeles Lakers game last Saturday.

3. Have you seen the Martin Luther King, jr. National historic site in Atlanta, ga?

   Have you seen the Martin Luther King, Jr. National Historic Site in Atlanta, GA?

Writer's Companion • UNIT 3
Lesson 11 *Sentence Beginnings*   **72**

Reaching All Learners

BELOW LEVEL

Discuss how common nouns can become proper nouns when they are part of titles. List words such as *aunt* and ask students to name additional examples.

ADVANCED

Challenge students to write sentences that include dialogue. Remind them that common nouns are capitalized when they begin a quotation. Have students share their work.

ENGLISH-LANGUAGE LEARNERS

Different languages often have different grammar rules. Challenge students to make charts comparing capitalization rules in their first language with the rules in English. Invite students to share their work.

© Harcourt

Revise: Changing Word Order

OBJECTIVES

- To revise the Student Model by changing word order
- To revise a descriptive paragraph by changing word order

Standard: LA.5.3.3.3 add supporting details/modify word choice

Teach/Model Discuss revising, explaining that it means changing writing to make it better. Explain that there are many types of changes writers can make. One is changing word order. Writers can change word order to introduce variety into their sentence beginnings.

Guided Practice Read aloud the introduction and the example sentences. Discuss how the changed word order adds interest for readers. Then read the directions for Part A and guide students to find one way to revise the sentence in Item 1. Tell students that there may be other ways to change the word order to make different sentence beginnings. Remind students that they may introduce new words and phrases when they rewrite.

Independent Writing Practice Have students revise the sentences in Items 2 and 3 of Part A. Then read the directions to Part B and ask students to complete their revisions independently.

LESSON 11: SENTENCE BEGINNINGS

Name _____

Revising the Student Model

Revise: Changing Word Order

One thing the writer might have done better is to start her sentences in different ways. Here is an example of how the writer might have changed the order of her words in the Student Model.

Example Original: The empty lot is surrounded by silver metal fencing on all four sides.

Revision: _Silver metal fencing surrounds the empty lot on all four sides._

A. Revise these sentences. Change word order and add words or phrases.

1. The smell of trash occasionally blends with the scent of the purple flowers growing on the chain fence.

   Possible response: Occasionally, when the air is warm, the smell of trash blends

   with the scent of the purple flowers growing on the chain fence.

2. I turn to look with distaste at the plastic bag blowing in a far corner.

   Possible response: With distaste, I turn to look at the plastic bag blowing in

   circles in a far corner.

3. I drop my hand from the sticky fence, and I turn to leave.

   Possible responses: Dropping my hand from the sticky fence, I turn to leave.

B. Revise the draft you wrote on page 70. Change word order to add variety to your sentence beginnings. Use another sheet of paper if necessary.

_____

_____

_____

_____

_____

_____

73

Writer's Companion ▪ UNIT 3
Lesson 11 *Sentence Beginnings*

WRITER'S STRATEGY: REVISING IN STAGES

Tell students that before they revise their writing, they should decide what areas they want to focus on improving. Explain that they may wish to revise their writing to add variety to sentences, to use more sensory details, and to check their spelling and grammar. Suggest that they focus their revision process by working in stages, revising one element of their writing before moving on to the next. Invite students to develop their own revision checklists and use them to guide their revisions.

© Harcourt

Identify: Making Clear Comparisons and Contrasts

OBJECTIVES

- To understand the terms *compare* and *contrast*
- To identify comparisons and contrasts in literature

Standard: LA.5.3.1.1 generate ideas

Teach/Model Tell students that there are different ways to organize their writing. Explain that, in this lesson, students will learn about using comparisons and contrasts. Read aloud the introduction and the directions to Part A. Then read the selection from *Ultimate Field Trip 3: Wading into Marine Biology*. Have students listen for the comparisons and contrasts that the writer describes.

Guided Practice Ask students to summarize what they learned from the passage. Then read aloud the directions for Part B. Guide students to identify *also* as a word that signals a comparison. Then ask them to find the sentences that tell how each animal avoids being swept away by the tides.

Independent Writing Practice Read aloud the directions to Part C and have students complete the exercise on their own. Ask students to explain where they got the information for their sentences.

Use a Literature Model

LESSON 12: CLEAR COMPARISONS AND CONTRASTS

Name _____

Writer's Craft in Literature

Identify: Making Clear Comparisons and Contrasts

When you **compare,** you focus on likenesses. When you **contrast,** you examine differences. Writing that compares and contrasts look at how the people, objects, places, or events in the text are alike and different.

A. Read this passage from *Ultimate Field Trip 3: Wading into Marine Biology*. Notice how the writer suggests similarities and differences in the animals she describes.

Literature Model

This is the tidal zone—land covered and uncovered by the ocean as the tide climbs up and down the shore. To survive, the plants and animals of the tidal zone must be able to adjust to many different conditions. Snails creep along, for example, until the waves roll in. Then they attach themselves to rocks, using their single foot like a suction cup. Barnacles also avoid being swept out to sea by cementing themselves to rocks. Then, when the tide retreats, these barnacles close their shells tight to keep their wet world safely inside. Clams dig into the sand and wait for the water's return.

—from *Ultimate Field Trip 3: Wading into Marine Biology* by Susan E. Goodman

B. Identify the compare-and-contrast text structure in the passage.

1. Look for a word that signals a likeness between snails and barnacles. Underline it.
2. Draw boxes around the sentences that tell how snails, barnacles, and clams avoid being drawn out to sea with the tides.

C. Write one sentence that compares snails and barnacles.

Possible response: Both attach themselves to rocks during high tide to avoid being

washed out to sea.

_____

_____

Writer's Companion ▪ UNIT 3
Lesson 12 *Clear Comparisons and Contrasts*   74

EXTENDING THE CONCEPT: SIGNALING COMPARISONS AND CONTRASTS

Explain that writers often use clue words to signal that a comparison or a contrast is being made. For example, words that signal comparisons include *also, in the same way,* and *similarly*. Words that signal contrasts include *unlike, however,* and *but*. Ask students to think of other words they know that signal comparisons and contrasts. Record students' responses on the board. Ask students to look through a magazine or newspaper to find signal words. Have them share the comparisons and contrasts they find. Ask them to name the signal words that helped them recognize each comparison or contrast.

Explore: Clear Comparisons and Contrasts

OBJECTIVES

- To deepen students' understanding of comparisons and contrasts
- To explore ways to compare and contrast things

Teach/Model Use the introduction and graphic organizer to help students understand how to use comparisons and contrasts in writing. Read each section of the graphic organizer. You may wish to draw a copy of the organizer on the board and complete it with a specific example.

Guided Practice Read aloud the directions for Part A and use the example to model how to find the information that is being compared or contrasted. Guide students through the steps to complete Items 1–3.

Independent Writing Practice Read aloud the directions to Part B. Then ask students to read the paragraph silently and complete the exercise on their own.

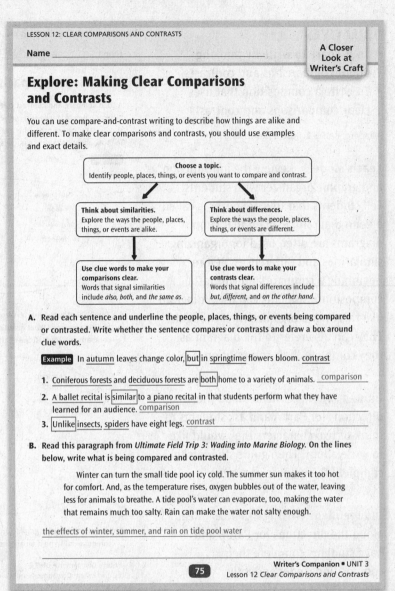

LESSON 12: CLEAR COMPARISONS AND CONTRASTS

Name _____

A Closer Look at Writer's Craft

Explore: Making Clear Comparisons and Contrasts

You can use compare-and-contrast writing to describe how things are alike and different. To make clear comparisons and contrasts, you should use examples and exact details.

Choose a topic.
Identify people, places, things, or events you want to compare and contrast.

Think about similarities.
Explore the ways the people, places, things, or events are alike.

Think about differences.
Explore the ways the people, places, things, or events are different.

Use clue words to make your comparisons clear.
Words that signal similarities include *also*, *both*, and *the same as*.

Use clue words to make your contrasts clear.
Words that signal differences include *but*, *different*, and *on the other hand*.

A. Read each sentence and underline the people, places, things, or events being compared or contrasted. Write whether the sentence compares or contrasts and draw a box around clue words.

Example In autumn leaves change color, but in springtime flowers bloom. contrast

1. Coniferous forests and deciduous forests are both home to a variety of animals. comparison

2. A ballet recital is similar to a piano recital in that students perform what they have learned for an audience. comparison

3. Unlike insects, spiders have eight legs. contrast

B. Read this paragraph from *Ultimate Field Trip 3: Wading into Marine Biology*. On the lines below, write what is being compared and contrasted.

Winter can turn the small tide pool icy cold. The summer sun makes it too hot for comfort. And, as the temperature rises, oxygen bubbles out of the water, leaving less for animals to breathe. A tide pool's water can evaporate, too, making the water that remains much too salty. Rain can make the water not salty enough.

the effects of winter, summer, and rain on tide pool water

Writer's Companion ▪ UNIT 3
75
Lesson 12 *Clear Comparisons and Contrasts*

SHARING AND DISCUSSING

Tell students that people make comparisons and contrasts every day. Explain that people often use comparisons and contrasts when they make decisions. Ask students to keep a record of the decisions they make over the course of a day, such as what to eat for lunch, which shirt to wear, or what to do for fun. Invite volunteers to share their decisions and explain how making comparisons and contrasts helped them make their decisions.

© Harcourt

Use: Clear Comparisons and Contrasts

OBJECTIVES

- To prepare to write by thinking about comparisons and contrasts
- To write a composition that uses clear comparisons and contrasts

Standard: LA.5.3.2.1 use a pre-writing plan

Teach/Model Review the introduction and graphic organizer with students. Tell students that this organizer is called a Venn diagram. Explain that Venn diagrams are often used for organizing similarities and differences. Before beginning a compare-and-contrast composition, students can use a diagram like this one to organize their thoughts. They can also refer to the diagram as they complete their composition.

Guided Practice Read aloud the directions for Part A and ask students to think of two characters they would like to write about. Then guide students to complete the graphic organizer.

Independent Writing Practice Read aloud the directions for Part B and have students complete their compositions independently.

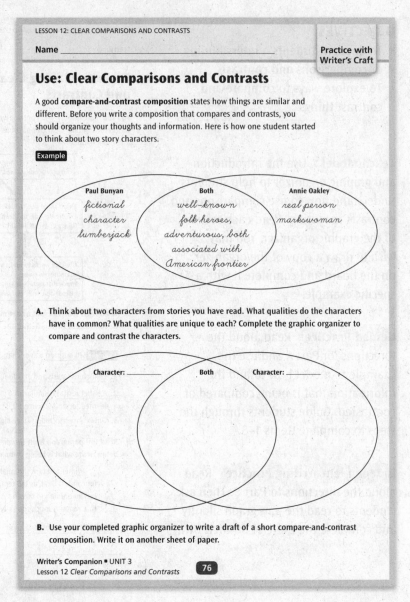

LESSON 12: CLEAR COMPARISONS AND CONTRASTS

Name _____

Practice with Writer's Craft

Use: Clear Comparisons and Contrasts

A good **compare-and-contrast composition** states how things are similar and different. Before you write a composition that compares and contrasts, you should organize your thoughts and information. Here is how one student started to think about two story characters.

Example

Paul Bunyan — fictional character, lumberjack

Both — well-known folk heroes, adventurous, both associated with American frontier

Annie Oakley — real person, markswoman

A. Think about two characters from stories you have read. What qualities do the characters have in common? What qualities are unique to each? Complete the graphic organizer to compare and contrast the characters.

Character: _____   Both   Character: _____

B. Use your completed graphic organizer to write a draft of a short compare-and-contrast composition. Write it on another sheet of paper.

Writer's Companion • UNIT 3
Lesson 12 *Clear Comparisons and Contrasts*   76

Reaching All Learners

BELOW LEVEL

Have students describe the characters they chose to a partner. Have partners decide what is the most important information. Then have them work together to put it into the graphic organizer.

ADVANCED

Challenge students to incorporate a third character into their composition. Show students how to add a third oval to the Venn diagram and have them use the revised diagram to compare and contrast the three characters.

ENGLISH-LANGUAGE LEARNERS

Suggest that English language learners start by completing the Venn diagram in their first language. Then have them work with a partner to create an English version that accurately reflects the comparisons and contrasts they have described.

© Harcourt

The Parts of a Compare-and-Contrast Composition

OBJECTIVES

- To understand the parts of a compare-and-contrast composition
- To analyze a Student Model

Standard: LA.5.3.3.1 evaluate for writing traits

Teach/Model Explain that the writing model on this page is a first draft of a student's compare-and-contrast composition. Read aloud the introductory text and the boxed call-outs. Then read the Student Model. As students listen, have them pay careful attention to how the composition is organized. After you have read the model, ask a volunteer to summarize the composition orally.

Guided Practice Point out the questions below the model. Read aloud Item 1 and guide students to find the sentence that introduces the topic of the composition. Then read aloud Items 2 and 3 and ask students to reread the composition to find the paragraph that compares and the paragraph that contrasts.

Independent Writing Practice Have students complete Item 4 independently. Remind them that the writer's purpose answers the question: "Why did the writer write this composition?"

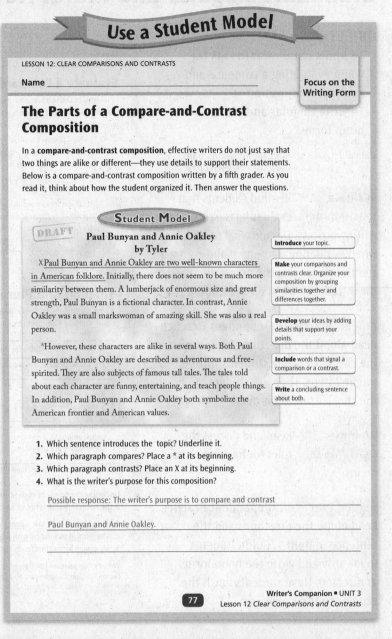

Use a Student Model

LESSON 12: CLEAR COMPARISONS AND CONTRASTS

Name _____

Focus on the Writing Form

The Parts of a Compare-and-Contrast Composition

In a **compare-and-contrast composition**, effective writers do not just say that two things are alike or different—they use details to support their statements. Below is a compare-and-contrast composition written by a fifth grader. As you read it, think about how the student organized it. Then answer the questions.

Student Model

DRAFT

Paul Bunyan and Annie Oakley
by Tyler

X Paul Bunyan and Annie Oakley are two well-known characters in American folklore. Initially, there does not seem to be much more similarity between them. A lumberjack of enormous size and great strength, Paul Bunyan is a fictional character. In contrast, Annie Oakley was a small markswoman of amazing skill. She was also a real person.

*However, these characters are alike in several ways. Both Paul Bunyan and Annie Oakley are described as adventurous and free-spirited. They are also subjects of famous tall tales. The tales told about each character are funny, entertaining, and teach people things. In addition, Paul Bunyan and Annie Oakley both symbolize the American frontier and American values.

Introduce your topic.

Make your comparisons and contrasts clear. Organize your composition by grouping similarities together and differences together.

Develop your ideas by adding details that support your points.

Include words that signal a comparison or a contrast.

Write a concluding sentence about both.

1. Which sentence introduces the topic? Underline it.
2. Which paragraph compares? Place a * at its beginning.
3. Which paragraph contrasts? Place an X at its beginning.
4. What is the writer's purpose for this composition?

   Possible response: The writer's purpose is to compare and contrast

   Paul Bunyan and Annie Oakley.

Writer's Companion • UNIT 3
77
Lesson 12 *Clear Comparisons and Contrasts*

WRITER'S STRATEGY: ORGANIZING COMPARE-AND-CONTRAST COMPOSITIONS

Explain to students that there are several ways to organize a compare-and-contrast composition. Point out that three organizational strategies are: *whole-to-whole, similarities-to-differences,* and *point-to-point.* In the whole-to-whole strategy, you say everything about one item and then say everything about the other. In the similarities-to-differences strategy, you discuss all of the similarities about the items, and then you discuss all of the differences. (The Student Model follows this organizational pattern.) In the point-to-point strategy, you compare and contrast one point and then move on to the next. Ask students to work in groups to write an outline for a composition using one of the three strategies you have discussed. Ask groups to share and discuss their work.

© Harcourt

Evaluate a Compare-and-Contrast Composition/ Grammar: Singular and Plural Nouns

OBJECTIVES

- To understand what to look for when evaluating a compare-and-contrast composition
- To write singular and plural noun forms

Standard: LA.5.3.3.1 evaluate for writing traits; LA.5.3.4.4 use parts of speech correctly

Evaluate Teach/Model Remind students that evaluating is part of the writing process. Discuss what to look for when evaluating a compare-and-contrast composition, using the points discussed in the introductory text on the student page.

Guided Practice/Independent Practice
Read aloud the directions for completing the checklist. Guide students through the first item. Then ask students to finish the checklist on their own.

Grammar Teach/Model Read and discuss the rules for forming plural nouns.

Guided Practice/Independent Practice
Read aloud the directions and the sentence in Item 1. Guide students to identify and write the noun forms as directed. Have students finish the activity on their own.

LESSON 12: CLEAR COMPARISONS AND CONTRASTS

Name _____

Evaluating the Student Model

Evaluate a Compare-and-Contrast Composition

When you evaluate a compare-and-contrast composition, ask yourself how clear the comparisons and contrasts were. You should also consider whether the writer gave details to support the comparisons or contrasts.

Now use the checklist to evaluate the Student Model. Put a check in the box next to each thing the writer did well. If you do not think the writer did a good job, do not check the box.

- ☐ The writer introduced the topic.
- ☐ The writer made clear comparisons and contrasts.
- ☐ The similarities and differences were well organized.
- ☐ The writer used details to support the main idea.
- ☐ The writer included words that signal comparisons and words that signal contrasts.

Writer's Grammar
Singular and Plural Nouns

A *singular noun* refers to one person, place, thing, or idea. Plural nouns refer to more than one noun. Following are the rules for how to change singular nouns into plural nouns.

Rules for Forming Plural Nouns	Examples	
1. The plural of a noun is usually formed by adding –s to a singular noun.	cat cats	field fields
2. Nouns ending in s, x, z, ch, sh, and most nouns ending in o form the plural by adding –es.	dress dresses	hero heroes
3. Some nouns ending in f or fe form the plural by changing –f or –fe to –ves.	knife knives	calf calves
4. Nouns ending in y preceded by a vowel form the plural by adding –s; nouns ending in a consonant + y form the plural by changing y to –ies.	day days	lady ladies
5. Some nouns are irregular.	person people	foot feet
6. Some nouns have no singular form. Others are always singular.	pants pants	sugar sugar

Underline the nouns in each sentence. If the noun is singular, write its plural form. If the noun is plural, write its singular form.

1. The child said she saw a deer run into the field. children, deer, fields
2. The woman put the corn on a shelf. women, corn, shelves
3. My puppy lost its first tooth last week. puppies, teeth, weeks

Writer's Companion ▪ UNIT 3
Lesson 12 *Clear Comparisons and Contrasts* 78

SHARING AND DISCUSSING

Have students work in small groups to discuss their evaluations of the Student Model. Suggest that groups ask themselves whether they think the model is well developed. Write these questions on the board for students to discuss: **How thorough is the composition? Does the composition include similarities and differences to make the comparisons and contrasts clear for readers? Why or why not? What conclusions does the writer draw about the two characters? How do you know?** Have groups report their discussions to the class. Encourage students to justify their responses.

© Harcourt

Revise: Creating Parallel Phrasing

OBJECTIVES
- To revise sentences by creating parallel phrasing
- To revise a compare-and-contrast composition by using parallel phrasing

Standard: LA.5.3.3.3 add supporting details/modify word choice

Teach/Model   Ask students to discuss the different ways they have learned to revise their writing. Tell students that, in this activity, they will revise their writing by creating parallel phrasing. Explain that parallel phrasing means using the same kind of phrasing to express related ideas. This type of phrasing is helpful in making comparisons and contrasts clear for the reader.

Guided Practice   Read aloud the introduction and the example sentences. Discuss how the change to parallel phrasing makes the ideas clearer for readers. Then read the directions to Part A. Guide students to create parallel phrasing for Item 1 by making all of the verbs end in –ing. Ask students if there is another way to create parallel phrasing. (The verbs can be changed to "to write," "to draw," and "to play.")

Independent Writing Practice   Direct students to revise the sentences in Items 2 and 3 of Part A on their own. Then read the directions to Part B and ask them to complete their revisions independently.

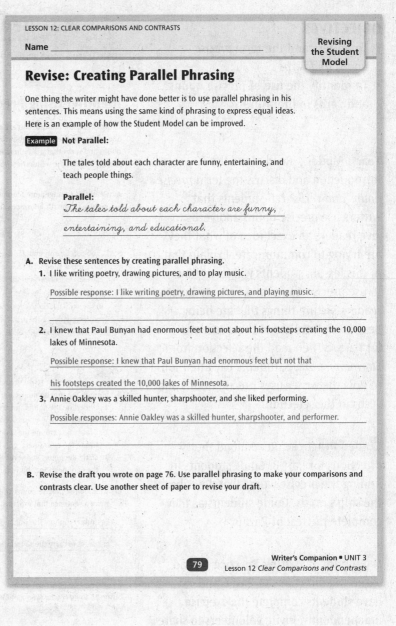

WRITER'S STRATEGY: PROOFREADING

Tell students that an important part of any revision is proofreading their work. Explain that proofreading means rereading their writing to look for mistakes in spelling and grammar. Suggest that students have another person—a family member or friend—proofread their work, too. Explain that it is sometimes easier to see mistakes when you are not already familiar with a piece of writing. Have students proofread their revised compositions. Then ask them to exchange papers with a partner and proofread each other's work.

Identify: Using Precise Nouns and Verbs

OBJECTIVES

- To understand the term *precise nouns and verbs*
- To identify the use of precise nouns and verbs in literature

Teach/Model Read aloud the introduction and discuss the term *precise nouns and verbs*. Tell students that writers use precise nouns and verbs to give readers an exact idea of what they are trying to communicate. Explain that, in this lesson, students will learn how to use precise nouns and verbs to help readers picture things that are being described. Read aloud the directions for Part A. Then read the selection from *Stormalong*. Have students pay attention to how the writer uses precise nouns and verbs in the selection.

Guided Practice Read aloud the directions for Part B. Guide students in finding the precise words that describe the ship's masts. Guide students as they complete the rest of Part B.

Independent Writing Practice Read aloud the directions to Part C and have students complete the exercise independently. Invite volunteers to share their responses.

Use a Literature Model

LESSON 13: USING PRECISE NOUNS AND VERBS

Name _____

Writer's Craft in Literature

Identify: Using Precise Nouns and Verbs

In order to communicate successfully to their readers, writers use **precise nouns and verbs.** Precise nouns and verbs are chosen carefully. They are the exact nouns and verbs that will help readers better understand the people, places, events, or ideas the writers describe.

A. Read this passage from *Stormalong*. Notice how the writer uses precise words to help readers picture the boat's enormous size.

Literature Model

Soon Stormy and *The Courser* were taking cargoes all over the world—to India, China, and Europe. It took four weeks to get all hands on deck. Teams of white horses carried sailors from stem to stern. The ship's towering masts had to be hinged to let the sun and moon go by. The tips of the masts were padded so they wouldn't punch holes in the sky. The trip to the crow's nest took so long, the sailors who climbed to the top returned with gray beards. The vessel was so big that once, when she hit an island in the Caribbean Sea, she knocked it clear into the Gulf of Mexico!

—from *Stormalong*
by Mary Pope Osborne

B. Identify the precise nouns and verbs used in the passage. Possible responses are given.
1. Underline the nouns and verbs that tell exactly how the boat was protected so it would not damage the sky. masts, hinged, tips, padded, punch holes
2. Draw a box around the words that describe how sailors looked when they returned from a trip to the crow's nest. gray beards
3. Circle the nouns and verbs that describe precisely what happened when the ship sailed in the Caribbean Sea. hit island, knocked, Gulf of Mexico

C. What do the precise nouns and verbs in the third sentence tell you about the ship? Write a sentence that explains.

Possible response: The words give readers an idea of how long the ship is—it takes teams

of horses to carry the sailors the length of the ship.

_____

Writer's Companion • UNIT 3
Lesson 13 *Using Precise Nouns and Verbs*   80

EXTENDING THE CONCEPT: PRECISE WORD CHOICE

Tell students that effective word choice can entail using lively, descriptive, precise language in a piece of writing. Explain that successful word choice helps communicate ideas to readers. It also creates a response in readers. Have groups make a list of all the methods they have learned to develop their ability to choose precise words. Clarify that strong and precise word choice does not always mean using big vocabulary words. It can also mean using everyday words in a meaningful way.

Explore: Using Precise Nouns and Verbs

OBJECTIVES
- To increase students' understanding of precise nouns and verbs
- To write sentences with precise nouns and verbs

Teach/Model Tell students that writers use precise nouns and verbs to communicate actions, thoughts, feelings, and ideas. Use the introduction and the graphic organizer to increase students' understanding of the importance of precise nouns and verbs. Review the graphic organizer and read each list of general and precise nouns. Ask students to discuss the different mental images given by each precise noun or verb.

Guided Practice Read aloud the directions for Part A and ask a volunteer to read the two sentences used in the example. Ask students to compare the original sentence with the rewritten one. Guide students through completing Items 1–3.

Independent Writing Practice Read aloud the directions to Part B. Guide students to choose a word with which to fill in the first blank. Then ask students to complete the exercise on their own.

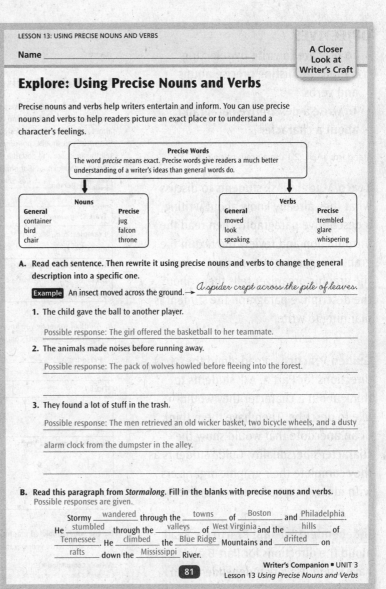

© Harcourt

SHARING AND DISCUSSING

Invite students to read aloud their responses to Part B. Have them read the entire paragraph from start to finish, substituting their chosen words for the blank spaces. Ask students to explain why they chose the words they did. What image or feeling did they hope to convey? As students read and explain their paragraphs, facilitate a broader discussion with the class. Ask them to discuss how different precise nouns and verbs yield different meanings.

Use: Using Precise Nouns and Verbs

OBJECTIVES

- To prepare to write by selecting a topic and listing precise nouns and verbs
- To write a descriptive paragraph about a character

Standard: LA.5.3.2.1 use a pre-writing plan

Teach/Model Ask students to discuss what they already know about writing a descriptive paragraph. Then read the introduction and review the text in the graphic organizer. Ask students what the graphic organizer tells them about the descriptive paragraph the student is planning to write.

Guided Practice Read aloud the directions for Part A. Ask students to think about a character they would like to describe. Then have them think of an anecdote that would show the character's personality. Guide students as they complete their graphic organizers with ideas for specific nouns and verbs.

Independent Writing Practice Read aloud the directions for Part B and have students work independently to complete the activity.

LESSON 13: USING PRECISE NOUNS AND VERBS

Name _____

Practice with Writer's Craft

Use: Using Precise Nouns and Verbs

When you write a **descriptive paragraph** about a character, you focus on that person's individual traits. One way to do this is to tell an anecdote, or short story, about the person that illustrates the characteristics you want to describe. Before you write, you should choose some precise nouns and verbs that will help you tell the anecdote and describe the character accurately. Here is how one student started to think about planning a character sketch.

Example Person: *Uncle Max*   Anecdote: *my visit to workshop*

Trait 1: *messy*	Trait 2: *energetic*	Trait 3: *supportive*
Examples: *trash in workshop*	**Examples:** *quick movements*	**Examples:** *helps me practice for play*
Specific Nouns and Verbs: *piles of paper, lumber, and recycling*	**Specific Nouns and Verbs:** *flings arms, knocks over bucket*	**Specific Nouns and Verbs:** *encourages, cheers*

A. Think of someone you know well. What characteristics or personality traits would you list to describe this person? Complete the graphic organizer.

Person: _____   Anecdote: _____

Trait 1:	Trait 2:	Trait 3:
Examples:	**Examples:**	**Examples:**
Specific Nouns and Verbs:	**Specific Nouns and Verbs:**	**Specific Nouns and Verbs:**

B. Use your completed graphic organizer to write a paragraph describing someone you know very well. Write your paragraph on another sheet of paper.

Writer's Companion ▪ UNIT 3
Lesson 13 *Using Precise Nouns and Verbs*   82

WRITER'S STRATEGY: WORD SURVEY

After they have completed their graphic organizers, but before they begin to write, encourage students to reread the completed organizer and think critically about their word choices. Have them ask themselves if the words they have chosen are as colorful and specific as possible. Ask students to read each word and consider the following questions:

- Is this an everyday word, or is it an unusual word that will catch readers' attention?
- Does this word create a vivid picture for readers, or can I think of a more interesting one?

The Parts of a Descriptive Paragraph

OBJECTIVES
- To understand the parts of a descriptive paragraph
- To analyze a Student Model

Teach/Model   Read aloud the introduction. Tell students that the writing model on this page is a first draft of a student's descriptive paragraph about a character. Read the boxed call-outs aloud. Then read the model, asking students to pay careful attention to how the description is developed. After you have read the model, ask students to explain what they know about Uncle Max.

Guided Practice   Point out the first two Items below the model. Read aloud Item 1 and guide students to find the sentence that introduces the setting for the description. Then read aloud Item 2 and guide students to identify precise nouns and verbs in the passage.

Independent Writing Practice   Have students complete Items 3 and 4 independently. Invite them to share and discuss their responses.

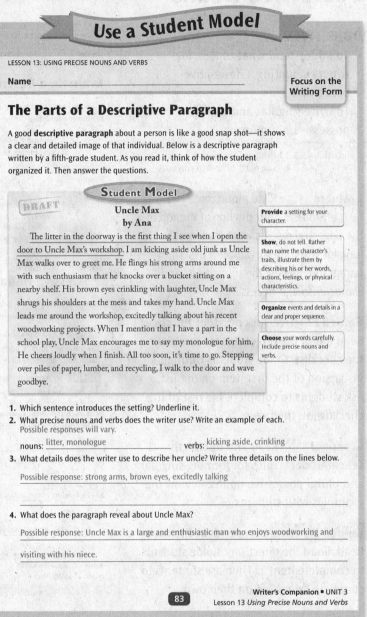

EXTENDING THE CONCEPT: SHOW, DON'T TELL

Tell students that a maxim often used by writers is *show, don't tell*. Explain that this means that writers should aim to show readers what something is like rather than telling them what it is like. For example, rather than say, "The sunset was pretty" it is better to say, "As the sun set, the sky exploded into clouds of pink and gold." Ask students to compare these two sentences and discuss why the second one is more effective than the first. Ask students for other examples that illustrate the importance of showing instead of telling. Record students' ideas on chart paper and display them in the classroom under the heading *Show, Don't Tell*.

Writer's Companion • UNIT 3
Lesson 13 *Using Precise Nouns and Verbs*

© Harcourt

Evaluate a Descriptive Paragraph/Grammar: Possessive Nouns

OBJECTIVES

- To understand what to look for when evaluating a descriptive paragraph
- To write singular and plural possessive noun forms

Standard: LA.5.3.3.1 evaluate for writing traits;
LA.5.3.4.4 use parts of speech correctly

Evaluate Teach/Model   Read aloud the introduction at the top of the page and discuss what students should look for when they evaluate a descriptive paragraph. Review the terms *traits* and *characteristics,* if necessary.

Guided Practice/Independent Practice

Read aloud the directions for completing the checklist. Guide students through a discussion of the first item on the list. Ask students to complete the rest of the checklist on their own.

Grammar Teach/Model   Read and discuss the rules for forming singular and plural possessive nouns. Review the examples with students.

Guided Practice/Independent Practice

Read aloud the directions. Guide students to complete Item 1. Then ask students to complete Items 2–4 on their own.

LESSON 13: USING PRECISE NOUNS AND VERBS

Name _____

Evaluating the Student Model

Evaluate a Descriptive Paragraph

When you evaluate a descriptive paragraph of a character, ask yourself how well the writer established the person's traits and characteristics.

Now use the checklist to evaluate the Student Model. Put a check in the box next to each thing the writer did well. If you do not think the writer did a good job, do not check the box.

- ☐ The writer described the character within an appropriate setting.
- ☐ The writer illustrated, rather than told, the character's traits.
- ☐ The events and details flowed in an order that made sense.
- ☐ The writer used precise nouns and verbs.

Writer's Grammar
Possessive Nouns

A possessive noun shows ownership.
The possessive form of singular nouns is formed by adding an *apostrophe* and an *s.*

Example   the food of the dog   the dog's food

The possessive form of plural nouns is formed by adding an *apostrophe.* If the plural noun does not end in *s,* then an *apostrophe* and an *s* are added.

Example   the food of the dogs   the dogs' food
         the books of the women   the women's books

Read each sentence. Rewrite the underlined word group as a possessive noun.

1. The Environmental Protection Agency is checking the water of the city.

   the city's water

2. When they went outside, they saw that the wheels of the trucks were flat.

   the trucks' wheels

3. The howling of the wolf woke up the entire camp last night.

   The wolf's howling

4. The children of the Smiths know all of the lyrics to the song.

   The Smiths' children

Writer's Companion • UNIT 3
Lesson 13 *Using Precise Nouns and Verbs*   84

Reaching All Learners

BELOW LEVEL

Possessive nouns can be confusing for some students. Caution students to look carefully and decide whether each noun is plural or singular before writing it in possessive form.

ADVANCED

For extra practice, have students write their own sentences with word groups that can be rewritten as possessive nouns. Have pairs exchange papers and rewrite sentences.

ENGLISH-LANGUAGE LEARNERS

In many languages, ownership is shown differently than it is in English. Work with students to clarify rules for forming possessive nouns in English.

© Harcourt

Revise: Adding Precise Nouns and Verbs

OBJECTIVES
- To revise sentences by adding precise nouns and verbs
- To revise a descriptive paragraph

Standard: LA.5.3.3.3 add supporting details/modify word choice

Teach/Model Tell students that revising their writing gives them an opportunity to correct mistakes and improve their word choice. Explain that one way to revise writing is to add precise nouns and verbs. Adding precise vocabulary can help make writing clearer and more interesting.

Guided Practice Read aloud the introduction and the example revision. Ask students to identify the noun and verb that were added to the revised sentence. Explain that these precise words make a more vivid picture for readers. Read aloud the directions for Part A and guide students to revise the sentence in Item 1 by adding precise nouns and verbs. Ask students to suggest other revisions. Remind students that they can use the Word Bank as a resource as they revise the sentences.

Independent Writing Practice Have students complete Items 2 and 3 independently. Then read the directions for Part B and ask students to revise their descriptive paragraphs on their own.

LESSON 13: USING PRECISE NOUNS AND VERBS

Revising the Student Model

Name _____

Revise: Adding Precise Nouns and Verbs

One thing the writer might have done better is to use more precise nouns and verbs. Here is an example of how the Student Model can be improved.

Example I am kicking aside old junk as Uncle Max walks over to greet me.

I am kicking aside a week-old pizza box as Uncle Max strides over to greet me.

A. Revise these sentences by adding precise nouns and verbs. Use the Word Bank to help you.

1. Daryl put his stuff in his bag.

   Possible response: Daryl crammed his clothing and souvenirs into his suitcase.

2. The children ate their dinner.

   Possible response: The three boys gulped down the chicken noodle soup and swallowed their bread quickly.

3. Looking over her shoulder, Gertrude saw something.

   Possible responses: Looking over her shoulder, Gertrude noticed a dark shadow inching its way along the garden wall.

Word Bank
cram
gulp
garden
souvenir
suitcase

B. Revise the draft you wrote on page 82. Add precise nouns and verbs to make a clear mental picture for readers. Use another sheet of paper if you need more space.

_____
_____
_____
_____
_____
_____
_____

85   **Writer's Companion • UNIT 3**
Lesson 13 *Using Precise Nouns and Verbs*

WRITER'S STRATEGY: REVISING FOR PRECISION

Before students begin revising their descriptive paragraphs, have them read their drafts aloud to a partner. Have them ask the partner to describe what picture the paragraph creates. Explain that the more precise the writer's language is, the clearer the picture will be. Tell students to use what they have learned from their partners to revise their drafts. Suggest that students go back and circle words or phrases that could be more precise. Tell them to ask themselves, "What exact image do I want readers to see when reading this?"

© Harcourt

Review Writer's Craft

OBJECTIVES

- To review sentence fluency and word choice
- To identify characteristics of clear writing in literature

Teach/Model Read aloud the introduction. Explain that, in this lesson, students will review what they have learned about sentence fluency and word choice. Read the directions for Part A aloud. Then read the passage from *A Drop of Water* and ask students to listen carefully. Tell them to listen for the use of variety in sentence beginnings, precise nouns and verbs, and compare-and-contrast text structure.

Guided Practice Ask students to discuss what they know about sentence fluency and writing conventions. Invite students to read aloud passages from the selection that they feel illustrate some aspect of effective writing. Then guide students to complete Part B.

Independent Writing Practice Read aloud the question in Part C. Remind students that the main idea is the most important idea. Have students answer the question on their own.

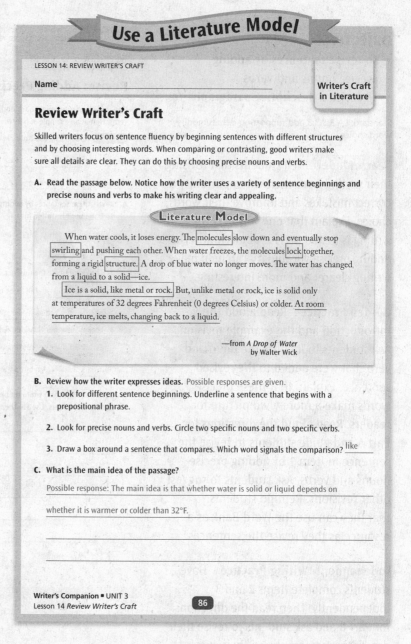

Use a Literature Model

LESSON 14: REVIEW WRITER'S CRAFT

Name _____

Writer's Craft in Literature

Review Writer's Craft

Skilled writers focus on sentence fluency by beginning sentences with different structures and by choosing interesting words. When comparing or contrasting, good writers make sure all details are clear. They can do this by choosing precise nouns and verbs.

A. Read the passage below. Notice how the writer uses a variety of sentence beginnings and precise nouns and verbs to make his writing clear and appealing.

Literature Model

When water cools, it loses energy. The molecules slow down and eventually stop swirling and pushing each other. When water freezes, the molecules lock together, forming a rigid structure. A drop of blue water no longer moves. The water has changed from a liquid to a solid—ice.

Ice is a solid, like metal or rock. But, unlike metal or rock, ice is solid only at temperatures of 32 degrees Fahrenheit (0 degrees Celsius) or colder. At room temperature, ice melts, changing back to a liquid.

—from *A Drop of Water* by Walter Wick

B. Review how the writer expresses ideas. Possible responses are given.

1. Look for different sentence beginnings. Underline a sentence that begins with a prepositional phrase.

2. Look for precise nouns and verbs. Circle two specific nouns and two specific verbs.

3. Draw a box around a sentence that compares. Which word signals the comparison? like

C. What is the main idea of the passage?

Possible response: The main idea is that whether water is solid or liquid depends on

whether it is warmer or colder than 32°F.

Writer's Companion • UNIT 3
Lesson 14 *Review Writer's Craft*

86

WRITER'S STRATEGY: PRACTICE MAKES PERFECT

Tell students that skilled writers develop their craft with practice. Ask students to consider which of their writing skills they would like to improve. Have students name various skills (grammar, sentence fluency, organization, etc.). Have students divide into small groups and assign each group one of the writing skills named. Have each group make a list of all the methods they have learned to develop that skill. Remind students to refer to previous lessons to help them develop their lists. Have groups share their work.

© Harcourt

Review Writer's Craft

OBJECTIVES

- To deepen students' understanding of sentence fluency and word choice
- To analyze writing for sentence fluency and word choice

Teach/Model Use the graphic organizer to review ways to use the writing traits of sentence fluency and word choice. Remind students to vary their sentence beginnings, use parallel phrasing, and use precise vocabulary. Stress that skillful use of sentence fluency and word choice will make writing both interesting and clear.

Guided Practice Read aloud the directions for Part A. Tell students that the example passage has many of the ingredients of effective writing. Then read the passage aloud. Read the directions for Part B and use the example to show students how to describe sentence beginnings and identify precise nouns and verbs.

Independent Writing Practice Have students complete Part B on their own.

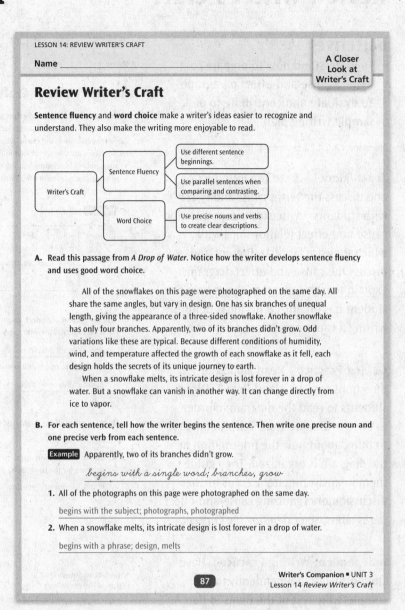

LESSON 14: REVIEW WRITER'S CRAFT

Name _____

A Closer Look at Writer's Craft

Review Writer's Craft

Sentence fluency and **word choice** make a writer's ideas easier to recognize and understand. They also make the writing more enjoyable to read.

Writer's Craft → Sentence Fluency → Use different sentence beginnings. / Use parallel sentences when comparing and contrasting.

Word Choice → Use precise nouns and verbs to create clear descriptions.

A. Read this passage from *A Drop of Water*. Notice how the writer develops sentence fluency and uses good word choice.

> All of the snowflakes on this page were photographed on the same day. All share the same angles, but vary in design. One has six branches of unequal length, giving the appearance of a three-sided snowflake. Another snowflake has only four branches. Apparently, two of its branches didn't grow. Odd variations like these are typical. Because different conditions of humidity, wind, and temperature affected the growth of each snowflake as it fell, each design holds the secrets of its unique journey to earth.
>
> When a snowflake melts, its intricate design is lost forever in a drop of water. But a snowflake can vanish in another way. It can change directly from ice to vapor.

B. For each sentence, tell how the writer begins the sentence. Then write one precise noun and one precise verb from each sentence.

Example Apparently, two of its branches didn't grow.

begins with a single word; branches, grow

1. All of the photographs on this page were photographed on the same day.

   begins with the subject; photographs, photographed

2. When a snowflake melts, its intricate design is lost forever in a drop of water.

   begins with a phrase; design, melts

87   **Writer's Companion** • UNIT 3
Lesson 14 *Review Writer's Craft*

EXTENDING THE CONCEPT: COMPARE AND CONTRAST

Tell students to look at the passage in Part A. Explain that the passage tells about some similarities and differences among snowflakes. Draw a two-column chart on the board. Title the left-hand column *Comparisons* and the right-hand column *Contrasts*. Ask students to look through the passage to find characteristics that all snowflakes have in common. Then have them look for characteristics that can vary among snowflakes. Have students name these as you write them on the board under the correct heading. Finally, have students search the passage for words that signal comparisons and contrasts, such as *all*, *each*, and *different*.

© Harcourt

Review Writer's Craft

OBJECTIVES
- To understand how to prepare to write a cause-and-effect paragraph
- To evaluate and contribute to a sample writing plan

Standard: LA.5.4.2.2 record information

Teach/Model   Read the introduction and discuss the terms *cause* and *effect* with students. Invite students to describe cause-and-effect relationships with which they are familiar. Present and discuss the cause-and-effect diagram. Explain that this diagram shows how one student has organized his ideas before writing a cause-and-effect paragraph.

Guided Practice   Read aloud the directions for Part A and Item 1. Direct students to read the diagram in order to answer the question. Tell students to think about how the information in the diagram is organized. Then guide them in answering Item 2. For further discussion of organizing cause-and-effect paragraphs, see *Extending the Concept.*

Independent Writing Practice   Have students work independently to complete the rest of the items in Part A.

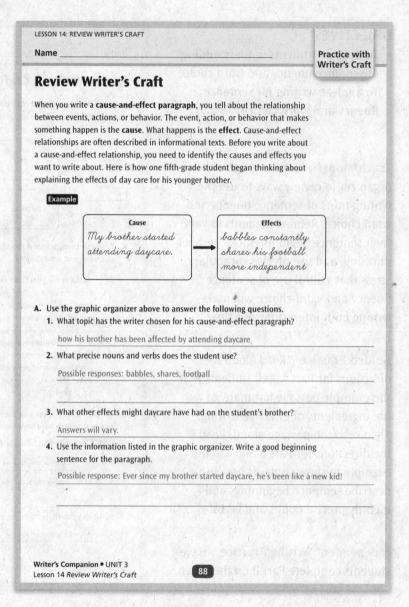

LESSON 14: REVIEW WRITER'S CRAFT

Name _____

Practice with Writer's Craft

Review Writer's Craft

When you write a **cause-and-effect paragraph**, you tell about the relationship between events, actions, or behavior. The event, action, or behavior that makes something happen is the **cause**. What happens is the **effect**. Cause-and-effect relationships are often described in informational texts. Before you write about a cause-and-effect relationship, you need to identify the causes and effects you want to write about. Here is how one fifth-grade student began thinking about explaining the effects of day care for his younger brother.

Example

Cause	Effects
My brother started attending daycare.	babbles constantly shares his football more independent

A. Use the graphic organizer above to answer the following questions.

1. What topic has the writer chosen for his cause-and-effect paragraph?

   how his brother has been affected by attending daycare

2. What precise nouns and verbs does the student use?

   Possible responses: babbles, shares, football

3. What other effects might daycare have had on the student's brother?

   Answers will vary.

4. Use the information listed in the graphic organizer. Write a good beginning sentence for the paragraph.

   Possible response: Ever since my brother started daycare, he's been like a new kid!

Writer's Companion • UNIT 3
Lesson 14 *Review Writer's Craft*   88

EXTENDING THE CONCEPT: ORGANIZING CAUSE-AND-EFFECT PARAGRAPHS

Tell students that cause-and-effect paragraphs follow basic rules of organization. That is, they express a main idea in a topic sentence and follow up with specific supporting details. However, the purpose of a cause-and-effect paragraph is to discuss the relationship between causes and effects. So, if the paragraph states an effect and discusses its causes, the topic sentence introduces the effect and the supporting sentences describe the causes. On the other hand, if the paragraph states a cause and discusses its effects, the topic sentence introduces the cause and the supporting sentences describe the effects.

© Harcourt

The Parts of a Cause-and-Effect Paragraph

OBJECTIVES

- To understand how the elements of a cause-and-effect paragraph are organized
- To analyze a Student Model

Standard: LA.5.3.3.1 evaluate for writing traits

Teach/Model   Tell students that the writing model on this page is a draft of a cause-and-effect paragraph written by a student. Read aloud the introduction, taking care to present and discuss the signal words mentioned. Then read the boxed call-outs for how to organize a cause-and-effect paragraph. Finally read the model aloud and ask students to pay careful attention to how the paragraph is organized.

Guided Practice   Point out the questions below the Student Model. Read the first question aloud. Guide students to find the topic sentence of the paragraph.

Independent Writing Practice   Direct students to answer Questions 2–4 on their own. For additional discussion of words used to signal cause-and-effect relationships, see *Extending the Concept.*

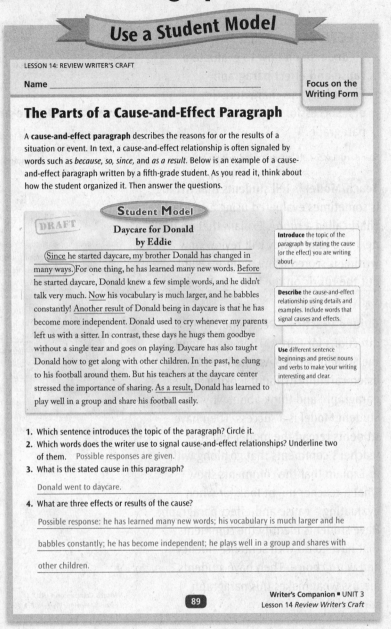

Use a Student Model

LESSON 14: REVIEW WRITER'S CRAFT

Name _____

Focus on the Writing Form

The Parts of a Cause-and-Effect Paragraph

A **cause-and-effect paragraph** describes the reasons for or the results of a situation or event. In text, a cause-and-effect relationship is often signaled by words such as *because, so, since,* and *as a result*. Below is an example of a cause-and-effect paragraph written by a fifth-grade student. As you read it, think about how the student organized it. Then answer the questions.

Student Model

DRAFT

Daycare for Donald
by Eddie

(Since he started daycare, my brother Donald has changed in many ways.) For one thing, he has learned many new words. Before he started daycare, Donald knew a few simple words, and he didn't talk very much. Now his vocabulary is much larger, and he babbles constantly! Another result of Donald being in daycare is that he has become more independent. Donald used to cry whenever my parents left us with a sitter. In contrast, these days he hugs them goodbye without a single tear and goes on playing. Daycare has also taught Donald how to get along with other children. In the past, he clung to his football around them. But his teachers at the daycare center stressed the importance of sharing. As a result, Donald has learned to play well in a group and share his football easily.

Introduce the topic of the paragraph by stating the cause (or the effect) you are writing about.

Describe the cause-and-effect relationship using details and examples. Include words that signal causes and effects.

Use different sentence beginnings and precise nouns and verbs to make your writing interesting and clear.

1. Which sentence introduces the topic of the paragraph? Circle it.
2. Which words does the writer use to signal cause-and-effect relationships? Underline two of them.   Possible responses are given.
3. What is the stated cause in this paragraph?

   Donald went to daycare.

4. What are three effects or results of the cause?

   Possible response: he has learned many new words; his vocabulary is much larger and he

   babbles constantly; he has become independent; he plays well in a group and shares with

   other children.

89

Writer's Companion • UNIT 3
Lesson 14 *Review Writer's Craft*

EXTENDING THE CONCEPT: IDENTIFYING CAUSE-AND-EFFECT RELATIONSHIPS

Explain to students that certain words can signal that a cause-and-effect relationship is being described. Reread the signal words mentioned in the introductory text on this page and record them on the board. Ask students if they know any other signal words. Elicit responses, and add the words to the list. Ask students to work in pairs to select and read a passage from a piece of writing. Have students search for signal words that will help them identify cause-and-effect relationships. Invite students to share what they discovered with the class.

Evaluate a Cause-and-Effect Paragraph

OBJECTIVES

- To understand how to evaluate a cause-and-effect paragraph
- To identify the characteristics of a successful cause-and-effect paragraph

Standard: LA.5.3.3.1 evaluate for writing traits

Teach/Model   Tell students that writing is sometimes evaluated using a special chart called a *rubric*. Explain that on the next two pages, they will review how writing is scored using a rubric. Point out the rubric on the following page.

Guided Practice   Read aloud the directions for Part A. Then read aloud the Student Model. Ask students to listen carefully (without looking at the paragraph) and think about why the Student Model is a success. Then have students reread the model and the teacher's comments that go along with it. Explain that the comments show what a teacher might look for when evaluating a cause-and-effect paragraph. Have students identify the comments that have to do with sentence fluency and word choice. Then have students discuss what makes this paragraph successful.

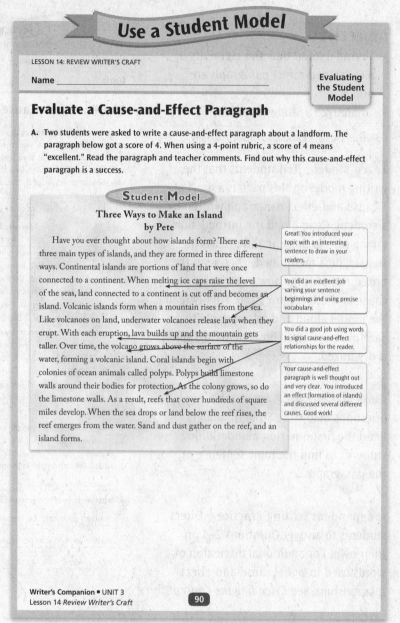

Use a Student Model

LESSON 14: REVIEW WRITER'S CRAFT

Name _____

Evaluating the Student Model

Evaluate a Cause-and-Effect Paragraph

A. Two students were asked to write a cause-and-effect paragraph about a landform. The paragraph below got a score of 4. When using a 4-point rubric, a score of 4 means "excellent." Read the paragraph and teacher comments. Find out why this cause-and-effect paragraph is a success.

Student Model

Three Ways to Make an Island
by Pete

Have you ever thought about how islands form? There are three main types of islands, and they are formed in three different ways. Continental islands are portions of land that were once connected to a continent. When melting ice caps raise the level of the seas, land connected to a continent is cut off and becomes an island. Volcanic islands form when a mountain rises from the sea. Like volcanoes on land, underwater volcanoes release lava when they erupt. With each eruption, lava builds up and the mountain gets taller. Over time, the volcano grows above the surface of the water, forming a volcanic island. Coral islands begin with colonies of ocean animals called polyps. Polyps build limestone walls around their bodies for protection. As the colony grows, so do the limestone walls. As a result, reefs that cover hundreds of square miles develop. When the sea drops or land below the reef rises, the reef emerges from the water. Sand and dust gather on the reef, and an island forms.

Great! You introduced your topic with an interesting sentence to draw in your readers.

You did an excellent job varying your sentence beginnings and using precise vocabulary.

You did a good job using words to signal cause-and-effect relationships for the reader.

Your cause-and-effect paragraph is well thought out and very clear. You introduced an effect (formation of islands) and discussed several different causes. Good work!

SHARING AND DISCUSSING

Ask students to work in small groups to discuss the Student Model. Have students focus their discussions on sentence fluency and word choice. Ask one group member to read the paragraph aloud while other group members listen and take notes to aid them in their discussion. After some discussion, ask groups to decide whether they agree with the paragraph's score. Ask groups to report their decisions. Have students explain their reasoning by citing examples from the text.

Evaluate a Cause-and-Effect Paragraph

OBJECTIVES

- To understand why a cause-and-effect paragraph received a low score on a rubric
- To use a rubric to evaluate a cause-and-effect paragraph

Standard: LA.5.3.3.1 evaluate for writing traits

Teach/Model Tell students that they will now read a cause-and-effect paragraph that received a score of 2 on a 4-point rubric. Read aloud the Student Model. Ask students to listen (without looking at the paragraph) and think about ways in which the paragraph could be improved.

Guided Practice Ask students to comment on any strengths or weaknesses they noticed in the cause-and-effect paragraph. Then have them read the Student Model and teacher's comments to themselves. Ask students to summarize how the cause-and-effect paragraph could be improved.

Independent Writing Practice Discuss how to use the 4-point rubric at the bottom of the page. For additional instruction, see *Writer's Strategy* below. Ask students to complete the rubric to show what score they would give the cause-and-effect paragraph on page 89.

Use a Student Model

LESSON 14: REVIEW WRITER'S CRAFT

Name _____

Evaluating the Student Model

B. This summary got a score of 2. Why did it get a low score?

Student Model

How Rivers Form
by Ellie

Rivers form over a long period of time. Water flows from higher places to lower places. Here is the series of actions that make them. Rain falls on mountains, and sometimes it collects in depressions in the rocks. When it gets cold, the water freezes, and erosion occurs. Water continues to wear away rock over time. Wind and weather does, too. After some time, small streams form. The streams cause further erosion. The stream grows larger and becomes a river.

> Focus your introductory sentence. A cause-and-effect relationship is not set up here.

> Are the causes and effects clear? You could use signal words and vary your sentence beginnings more to help readers follow the flow of ideas.

> Good work including the term *depressions*. But what kind of weather erodes rock? You could use more precise vocabulary to help readers understand these processes better.

C. What score would you give the student's paragraph? Put a number on each line.

	4	3	2	1
Sentence Fluency _____	☐ There is a lot of variety in sentence beginnings, and the writer uses many precise nouns and verbs.	☐ There is some variety in sentence beginnings, and the writer uses some precise nouns and verbs.	☐ There is almost no variety in sentence beginnings, but the writer uses some precise nouns and verbs.	☐ There is little or no variety in sentence beginnings, and the vocabulary is lacking in precision.
Conventions _____	☐ The writer uses a clear, correct cause-and-effect paragraph structure with strong reasons and results.	☐ The writer uses a clear, correct cause-and-effect paragraph structure with some reasons and results.	☐ The cause-and-effect structure is clear but there are not enough reasons and results.	☐ The cause-and-effect structure is unclear and there are little or no reasons and results.
Word Choice _____	☐ The writer always uses precise nouns and verbs.	☐ The writer usually uses precise nouns and verbs.	☐ The writer uses some precise nouns and verbs.	☐ The writer does not use precise nouns and verbs.

WRITER'S STRATEGY: USING CHARTS AND TABLES AS EVALUATION TOOLS

Remind students that they often use diagrams or other organizational tools in the prewriting stage of the writing process. Tell students that sometimes it is helpful to use an organizational tool in the evaluation process, too. Explain that a rubric is a writing evaluation tool in which particular writing traits are listed and described. Rubrics can be adjusted to fit a particular writing mode or to evaluate particular writing traits. Ask students to read through the rubric on their own. Answer any questions they may have about its organization or use.

© Harcourt

Extended Writing/Test Prep

OBJECTIVES

- To apply sentence fluency and word choice to a longer piece of writing
- To become familiar with writing prompts

Standard: LA.5.3.1.3 organize ideas

Teach/Model Tell students that the next two pages will give them an opportunity to select a topic for a longer piece of writing. Explain that they can choose from several possible writing activities. Read aloud the introduction, the directions in Part A, and Items 1–3. Ask students to name the writing forms they hear mentioned. Then review each writing form by directing students to reread the Student Model tips from the lesson in which that form appears.

- A Descriptive Paragraph, Setting: Lesson 11, page 71
- A Compare-and-Contrast Composition: Lesson 12, page 77
- A Descriptive Paragraph, Character: Lesson 13, page 83
- A Cause-and-Effect Paragraph: Lesson 14, page 89

Guided Practice Have students select one of the writing choices and begin the prewriting process by completing Part B independently.

LESSON 15: WRITING TEST PRACTICE

Name _____

Extended Writing/Test Prep

Extended Writing/Test Prep

On the first two pages of this lesson, you will use what you have learned about different kinds of paragraphs to write a longer written work.

A. Read the three choices below. Put a star by the writing activity you would like to do.

1. Respond to a Writing Prompt.

   Writing Situation: A friend tells you that she doesn't think her poor eating habits and lack of exercise affect her overall health that much.

   Directions for Writing: Think about what you know about being healthy. Now, write a cause-and-effect essay that shows how healthy eating and exercise affect people. Remember to use different sentence beginnings and precise nouns and verbs in your essay.

2. Choose one of the pieces of writing you started in this unit:
   - a descriptive paragraph, setting (page 70)
   - a compare-and-contrast composition (page 76)
   - a descriptive paragraph, character (page 82)

   Revise and expand your work into a complete piece of writing. Use what you have learned about sentence fluency and word choice to help readers understand the people, places, events, or ideas you write about.

3. Choose a topic you would like to write about. Write a cause-and-effect essay to describe a cause-and-effect relationship with which you are familiar.

B. Use the space below and on the next page to plan your writing.

TOPIC: _____

WRITING FORM: _____

HOW I WILL ORGANIZE MY WRITING: _____

_____

_____

_____

_____

Writer's Companion • UNIT 3
Lesson 15 *Writing Test Practice*   92

Reaching All Learners

BELOW LEVEL	ADVANCED	ENGLISH-LANGUAGE LEARNERS
Help students to develop an organizational plan that includes the essential elements of their chosen writing form.	Ask students to plan how they will incorporate other literary elements (such as metaphor or dialogue) into their writing.	Ask English-Language Learners to state their chosen topic, writing form, and organizational plan in their own words, orally, before committing it to paper.

© Harcourt

Extended Writing/Test Prep

OBJECTIVES

- To use a graphic organizer to plan a piece of writing
- To use the writing process to complete a longer written work

Standard: LA.5.3.2.1 use a pre-writing plan

Teach/Model Explain to students that in Part C they will select a graphic organizer and use it to plan their writing. Tell students they can pick a new organizer or reuse one from one of the lessons that has been reviewed. Model how to complete one of the graphic organizers for students. Ask students to discuss how they can use the organizer when they develop their writing plan.

Guided Practice Help students complete their graphic organizers and develop a writing plan. For additional prewriting help, see *Sharing and Discussing.*

Independent Writing Draft, Revise, and Publish Review the steps of the writing process. After students have finished their drafts, ask them to revise their work. Suggest that students publish their work by adding their finished papers to the class reading library.

© Harcourt

LESSON 15: WRITING TEST PRACTICE

Name _____

Extended Writing/Test Prep

C. In the space below, draw a graphic organizer that will help you plan your writing. Fill in the graphic organizer. Write additional notes on the lines below.

Notes

_____

_____

_____

_____

_____

_____

_____

D. Do your writing on another sheet of paper.

93

Writer's Companion ■ UNIT 3
Lesson 15 *Writing Test Practice*

SHARING AND DISCUSSING

Have students work in small groups to discuss the organizational features of descriptive paragraphs, compare-and-contrast compositions, and cause-and-effect paragraphs. Ask them also to review the importance of using different sentence beginnings and precise nouns and verbs. Then ask students to apply the skills they have reviewed as they complete their writing tasks independently.

Answering Multiple-Choice Questions

OBJECTIVES

- To answer questions that involve reading and evaluating a writing plan
- To use knowledge of the Venn diagram structure to answer test questions

Standard: LA.5.3.1.1 generate ideas

Teach/Model Tell students that on this page they will read and evaluate a writing plan. They will then answer multiple-choice questions about that plan. Read aloud the directions and the Test Tip. Then model how to answer the first item. Read each part of the writing plan aloud. Then recount what students have learned about the organization of information in a Venn diagram. Say: **Venn diagrams are used to compare and contrast categories. So, the best answer is choice D.**

Guided Practice Read Item 2 aloud and ask students to read the answer choices silently. Remind students to consider what they know about the different sections of the Venn diagram when selecting their answer. Have students mark the correct answer.

Independent Practice Ask students to complete the last test item on their own.

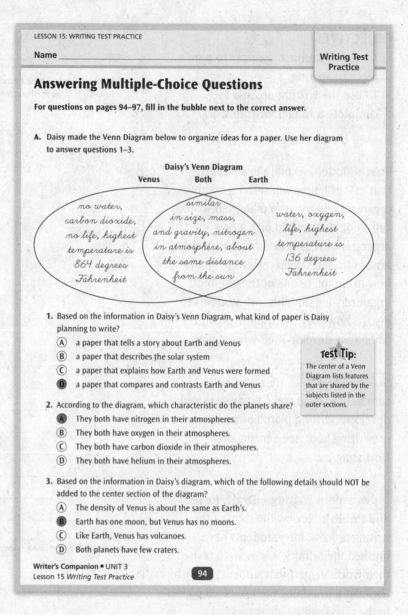

LESSON 15: WRITING TEST PRACTICE

Name _____

Writing Test Practice

Answering Multiple-Choice Questions

For questions on pages 94–97, fill in the bubble next to the correct answer.

A. Daisy made the Venn Diagram below to organize ideas for a paper. Use her diagram to answer questions 1–3.

Daisy's Venn Diagram

Venus   Both   Earth

no water, carbon dioxide, no life, highest temperature is 864 degrees Fahrenheit

similar in size, mass, and gravity, nitrogen in atmosphere, about the same distance from the sun

water, oxygen, life, highest temperature is 136 degrees Fahrenheit

1. Based on the information in Daisy's Venn Diagram, what kind of paper is Daisy planning to write?
   - Ⓐ a paper that tells a story about Earth and Venus
   - Ⓑ a paper that describes the solar system
   - Ⓒ a paper that explains how Earth and Venus were formed
   - Ⓓ a paper that compares and contrasts Earth and Venus

   Test Tip: The center of a Venn Diagram lists features that are shared by the subjects listed in the outer sections.

2. According to the diagram, which characteristic do the planets share?
   - Ⓐ They both have nitrogen in their atmospheres.
   - Ⓑ They both have oxygen in their atmospheres.
   - Ⓒ They both have carbon dioxide in their atmospheres.
   - Ⓓ They both have helium in their atmospheres.

3. Based on the information in Daisy's diagram, which of the following details should NOT be added to the center section of the diagram?
   - Ⓐ The density of Venus is about the same as Earth's.
   - Ⓑ Earth has one moon, but Venus has no moons.
   - Ⓒ Like Earth, Venus has volcanoes.
   - Ⓓ Both planets have few craters.

Writer's Companion • UNIT 3
Lesson 15 *Writing Test Practice*   94

Reaching All Learners

BELOW LEVEL	ADVANCED	ENGLISH-LANGUAGE LEARNERS
Help students read each question and restate what it asks them to do. For example: "This question asks me to find the detail that describes a feature of just one planet, not both planets."	Encourage students to write each of the answer choices from Item 3 in the appropriate section of the Venn diagram. Have students share and explain their responses.	Pair less fluent English speakers with more fluent English speakers. Have students discuss each answer choice in Item 3 in turn. Then guide them to see where each answer choice would be placed in the Venn diagram.

© Harcourt

Answering Multiple-Choice Questions (cont.)

OBJECTIVES
- To answer questions that involve reading a passage
- To change word order to revise the beginning of a sentence

Teach/Model Tell students that some multiple-choice question formats ask them to read a passage and then answer questions about it. Read aloud the directions for Part B. Then have students read the passage to themselves. Read aloud the first test item and model reading each sentence to determine whether it is on topic or not. Model marking the correct answer choice.

Guided Practice Guide students to answer Item 2. Emphasize the importance of rereading the passage to determine which of the possible placements listed in the answer choices makes the most sense. Guide students to see that answer choice C describes the best placement for the new sentence.

Independent Practice Read aloud the Test Tip to students. Then direct students to answer Item 3 on their own. Remind them to consider what they know about using different sentence beginnings.

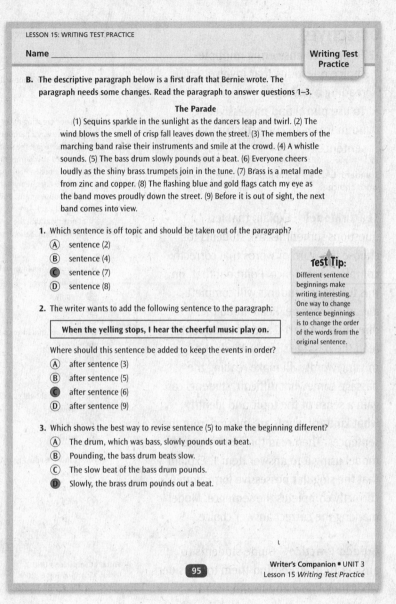

LESSON 15: WRITING TEST PRACTICE

Name _____

Writing Test Practice

B. The descriptive paragraph below is a first draft that Bernie wrote. The paragraph needs some changes. Read the paragraph to answer questions 1–3.

The Parade
(1) Sequins sparkle in the sunlight as the dancers leap and twirl. (2) The wind blows the smell of crisp fall leaves down the street. (3) The members of the marching band raise their instruments and smile at the crowd. (4) A whistle sounds. (5) The bass drum slowly pounds out a beat. (6) Everyone cheers loudly as the shiny brass trumpets join in the tune. (7) Brass is a metal made from zinc and copper. (8) The flashing blue and gold flags catch my eye as the band moves proudly down the street. (9) Before it is out of sight, the next band comes into view.

1. Which sentence is off topic and should be taken out of the paragraph?
   - (A) sentence (2)
   - (B) sentence (4)
   - (C) sentence (7)
   - (D) sentence (8)

Test Tip: Different sentence beginnings make writing interesting. One way to change sentence beginnings is to change the order of the words from the original sentence.

2. The writer wants to add the following sentence to the paragraph:

   > When the yelling stops, I hear the cheerful music play on.

   Where should this sentence be added to keep the events in order?
   - (A) after sentence (3)
   - (B) after sentence (5)
   - (C) after sentence (6)
   - (D) after sentence (9)

3. Which shows the best way to revise sentence (5) to make the beginning different?
   - (A) The drum, which was bass, slowly pounds out a beat.
   - (B) Pounding, the bass drum beats slow.
   - (C) The slow beat of the bass drum pounds.
   - (D) Slowly, the brass drum pounds out a beat.

95

Writer's Companion • UNIT 3
Lesson 15 *Writing Test Practice*

© Harcourt

USING ACADEMIC LANGUAGE

Tell students that tests often contain academic language—words they may not see in their regular reading. Before students complete the test items on this page, review academic words and phrases such as *off topic, keep events in order, revise,* and *different sentence beginnings*. Remind students to read each question and all of its answer choices before marking their answers.

Answering Multiple-Choice Questions (cont.)

OBJECTIVES

- To practice answering multiple-choice questions that involve reading a passage
- To use plural and possessive noun forms to correctly complete sentences

Standard: LA.5.3.3.3 add supporting details/modify word choice

Teach/Model Explain that test questions sometimes ask students to choose the word or words that correctly complete a sentence. Point out that, on this test page, students will complete a reading passage. Read aloud the directions for Part C and have students read the passage silently. While the missing words will make reading the passage somewhat difficult, students can gain a sense of the topic and identify what kinds of words are missing from the sentences. Then read the Test Tip and model using it to answer Item 1. Explain that the singular possessive form (*family's*) correctly completes the sentence. Model marking the correct answer choice.

Guided Practice Guide students to answer Item 2. Remind them to consider what they know about plural and possessive noun forms before they mark their answers.

Independent Practice Have students complete Items 3 and 4 independently.

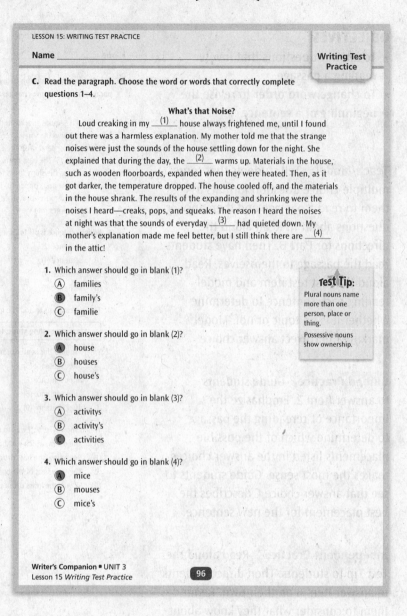

LESSON 15: WRITING TEST PRACTICE

Name _____

Writing Test Practice

C. Read the paragraph. Choose the word or words that correctly complete questions 1–4.

What's that Noise?

Loud creaking in my ___(1)___ house always frightened me, until I found out there was a harmless explanation. My mother told me that the strange noises were just the sounds of the house settling down for the night. She explained that during the day, the ___(2)___ warms up. Materials in the house, such as wooden floorboards, expanded when they were heated. Then, as it got darker, the temperature dropped. The house cooled off, and the materials in the house shrank. The results of the expanding and shrinking were the noises I heard—creaks, pops, and squeaks. The reason I heard the noises at night was that the sounds of everyday ___(3)___ had quieted down. My mother's explanation made me feel better, but I still think there are ___(4)___ in the attic!

1. Which answer should go in blank (1)?
   - Ⓐ families
   - Ⓑ family's
   - Ⓒ familie

2. Which answer should go in blank (2)?
   - Ⓐ house
   - Ⓑ houses
   - Ⓒ house's

3. Which answer should go in blank (3)?
   - Ⓐ activitys
   - Ⓑ activity's
   - Ⓒ activities

4. Which answer should go in blank (4)?
   - Ⓐ mice
   - Ⓑ mouses
   - Ⓒ mice's

Test Tip:
Plural nouns name more than one person, place or thing.
Possessive nouns show ownership.

Writer's Companion • UNIT 3
Lesson 15 *Writing Test Practice*

96

SHARING AND DISCUSSING

Have students work in pairs to discuss their answers and to analyze how they arrived at those answers. Ask partners to explain to each other how they approached each test question. Then have students compare their answers to each question and their methods for finding them. Was there a particular approach that resulted in more correct answers? If so, what was it?

© Harcourt

Answering Multiple-Choice Questions (cont.)

OBJECTIVES
- To answer questions that require choosing a correctly written sentence
- To use knowledge of capitalization rules to answer test questions

Standard: LA.5.3.4.2 capitalize proper nouns

Teach/Model Explain to students that some multiple-choice formats require them to read several sentences and decide which one is correctly written. Read the Test Tip to students, pointing out that the tip provides them with information that can help them determine which of the sentences is written correctly. Read Item 1 and each of the answer choices. Model using the information from the boxed tip to choose the correct answer. Be sure students understand that the name *Grand Canyon* is capitalized because it names a particular place. Mark the correct answer.

Guided Practice Ask a volunteer to read Item 2 and have students read the three answer choices to themselves. Remind them to look carefully to see which version of the sentences correctly capitalizes all of the proper nouns in the sentence. Have students mark the correct answer.

Independent Practice   Have students complete Items 3–5 on their own. Invite students to share their responses.

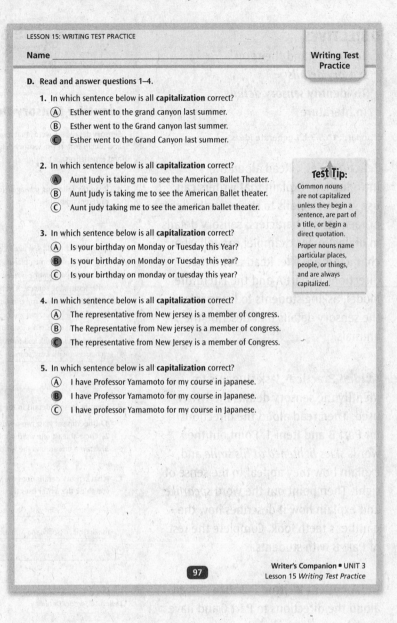

LESSON 15: WRITING TEST PRACTICE

Name _____

Writing Test Practice

D. Read and answer questions 1–4.

1. In which sentence below is all **capitalization** correct?
- (A) Esther went to the grand canyon last summer.
- (B) Esther went to the Grand canyon last summer.
- (C) Esther went to the Grand Canyon last summer.

2. In which sentence below is all **capitalization** correct?
- (A) Aunt Judy is taking me to see the American Ballet Theater.
- (B) Aunt Judy is taking me to see the American Ballet theater.
- (C) Aunt judy taking me to see the american ballet theater.

3. In which sentence below is all **capitalization** correct?
- (A) Is your birthday on Monday or Tuesday this Year?
- (B) Is your birthday on Monday or Tuesday this year?
- (C) Is your birthday on monday or tuesday this year?

4. In which sentence below is all **capitalization** correct?
- (A) The representative from New jersey is a member of congress.
- (B) The Representative from New jersey is a member of congress.
- (C) The representative from New Jersey is a member of Congress.

5. In which sentence below is all **capitalization** correct?
- (A) I have Professor Yamamoto for my course in japanese.
- (B) I have Professor Yamamoto for my course in Japanese.
- (C) I have professor Yamamoto for my course in Japanese.

Test Tip:
Common nouns are not capitalized unless they begin a sentence, are part of a title, or begin a direct quotation.

Proper nouns name particular places, people, or things, and are always capitalized.

97   Writer's Companion • UNIT 3
Lesson 15 *Writing Test Practice*

ASSESSING STUDENT RESPONSES

If students are consistently answering questions incorrectly, explore why they are struggling. Perhaps they are having a problem identifying errors in a sentence or identifying the correct sentence out of several choices. Reread the test tip with students. Then extend their understanding of the tip by giving them several different examples to illustrate the differences between common and proper nouns.

© Harcourt

Identify: Sensory Details

OBJECTIVES

- To understand the term *sensory details*
- To identify *sensory details* in literature

Standard: LA.5.3.1.1 generate ideas

Teach/Model Read aloud the introduction. Explain that writers can use sensory details to show the thoughts or feelings of characters; sensory details in dialogue, for example, can tell what characters are like. Read aloud the directions to part A and the Literature Model, asking students to listen for the sensory details that describe the animals.

Guided Practice Ask students to identify the sensory details the writer used. Then read aloud the directions for Part B and Item 1. Point out the words *skies lightened at his smile* and explain how they appeal to the sense of sight. Then point out the word *spearlike* and explain how it describes how the panther's teeth look. Complete the rest of Part B with students.

Independent Writing Practice Read aloud the directions to Part C and have students complete it independently.

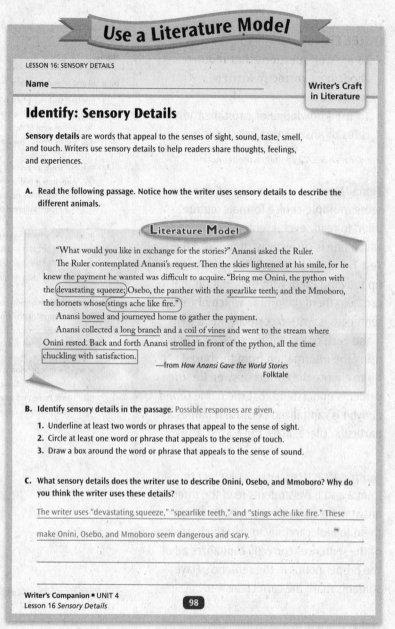

Use a Literature Model

LESSON 16: SENSORY DETAILS

Name _____

Writer's Craft in Literature

Identify: Sensory Details

Sensory details are words that appeal to the senses of sight, sound, taste, smell, and touch. Writers use sensory details to help readers share thoughts, feelings, and experiences.

A. Read the following passage. Notice how the writer uses sensory details to describe the different animals.

Literature Model

"What would you like in exchange for the stories?" Anansi asked the Ruler.

The Ruler contemplated Anansi's request. Then the skies lightened at his smile, for he knew the payment he wanted was difficult to acquire. "Bring me Onini, the python with the devastating squeeze; Osebo, the panther with the spearlike teeth; and the Mmoboro, the hornets whose stings ache like fire."

Anansi bowed and journeyed home to gather the payment.

Anansi collected a long branch and a coil of vines and went to the stream where Onini rested. Back and forth Anansi strolled in front of the python, all the time chuckling with satisfaction.

—from *How Anansi Gave the World Stories*
Folktale

B. Identify sensory details in the passage. Possible responses are given.

1. Underline at least two words or phrases that appeal to the sense of sight.
2. Circle at least one word or phrase that appeals to the sense of touch.
3. Draw a box around the word or phrase that appeals to the sense of sound.

C. What sensory details does the writer use to describe Onini, Osebo, and Mmoboro? Why do you think the writer uses these details?

The writer uses "devastating squeeze," "spearlike teeth," and "stings ache like fire." These

make Onini, Osebo, and Mmoboro seem dangerous and scary.

_____

_____

Writer's Companion • UNIT 4
Lesson 16 *Sensory Details*   98

EXTENDING THE CONCEPT: SENSORY DETAILS

After students complete Part C, invite them to share and discuss their responses. Point out that the writer uses sensory details to describe what the animals look like and to show how scary the animals are. To illustrate the point, ask students if they would be more afraid of a python with a *tight squeeze* or one with a *devastating squeeze.* Have students work in small groups and brainstorm sensory details that show how scary pythons, panthers, or hornets might be.

© Harcourt

Explore: Sensory Details

OBJECTIVES
- To reinforce students' understanding of sensory details
- To identify and use sensory details

Teach/Model Read aloud the introduction and point out the graphic organizer at the top of the page. Explain to students that the graphic organizer shows how they can use sensory details in their own writing. Read aloud the text in the diagram, emphasizing that each box at the bottom shows a step in the process.

Guided Practice Read aloud the directions and example sentence for Part A. Model completing the example, explaining that students should look for words that describe a sound. Guide students as they complete Item 1, asking them to find words that describe how the sunburn felt. Guide students through the remaining items of Part A. Read aloud the instructions and passage for Part A. Guide students to underline the sensory details.

Independent Writing Practice Have students complete Part C independently.

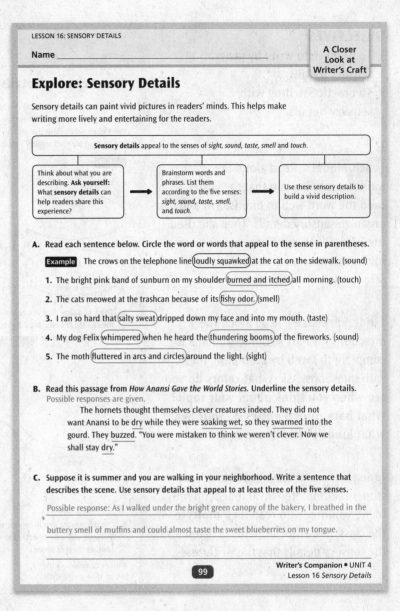

LESSON 16: SENSORY DETAILS

Name _____

A Closer Look at Writer's Craft

Explore: Sensory Details

Sensory details can paint vivid pictures in readers' minds. This helps make writing more lively and entertaining for the readers.

> **Sensory details** appeal to the senses of *sight, sound, taste, smell* and *touch.*
>
> Think about what you are describing. **Ask yourself:** What **sensory details** can help readers share this experience? → Brainstorm words and phrases. List them according to the five senses: *sight, sound, taste, smell,* and *touch.* → Use these sensory details to build a vivid description.

A. Read each sentence below. Circle the word or words that appeal to the sense in parentheses.

Example The crows on the telephone line (loudly squawked) at the cat on the sidewalk. (sound)

1. The bright pink band of sunburn on my shoulder (burned and itched) all morning. (touch)

2. The cats meowed at the trashcan because of its (fishy odor.) (smell)

3. I ran so hard that (salty sweat) dripped down my face and into my mouth. (taste)

4. My dog Felix (whimpered) when he heard the (thundering booms) of the fireworks. (sound)

5. The moth (fluttered in arcs and circles) around the light. (sight)

B. Read this passage from *How Anansi Gave the World Stories.* Underline the sensory details.
Possible responses are given.

> The hornets thought themselves clever creatures indeed. They did not want Anansi to be dry while they were soaking wet, so they swarmed into the gourd. They buzzed. "You were mistaken to think we weren't clever. Now we shall stay dry."

C. Suppose it is summer and you are walking in your neighborhood. Write a sentence that describes the scene. Use sensory details that appeal to at least three of the five senses.

Possible response: As I walked under the bright green canopy of the bakery, I breathed in the

buttery smell of muffins and could almost taste the sweet blueberries on my tongue.

99   Writer's Companion • UNIT 4
                   Lesson 16 *Sensory Details*

Reaching All Learners

BELOW LEVEL
Have students work with a partner or aide to complete Part C. Encourage students to first develop their ideas orally, describing their neighborhood scenes to a partner.

ADVANCED
Have students write a paragraph for Part C. Challenge students to use sensory details that appeal to all five senses.

ENGLISH-LANGUAGE LEARNERS
Have students work in small groups to discuss the meanings of words and phrases in Parts A and B.

© Harcourt

Use: Sensory Details

OBJECTIVES
- To prepare to write by generating sensory details
- To practice writing with sensory details

Teach/Model Read aloud the introduction. Explain that the writer used the word web to brainstorm and organize sensory details. Then she used these details to draft her narrative. Invite volunteers to read aloud the sensory details in the web.

Guided Practice Read aloud the directions for Part A. Guide students to complete the web by prompting them with questions. Ask: **What colors do you see when you think about your topic? What background noises do your hear? What kinds of smells are in the air?**

Independent Writing Practice Have students complete Part B independently. Invite volunteers to read their drafts to the class. Ask other students to listen for the sensory details that the writer uses.

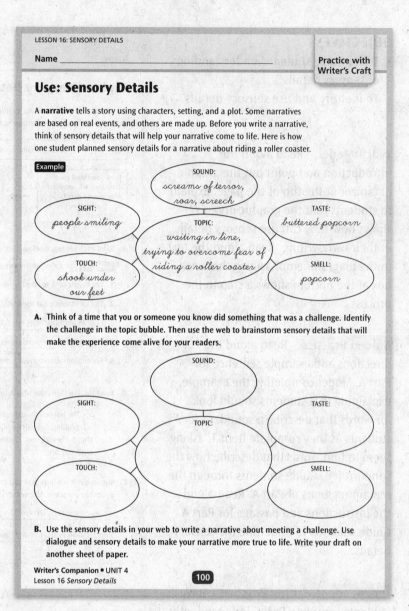

WRITER'S STRATEGY: FINDING A TOPIC

When students select a writing topic, they should look back at the writing they have done in their journals or notebooks. Tell students that they might be surprised to find that sometimes it only takes one word or phrase to give them a great idea for a writing topic. Explain that they might find ideas for a topic in unexpected ways. For example, they might read an entry about a day at school, which might remind them of the shoes they were wearing that day, which might make them think about their favorite sneakers, which they might discover makes a good writing topic!

© Harcourt

The Parts of a Narrative Paragraph

OBJECTIVES
- To understand the parts of a narrative paragraph
- To analyze a Student Model

Teach/Model   Read aloud the introduction, explaining that the Student Model is a narrative paragraph. It tells a story using characters, setting, and plot. Read aloud the call-outs to explain how a narrative paragraph is organized. Then read aloud the Student Model, asking students to listen for how the writer introduces the topic.

Guided Practice   Point out the questions below the Student Model. Guide students in completing Item 1, asking them which sentence introduces the topic with sensory details that help readers see, hear, and feel where the narrative takes place. Guide students in completing Item 2 by rereading the passage. After each sentence, ask: **Does this sentence relate to the roller coaster or to how the characters feel?** Point out that the sentence *A man was selling balloons* does not relate to either of these.

Independent Writing Practice   Have students complete Items 3–5 independently.

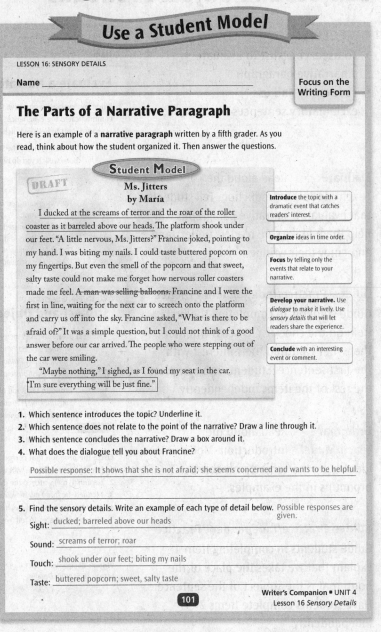

LESSON 16: SENSORY DETAILS

Name _____

Focus on the Writing Form

The Parts of a Narrative Paragraph

Here is an example of a **narrative paragraph** written by a fifth grader. As you read, think about how the student organized it. Then answer the questions.

Student Model

DRAFT

Ms. Jitters
by María

I ducked at the screams of terror and the roar of the roller coaster as it barreled above our heads. The platform shook under our feet. "A little nervous, Ms. Jitters?" Francine joked, pointing to my hand. I was biting my nails. I could taste buttered popcorn on my fingertips. But even the smell of the popcorn and that sweet, salty taste could not make me forget how nervous roller coasters made me feel. A man was selling balloons. Francine and I were the first in line, waiting for the next car to screech onto the platform and carry us off into the sky. Francine asked, "What is there to be afraid of?" It was a simple question, but I could not think of a good answer before our car arrived. The people who were stepping out of the car were smiling.

"Maybe nothing," I sighed, as I found my seat in the car. "I'm sure everything will be just fine."

Introduce the topic with a dramatic event that catches readers' interest.

Organize ideas in time order.

Focus by telling only the events that relate to your narrative.

Develop your narrative. Use *dialogue* to make it lively. Use *sensory details* that will let readers share the experience.

Conclude with an interesting event or comment.

1. Which sentence introduces the topic? Underline it.
2. Which sentence does not relate to the point of the narrative? Draw a line through it.
3. Which sentence concludes the narrative? Draw a box around it.
4. What does the dialogue tell you about Francine?

    Possible response: It shows that she is not afraid; she seems concerned and wants to be helpful.

5. Find the sensory details. Write an example of each type of detail below. Possible responses are given.

    Sight: ducked; barreled above our heads

    Sound: screams of terror; roar

    Touch: shook under our feet; biting my nails

    Taste: buttered popcorn; sweet, salty taste

101

Writer's Companion • UNIT 4
Lesson 16 *Sensory Details*

EXTENDING THE CONCEPT: USING DIALOGUE

Point out the dialogue in the Student Model. Tell students that the writer uses dialogue to show the words that the characters say. Explain that the writer also uses dialogue to make the narrative lively and to make the characters seem like real people. Invite volunteers to share and discuss their responses to Item 4. Have volunteers point to the lines of dialogue that tell them what Francine is like. Point out that the words in the last two lines of the Student Model are those of the narrator. Have students discuss what this dialogue tells them about the narrator.

© Harcourt

Evaluate a Narrative Paragraph/Grammar: Subject and Object Pronouns

OBJECTIVES

- To use a checklist to evaluate a narrative paragraph
- To identify and use exclamatory sentences

Evaluate Teach/Model Read aloud the introduction. Tell students that evaluating narrative paragraphs will help them make sure readers understand and enjoy their writing.

Guided Practice/Independent Practice

Guide students in completing the first item on the checklist. Discuss whether the writer captured their interest with the first sentence. Students can complete the rest of the items independently.

Grammar Teach/Model Read aloud the introduction. Model identifying the subject and object pronouns in the examples.

Guided Practice/Independent Practice

Guide students in completing Item 1. Explain that *We* takes the place of the noun that is the subject of the sentence. Have students complete Items 2–5 independently.

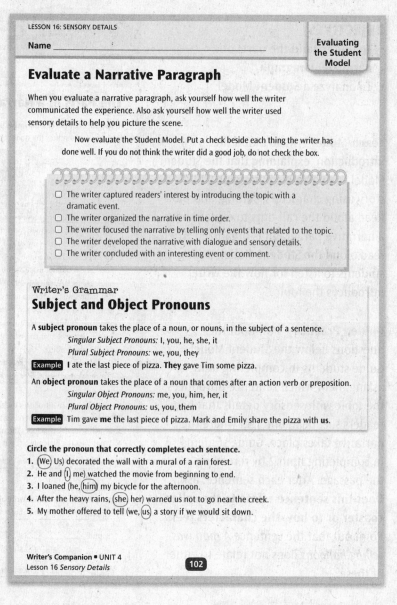

LESSON 16: SENSORY DETAILS

Name _____

Evaluating the Student Model

Evaluate a Narrative Paragraph

When you evaluate a narrative paragraph, ask yourself how well the writer communicated the experience. Also ask yourself how well the writer used sensory details to help you picture the scene.

Now evaluate the Student Model. Put a check beside each thing the writer has done well. If you do not think the writer did a good job, do not check the box.

- ☐ The writer captured readers' interest by introducing the topic with a dramatic event.
- ☐ The writer organized the narrative in time order.
- ☐ The writer focused the narrative by telling only events that related to the topic.
- ☐ The writer developed the narrative with dialogue and sensory details.
- ☐ The writer concluded with an interesting event or comment.

Writer's Grammar

Subject and Object Pronouns

A **subject pronoun** takes the place of a noun, or nouns, in the subject of a sentence.
   Singular Subject Pronouns: I, you, he, she, it
   Plural Subject Pronouns: we, you, they
   Example I ate the last piece of pizza. **They** gave Tim some pizza.

An **object pronoun** takes the place of a noun that comes after an action verb or preposition.
   Singular Object Pronouns: me, you, him, her, it
   Plural Object Pronouns: us, you, them
   Example Tim gave **me** the last piece of pizza. Mark and Emily share the pizza with **us**.

Circle the pronoun that correctly completes each sentence.
1. (We) Us) decorated the wall with a mural of a rain forest.
2. He and (I) me) watched the movie from beginning to end.
3. I loaned (he, (him) my bicycle for the afternoon.
4. After the heavy rains, (she) her) warned us not to go near the creek.
5. My mother offered to tell (we, (us) a story if we would sit down.

Writer's Companion • UNIT 4
Lesson 16 *Sensory Details*   102

SHARING AND DISCUSSING

After students have used the checklist to evaluate the Student Model, have them work in small groups to share and discuss the results of their evaluations. Model the process for evaluating the first item by saying: **First, I read the item on the checklist and looked back at the first sentence of the Student** **Model. Next, I decided that I liked how the writer used sensory details to show how thrilling roller coasters can seem.** Have students discuss how they might have have improved items they feel the writer did not do well.

© Harcourt

Revise: Adding Sensory Details

OBJECTIVES

- To understand the purpose of revising
- To revise a narrative paragraph by adding sensory details

Standard: LA.5.3.3.3 add supporting details/modify word choice

Teach/Model Tell students there is more to revising than simply correcting spelling and grammar errors. Explain that revising gives writers the chance to expand their ideas so that readers will better understand and enjoy their writing. Point out that one way writers can expand their ideas is by adding new sensory details.

Guided Practice Read aloud the introduction and the example. Point out that the writer added the phrase *smell of oil* to appeal to the sense of smell, as well as the word *shuddered* to appeal to the sense of touch. Have students discuss how the revisions improved the sentence. Then read aloud the directions to Part A. Model revising Item 1, pointing out that students could replace *dog* with the word *bulldog* from the Word Bank. Explain that the Word Bank can provide both words and ideas for their revisions.

Independent Writing Practice Have students complete Items 2–5 of Part A on their own. Then have them complete Part B independently.

LESSON 16: SENSORY DETAILS

Name _____

Revising the Student Model

Revise: Adding Sensory Details

One thing the writer could have done better is to add more sensory details. Those details would have helped her do a better job of describing the characters and narrative. Here is an example of how a sentence from the Student Model could be improved.

Example The platform shook under our feet.

The smell of oil came from the track as the platform shook and shuddered under our feet.

A. Revise these sentences. Add sensory details that will help readers share the experience. Use the Word Bank to help you. Possible responses are given.

1. The dog walked across the floor.

   My aunt's bulldog panted as its claws clicked across the wood floor.

2. I tried to keep myself from smelling the odor.

   I held my hand in front of my face to keep from smelling the foul exhaust

   that was puffing out of the old car.

3. My brother bit into a slice of lemon.

   My brother made a funny face and shook his head after he bit

   into the sour lemon.

4. The house looked old.

   The house looked worn down, as if it were ready to collapse.

5. Her grandmother's surfboard was decorated with many colors.

   Her grandmother's surfboard was covered with stickers and pictures of

   blue and purple dolphins.

B. Revise the draft of the narrative you wrote on page 100. Add sensory details to make the sentences more descriptive and entertaining for readers. Also pay close attention to subject and object pronouns. Write your revision on another sheet of paper.

Word Bank

blue
bulldog
clicked
collapse
foul
funny
panted
purple
sour
waved
wood
worn

103

Writer's Companion • UNIT 4
Lesson 16 *Sensory Details*

SHARING AND DISCUSSING

After students have completed their revisions, invite volunteers to read their narratives to the class. Encourage students to listen for the sensory details that the writer used to make the narratives interesting and entertaining. After each volunteer has finished reading, guide students in discussing which words and phrases stood out the most. Emphasize that this sharing activity is an opportunity to focus on what the writers did well.

© Harcourt

Identify: Creating Specific Voices

OBJECTIVES

- To understand how to *create specific voices*
- To identify *specific voices* in literature

Teach/Model Read aloud the introduction. Tell students that if they listen closely, they will notice that everyone–in real life and in stories–has an individual way of speaking and using words. Writers use dialogue and descriptive words to show this. Read aloud the Literature Model and ask students to listen for how the writer creates a voice for the character Eva.

Guided Practice Read aloud the directions to Part B and then guide students in completing Item 1. Reread Eva's line of dialogue and explain that the writer uses Eva's words to show that she wants to write about the events on her street but cannot seem to find a topic. Then guide students in completing Items 2 and 3, reading aloud Mr. Sims's response and having students discuss what they think Mr. Sims is like.

Independent Writing Practice Have students complete Part C independently.

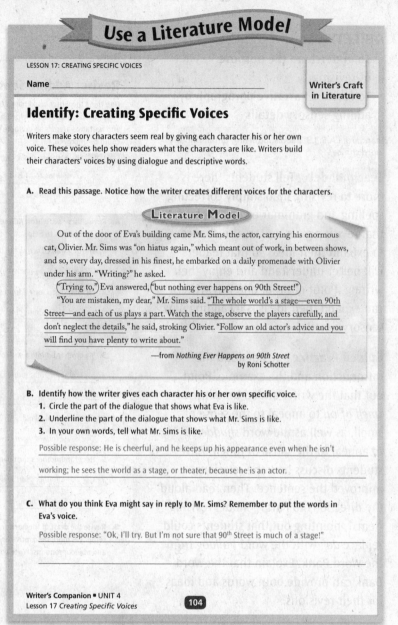

Use a Literature Model

LESSON 17: CREATING SPECIFIC VOICES

Name _____

Writer's Craft in Literature

Identify: Creating Specific Voices

Writers make story characters seem real by giving each character his or her own voice. These voices help show readers what the characters are like. Writers build their characters' voices by using dialogue and descriptive words.

A. Read this passage. Notice how the writer creates different voices for the characters.

Literature Model

Out of the door of Eva's building came Mr. Sims, the actor, carrying his enormous cat, Olivier. Mr. Sims was "on hiatus again," which meant out of work, in between shows, and so, every day, dressed in his finest, he embarked on a daily promenade with Olivier under his arm. "Writing?" he asked.

"Trying to," Eva answered, "but nothing ever happens on 90th Street!"

"You are mistaken, my dear," Mr. Sims said. "The whole world's a stage—even 90th Street—and each of us plays a part. Watch the stage, observe the players carefully, and don't neglect the details," he said, stroking Olivier. "Follow an old actor's advice and you will find you have plenty to write about."

—from *Nothing Ever Happens on 90th Street* by Roni Schotter

B. Identify how the writer gives each character his or her own specific voice.

1. Circle the part of the dialogue that shows what Eva is like.
2. Underline the part of the dialogue that shows what Mr. Sims is like.
3. In your own words, tell what Mr. Sims is like.

Possible response: He is cheerful, and he keeps up his appearance even when he isn't

working; he sees the world as a stage, or theater, because he is an actor.

C. What do you think Eva might say in reply to Mr. Sims? Remember to put the words in Eva's voice.

Possible response: "Ok, I'll try. But I'm not sure that 90th Street is much of a stage!"

_____

_____

Writer's Companion • UNIT 4
Lesson 17 *Creating Specific Voices*

104

EXTENDING THE CONCEPT: CREATING A SPECIFIC VOICE

Point out that the writer creates a specific voice for Mr. Sims by using metaphors that relate to the theater and to acting. Explain that writers often use metaphors, which compare one thing to another, without using the words *like* or *as*. Illustrate this by pointing out that Mr. Sims says, "The whole world's a stage." Ask: **What might Mr. Sims have said if he had been a professional baseball player?** Have students write a line of dialogue that might follow the line, "The whole world's a baseball diamond."

© Harcourt

Explore: Creating Specific Voices

OBJECTIVES

- To deepen students' understanding of creating specific voices
- To explore creating specific voices

Teach/Model   Read aloud the introduction. Tell students that the graphic organizers shows why writers create specific voices for characters, explaining that writers use these voices to bring characters to life. Explain that writers also use specific voices to show how characters are unique, using descriptive words that fit their personalities. Point out that writers can also create specific voices by using descriptive words that show exactly how characters think or feel.

Guided Practice   Read aloud the directions to Part A and the example. Model completing the example, explaining that these phrases are more likely to be used by the bus driver. Also point out that the example is an exclamation, which would more likely be spoken by someone who is easily excited. Guide students in completing Items 1–3 and review responses as a class.

Independent Writing Practice   Have students complete Part B independently.

LESSON 17: CREATING SPECIFIC VOICES

Name _____

A Closer Look at Writer's Craft

Explore: Creating Specific Voices

Writers create a **specific voice** for each character in a story or play.

Specific voices bring characters to life.	⟷	**Specific voices** show how each character is unique.	⟷	**Specific voices** show how each character thinks or feels.

A. Read each sentence of dialogue below. Put a check to show which character said the words. Underline the word or words that help create a specific voice for that character.

Example   "I'm all revved up and ready to roll!"

✓   Mr. Henry: a bus driver who is easily excited

____   Mrs. Hernández: a lawyer who rarely smiles

1. "I'm going to hit this one out of the park."

✓   Vanessa: a student who is good at sports

____   Theo: a student who prefers computers

2. "My thoughts branch in many directions but bloom only after I jot them down."

____   Michelle: a doctor who likes to go rock climbing

✓   Marcus: a writer who likes plants and trees

3. "That creepy little thing put its dirty feet on my book."

✓   Jorge: an older brother who does not like mice

____   Emma: an older sister who likes mice

B. Suppose that you are writing a story about a fifth grader who thinks her mother is going to throw a surprise picnic for her. Write at least two lines of dialogue that create a specific voice for the character.

Responses will vary.

_____

_____

_____

WRITER'S STRATEGY: FREEWRITING

Tell students that one way to generate ideas is to practice freewriting. Explain that freewriting involves writing down whatever comes to mind, without pausing to think about conventions or to plan what to write next. Tell students that they can generate ideas for developing a character's voice by freewriting from the character's point of view. Before students complete Part B, have them freewrite from the fifth grader's point of view. Then have students reread what they have written and underline the words that show the character's voice. Encourage them to use these words to complete Part B.

© Harcourt

Use: Creating Specific Voices

OBJECTIVES
- To prepare to write by generating ideas to create a specific voice
- To practice writing a skit using specific voices

Teach/Model Read aloud the introduction. Tell students that before they write a skit, they should generate ideas about their characters. Explain that when writers have ideas about a character's personality, they will know what their character might say in a certain situation. Have students read aloud the example chart.

Guided Practice Read aloud the directions for Part A. Guide students in completing the chart. Tell them that they might find it easier to generate ideas about their characters before choosing a setting. Prompt students to think about their characters with questions such as **What makes your characters laugh? How does your character act with his or her friends?**

Independent Writing Practice Have students complete Part B independently. Invite volunteers to share their skits with the class.

LESSON 17: CREATING SPECIFIC VOICES

Name _____

Practice with Writer's Craft

Use: Creating Specific Voices

A **skit** is a short play. It uses characters and dialogue to tell a story. Before you write a skit, organize your ideas so that each character has his or her own voice. Here is how one student started to plan his skit.

Example Setting: _outside_

Name of Character	Amy
Personality	funny likes to laugh and joke with her friends
Words that Character Might Use	"What's up?" "Tell me something funny."

A. Think about a setting and one character for a humorous skit. Then fill out the chart.

Setting: _____

Name of Character	
Personality	
Words that Character Might Use	

B. Use information from your chart to write a short, humorous skit with two or more characters. You may want to create a separate chart for each character. Then write your draft on another sheet of paper.

Writer's Companion • UNIT 4
Lesson 17 Creating Specific Voices   106

SHARING AND DISCUSSING

Have students work with partners to share and discuss the charts they completed for Part A. Ask partners to begin by telling each other about their characters. Then have them share what they have written in the charts. Encourage partners to brainstorm additional words and phrases that their characters might use. Have students add these additional words to their charts. After students have independently completed Part B, have them share the drafts of their skits.

The Parts of a Skit

OBJECTIVES
- To understand the parts of a skit
- To analyze a Student Model

Standard: LA.5.3.3.1 evaluate for writing traits

Teach/Model Read aloud the introduction. Tell students that the format of a skit or play is different from that of a story. Explain that, in a skit, each line of dialogue begins with the name of the character who is speaking. The writer also includes descriptions of how the characters should act that are called *stage directions*. Read aloud the call-outs. Then assign parts and have students read the Student Model. Ask other students to listen for how the writer uses dialogue to develop the plot.

Guided Practice Point out the items below the Student Model. Read aloud Item 1 and guide students to find the stage direction that tells where the skit takes place and who is on stage. Guide students in completing Item 2, having students pay attention to the stage directions to see who is on stage. Then point out that Tim speaks before he enters. Guide students in pointing to where Tim's line belongs.

Independent Writing Practice Have students complete Item 3 independently.

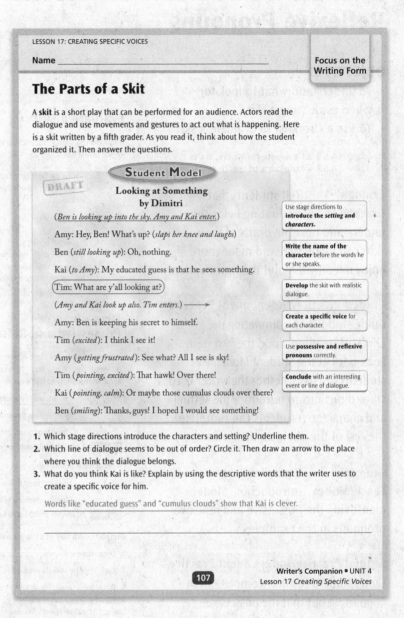

LESSON 17: CREATING SPECIFIC VOICES

Name _____

Focus on the Writing Form

The Parts of a Skit

A **skit** is a short play that can be performed for an audience. Actors read the dialogue and use movements and gestures to act out what is happening. Here is a skit written by a fifth grader. As you read it, think about how the student organized it. Then answer the questions.

Student Model

DRAFT

Looking at Something
by Dimitri

(*Ben is looking up into the sky. Amy and Kai enter.*)

Amy: Hey, Ben! What's up? (*slaps her knee and laughs*)

Ben (*still looking up*): Oh, nothing.

Kai (*to Amy*): My educated guess is that he sees something.

Tim: What are y'all looking at?

(*Amy and Kai look up also. Tim enters.*) ⟶

Amy: Ben is keeping his secret to himself.

Tim (*excited*): I think I see it!

Amy (*getting frustrated*): See what? All I see is sky!

Tim (*pointing, excited*): That hawk! Over there!

Kai (*pointing, calm*): Or maybe those cumulus clouds over there?

Ben (*smiling*): Thanks, guys! I hoped I would see something!

- Use stage directions to **introduce the *setting* and *characters*.**
- **Write the name of the character** before the words he or she speaks.
- **Develop** the skit with realistic dialogue.
- **Create a specific voice** for each character.
- Use **possessive and reflexive pronouns** correctly.
- **Conclude** with an interesting event or line of dialogue.

1. Which stage directions introduce the characters and setting? Underline them.
2. Which line of dialogue seems to be out of order? Circle it. Then draw an arrow to the place where you think the dialogue belongs.
3. What do you think Kai is like? Explain by using the descriptive words that the writer uses to create a specific voice for him.

   Words like "educated guess" and "cumulus clouds" show that Kai is clever.

   _____

   _____

107

Writer's Companion ▪ UNIT 4
Lesson 17 *Creating Specific Voices*

Reaching All Learners

BELOW LEVEL	ADVANCED	ENGLISH-LANGUAGE LEARNERS
Before students complete Item 3, have them discuss with a partner how the writer shows what Kai is like.	Have students work with a partner to brainstorm ideas for how the writer could have used more descriptive stage directions to make the setting clearer. Invite students to share their ideas.	Have students work in pairs to discuss how the terms that Kai uses, such as *cumulus clouds* and *educated guess,* show what he is like.

© Harcourt

Evaluate a Skit/Grammar: Possessive and Reflexive Pronouns

OBJECTIVES
- To understand what to look for when evaluating a skit
- To use a checklist to evaluate a skit

Standard: LA.5.3.3.1 evaluate for writing traits
LA.5.3.4.4 use parts of speech correctly

Evaluate
Teach/Model   Tell students that evaluating helps them understand how the drafts of their skits can be revised and made more enjoyable. Read aloud the introduction.

Guided Practice/Independent Practice
Guide students in completing the checklist, reading aloud the first item. Look back at the Student Model. Have students discuss whether the writer used stage directions to introduce the setting and characters. Students can complete the rest of the items on their own.

Grammar
Teach/Model   Read aloud the introduction. Model identifying the possessive and reflexive pronouns in the examples.

Guided Practice/Independent Practice
Guide students as they complete Item 1, pointing out that the possessive pronoun is used before the noun *friend*. Have students complete Items 2–3 independently.

LESSON 17: CREATING SPECIFIC VOICES

Name _____

Evaluating the Student Model

Evaluate a Skit

When you evaluate a skit, ask yourself how well the writer created specific voices for the characters.

Now evaluate the Student Model. Put a check beside each thing the writer did well. If you do not think the writer did a good job with something, do not check the box.

- ☐ The writer used stage directions to introduce the setting and characters.
- ☐ The writer wrote the name of the character before the words he or she speaks.
- ☐ The writer developed the skit with realistic dialogue.
- ☐ The writer created a specific voice for each character.
- ☐ The writer concluded with an interesting event or line of dialogue.

Writer's Grammar
Possessive and Reflexive Pronouns

A **pronoun** takes the place of one or more nouns. A **possessive pronoun** shows ownership. It takes the place of a possessive noun such as *María's* or *The boy's*. Some possessive pronouns come immediately before a noun. Others are used alone.

Possessive Pronouns Used Before a Noun	Possessive Pronouns Used Alone
Singular: my, your, his, her, its	*Singular:* mine, yours, his, hers
Plural: our, your, their	*Plural:* ours, yours, theirs

Example   Tess: I thought only **my** dog was cute, but **yours** is too.

A **reflexive pronoun** refers back to a noun or pronoun in the subject.

Singular: myself, yourself, himself, herself, itself

Plural: ourselves, yourselves, themselves

Example   Adam: We should give **ourselves** a big round of applause!

Complete each line of dialogue with the correct pronoun in parentheses.

1. Dina: Have you seen ____my____ friend Jessica? (my, mine)

2. Carl: Yes! She said she wanted to study by ____herself____. (her, herself)

3. Dina: She's smart. We should be studying by ____ourselves____, too. (ours, ourselves)

Writer's Companion • UNIT 4
Lesson 17 *Creating Specific Voices*   **108**

WRITER'S STRATEGY: EVALUATING VOICE

Often, the best way to evaluate dialogue and a character's voice is to hear the piece of writing read aloud. Suggest that students softly read aloud parts of the Student Model as they complete the checklist. Tell students that when they need to evaluate dialogue or characters' voices in their own writing, they should ask a partner to read aloud their writing to them. Explain that hearing their writing read by someone else will give them a better sense of which dialogue and characters' voices work well.

© Harcourt

Revise: Showing Characters' Traits

OBJECTIVES

- To understand the purpose of revising
- To revise a skit by showing character traits

Teach/Model Explain that when students write skits and stories, they can make as many revisions as they think are necessary to bring their characters to life. Tell students that in this activity they will learn how to revise their skits by showing characters' traits.

Guided Practice Read aloud the introduction and the example revision. Then direct students to page 106 and have them review the writer's description of Amy on the organizer. Then point out how the writer added the words *super-secretive* and the word *super* again to show that Amy likes to laugh and joke. Also point out how the writer added stage directions to show how Amy acts. Guide students in completing Item 1 by pointing out that the Word Bank can provide ideas for their revisions.

Independent Writing Practice Have students complete Items 2 and 3 of Part A independently. Then have them do Part B on their own.

LESSON 17: CREATING SPECIFIC VOICES

Name _____

Revising the Student Model

Revise: Showing Characters' Traits

One way the writer could have improved his skit is by showing the characters' traits more clearly. Writers can do this by creating a specific voice for each character. They also can include stage directions that make a characters' behavior more realistic. Here is how a line of dialogue from the Student Model could be improved.

Example Amy: Ben is keeping his secret to himself.

Amy: Super-secretive Ben is keeping his super secret to himself.

(nudges Kai and laughs)

A. Revise each line of dialogue by choosing the characters' traits and then showing them more clearly. Add stage directions to show what each character does while speaking. Use the Word Bank to help you.   Possible responses are given.

1. Miguel: You won't believe what I just did!

   Miguel (excitedly): Not in a billion, zillion years will you guess what I

   just did!

Word Bank
bushed
excitedly
exhausted
frowning
hate
running
yawning

2. Zoe: I am tired.

   Zoe (yawning): I'm so bushed, I'm ready to plant myself here.

   _____

3. Darla (*shaking her head*): No thanks. I don't like beets.

   Darla (shaking her head and turning up her nose): No THANK you!

   I hate beets!

   _____

B. Revise your skit from page 106. As you revise, make sure that you show the characters' traits clearly. Also make sure that you use possessive and reflexive pronouns correctly. Use another sheet of paper for your writing.

109

Writer's Companion • UNIT 4
Lesson 17 *Creating Specific Voices*

SHARING AND DISCUSSING

After they have completed their revisions in Part B, invite students to volunteer their skits for a dramatic reading. Assign the parts and have students "rehearse" for the performance by reading the skit aloud once or twice as a small group. When students are ready, have them present the dramatic reading for the class. After each performance, have students discuss how the writer used specific voices and stage directions to show the characters' traits.

© Harcourt

Identify: Vivid Words and Phrases

OBJECTIVES

- To understand the term *vivid words and phrases*
- To identify *vivid words and phrases* in literature

Standard: LA.5.3.1.1 generate ideas

Teach/Model   Read aloud the introduction. Tell students that writers use vivid words and phrases instead of plain ones to capture specific details, such as exactly how someone looks and acts. Read aloud the Literature Model, asking students to listen for the vivid words and phrases that make the passage lively and entertaining.

Guided Practice   Read aloud the directions to Part B. Guide students in completing Item 1. Point out that in the first sentence the writer used the word *constantly* to describe how the caterpillar moved its head. Then point out how the vivid words and phrases in the second sentence continue describing how the caterpillar constantly moved. Guide students in completing Items 2 and 3.

Independent Writing Practice   After reading aloud the directions, have students complete Part C independently.

Use a Literature Model

LESSON 18: VIVID WORDS AND PHRASES

Name _____

Writer's Craft in Literature

Identify: Vivid Words and Phrases

Writers use **vivid words and phrases** to create exact pictures of what they want to describe. Vivid words and phrases make writing lively and entertaining.

A. Read the following passage. Notice how the writer includes vivid words and phrases.

Literature Model

The caterpillar moved its head <u>constantly</u>. Sometimes fast, sometimes a little slower, but <u>never stopping</u>—it looked like really hard work. The silk came out of its mouth just as Patrick had said.

At first the silk was almost (invisible.) You (could see the strands only if you looked really hard.)

By the next morning, though, the caterpillar had already wrapped itself in a layer of silk. It looked like it was living inside a cloud. We could see its | black | mouth | moving, | moving, busy, busy, busy.

—from *Project Mulberry* by Linda Sue Park

B. Identify vivid words and phrases in the passage. Possible responses are given.
1. Underline words and phrases in the first paragraph that describe how the caterpillar moves.
2. Circle words and phrases in the second paragraph that describe the silk.
3. Put a box around the words in the last sentence that describe the caterpillar's mouth.

C. How does the appearance of the silk change overnight? Use details from the passage to answer in your own words.

Possible response: The silk went from being "strands" that were "almost invisible" to being in

a "layer" so that the caterpillar looked like it "was living inside a cloud."

_____

_____

EXTENDING THE CONCEPT: VIVID WORDS AND PHRASES

Explain the difference between vivid words and phrases and plain ones by writing the following sentence on the board: *The dog walks.* Point out that the words *dog* and *walks* are plain, because they do not provide a precise image of what the dog looks like or how it walks. Then write the following sentence: *The poodle prances.* Point out how the exact word *poodle* provides a clear kind of image of what dog it is. The vivid verb *prances* shows exactly how the poodle walks.

© Harcourt

Explore: Vivid Words and Phrases

OBJECTIVES
- To deepen students' understanding of vivid words and phrases
- To identify vivid words and phrases

Teach/Model Read aloud the introduction and explain that the graphic organizer shows how students can use specific and vivid nouns, adjectives, adverbs, and verbs to make their writing more descriptive and lively.

Guided Practice Read aloud the directions and passage in Part A. Point out that in the underlined phrase, the writer uses vivid words to describe what is on the mountain path where Eduardo sees the wildflowers. Guide students in completing Item 1 by pointing out the word *snow-capped* and by asking what word the writer uses to describe exactly how the mountain peak towered. Guide students in completing Items 2 and 3. Then read aloud the directions to Part B and the passage. Guide students in identifying the words and phrases that describe the caterpillars' motion.

Independent Writing Practice Have students complete Part C independently.

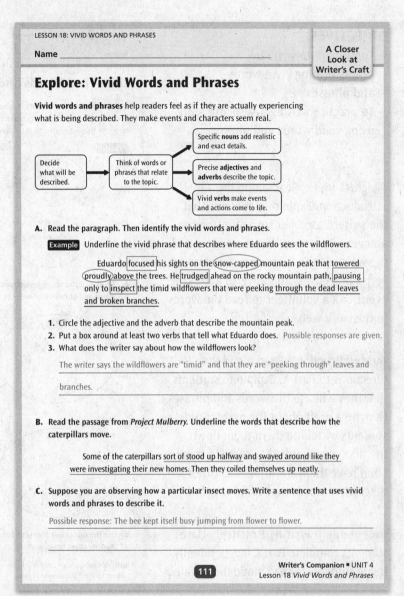

LESSON 18: VIVID WORDS AND PHRASES

Name _____

A Closer
Look at
Writer's Craft

Explore: Vivid Words and Phrases

Vivid words and phrases help readers feel as if they are actually experiencing what is being described. They make events and characters seem real.

Decide what will be described. → Think of words or phrases that relate to the topic. → Specific **nouns** add realistic and exact details.

Precise **adjectives** and **adverbs** describe the topic.

Vivid **verbs** make events and actions come to life.

A. Read the paragraph. Then identify the vivid words and phrases.

Example Underline the vivid phrase that describes where Eduardo sees the wildflowers.

> Eduardo focused his sights on the snow-capped mountain peak that towered proudly above the trees. He trudged ahead on the rocky mountain path, pausing only to inspect the timid wildflowers that were peeking through the dead leaves and broken branches.

1. Circle the adjective and the adverb that describe the mountain peak.

2. Put a box around at least two verbs that tell what Eduardo does. Possible responses are given.

3. What does the writer say about how the wildflowers look?

The writer says the wildflowers are "timid" and that they are "peeking through" leaves and

branches.

B. Read the passage from *Project Mulberry*. Underline the words that describe how the caterpillars move.

> Some of the caterpillars sort of stood up halfway and swayed around like they were investigating their new homes. Then they coiled themselves up neatly.

C. Suppose you are observing how a particular insect moves. Write a sentence that uses vivid words and phrases to describe it.

Possible response: The bee kept itself busy jumping from flower to flower.

_____

111

Writer's Companion • UNIT 4
Lesson 18 *Vivid Words and Phrases*

SHARING AND DISCUSSING

Have students read their responses for Part C to a partner. Tell students to listen for the vivid words and phrases that their partner uses to describe the insect. Then tell students to discuss how the vivid words and phrases helped them picture what the insect looks like and how the insect moves. Then have partners brainstorm additional vivid words and phrases. Encourage students to use these additional details to write a second sentence.

© Harcourt

Use: Vivid Words and Phrases

OBJECTIVES
- To prepare to write by brainstorming vivid words and phrases
- To practice writing a suspense story using vivid words and phrases

Teach/Model Read aloud the introduction. Explain to students that the writer based her suspense story on an event. Point out that the writer used the word web to brainstorm vivid nouns, verbs, adjectives, and adverbs about the event. Ask a volunteer to read the words in the word web.

Guided Practice Read aloud the directions to Part A. Explain to students that they will use the words and phrases to write a draft about the event. Guide students by telling them to jot down the first vivid words that come to mind. Then have them continue with other descriptive words that come to mind.

Independent Writing Practice Have students complete Part C independently. Invite students to read aloud their drafts.

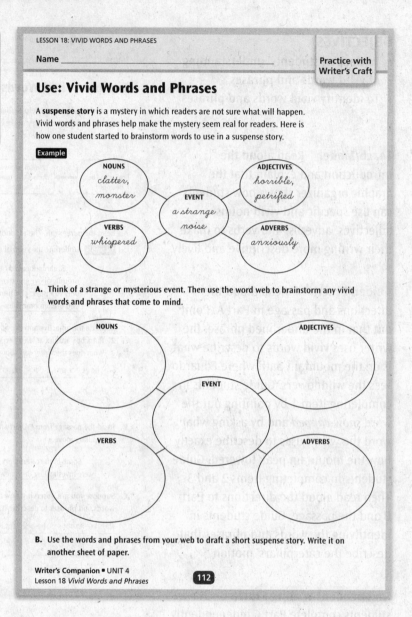

Reaching All Learners

BELOW LEVEL	ADVANCED	ENGLISH-LANGUAGE LEARNERS
Allow students to brainstorm vivid words without organizing them by the parts of speech. Then have students work with a partner or aide to use the words to build sentences for their drafts.	Encourage students writing above grade level to use additional word webs to focus their brainstorming on other elements of their suspense story, such as vivid words for characters or setting.	Pair less fluent English speakers with more fluent English speakers. Have students discuss a mysterious event and then collaborate to brainstorm vivid words and phrases for the web.

© Harcourt

The Parts of a Suspense Story

OBJECTIVES
- To understand the parts of a suspense story
- To analyze a Student Model

Standard: LA.5.3.3.1 evaluate for writing traits

Teach/Model   Read aloud the introduction and the call-outs. Explain that in a suspense story the writer develops the details and events in a way that makes readers eager to know what happens next. Then read aloud the Student Model, asking students to listen to find out how the writer develops the ideas and creates a feeling of suspense.

Guided Practice   Point out the items below the Student Model. Guide students in completing Item 1 by pointing out the first sentence. Explain that the word *anxiously* tells readers that Tina is nervous that something is going to happen. Explain that the writer uses this vivid word to create a sense of suspense and to make readers want to find out what will happen next. Guide students in completing Item 2 by asking students to find the detail that makes them think that something is about to happen.

Independent Writing Practice   Have students complete Items 3–4 independently.

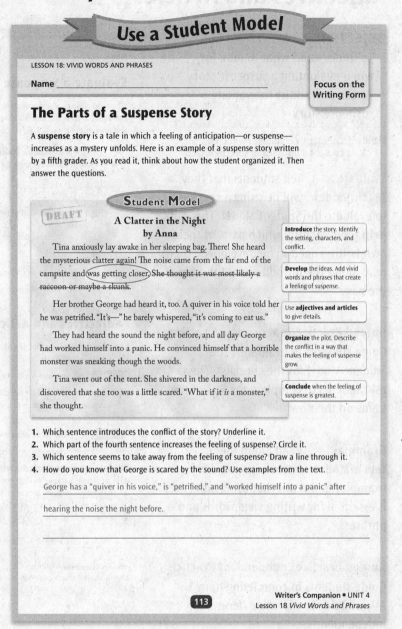

Use a Student Model

LESSON 18: VIVID WORDS AND PHRASES

Name _____

Focus on the Writing Form

The Parts of a Suspense Story

A **suspense story** is a tale in which a feeling of anticipation—or suspense—increases as a mystery unfolds. Here is an example of a suspense story written by a fifth grader. As you read it, think about how the student organized it. Then answer the questions.

Student Model

DRAFT

A Clatter in the Night
by Anna

Tina anxiously lay awake in her sleeping bag. There! She heard the mysterious clatter again! The noise came from the far end of the campsite and was getting closer. She thought it was most likely a raccoon or maybe a skunk.

Her brother George had heard it, too. A quiver in his voice told her he was petrified. "It's—" he barely whispered, "it's coming to eat us."

They had heard the sound the night before, and all day George had worked himself into a panic. He convinced himself that a horrible monster was sneaking though the woods.

Tina went out of the tent. She shivered in the darkness, and discovered that she too was a little scared. "What if it *is* a monster," she thought.

Call-outs:
- **Introduce** the story. Identify the setting, characters, and conflict.
- **Develop** the ideas. Add vivid words and phrases that create a feeling of suspense.
- Use **adjectives and articles** to give details.
- **Organize** the plot. Describe the conflict in a way that makes the feeling of suspense grow.
- **Conclude** when the feeling of suspense is greatest.

1. Which sentence introduces the conflict of the story? Underline it.
2. Which part of the fourth sentence increases the feeling of suspense? Circle it.
3. Which sentence seems to take away from the feeling of suspense? Draw a line through it.
4. How do you know that George is scared by the sound? Use examples from the text.

George has a "quiver in his voice," is "petrified," and "worked himself into a panic" after

hearing the noise the night before.

113

Writer's Companion • UNIT 4
Lesson 18 *Vivid Words and Phrases*

EXTENDING THE CONCEPT: DEVELOPING IDEAS

Invite volunteers to share and discuss their responses to Item 3. Explain that the sentence takes away from the sense of suspense by limiting readers' thoughts to the possibility that the noise was made by a harmless skunk or raccoon. Explain that a writer should develop ideas in a suspense story so that the vivid words provide enough details to spark interest, but not enough to spoil the mystery. Have students discuss the details the writer uses in the Student Model.

© Harcourt

Evaluate a Suspense Story/Grammar: Adjectives and Articles

OBJECTIVES

- To understand what to look for when evaluating a suspense story
- To use a checklist to evaluate a suspense story

Standard: LA.5.3.3.1 evaluate for writing traits; LA.5.3.4.4 use parts of speech correctly

Evaluate Teach/Model   Tell students that they will be using a checklist to evaluate the Student Model. This will help them identify which parts of their own writing need to be developed. Then read aloud the introduction at the top of the page.

Guided Practice/Independent Practice

Guide students in evaluating the Student Model for the checklist. Then ask students to complete the rest of the items on their own.

Grammar Teach/Model   Read aloud the introduction and examples. Point out that using adjectives is essential for writing vivid words and phrases.

Guided Practice/Independent Practice

Guide students in completing Item 1. Ask students to complete Items 2–4 independently.

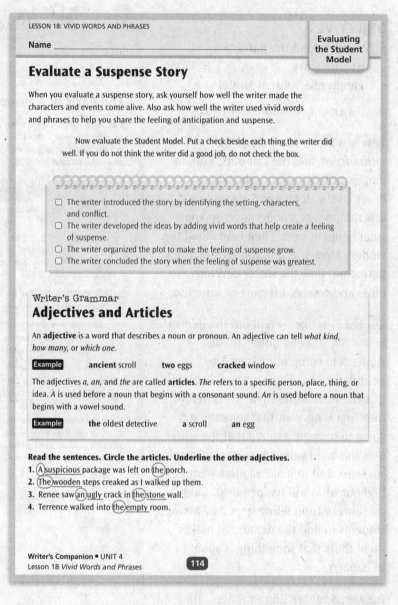

LESSON 18: VIVID WORDS AND PHRASES

Name _____

Evaluating the Student Model

Evaluate a Suspense Story

When you evaluate a suspense story, ask yourself how well the writer made the characters and events come alive. Also ask how well the writer used vivid words and phrases to help you share the feeling of anticipation and suspense.

Now evaluate the Student Model. Put a check beside each thing the writer did well. If you do not think the writer did a good job, do not check the box.

- ☐ The writer introduced the story by identifying the setting, characters, and conflict.
- ☐ The writer developed the ideas by adding vivid words that help create a feeling of suspense.
- ☐ The writer organized the plot to make the feeling of suspense grow.
- ☐ The writer concluded the story when the feeling of suspense was greatest.

Writer's Grammar
Adjectives and Articles

An **adjective** is a word that describes a noun or pronoun. An adjective can tell *what kind, how many,* or *which one.*

Example   **ancient** scroll   **two** eggs   **cracked** window

The adjectives *a, an,* and *the* are called **articles.** *The* refers to a specific person, place, thing, or idea. *A* is used before a noun that begins with a consonant sound. *An* is used before a noun that begins with a vowel sound.

Example   **the** oldest detective   **a** scroll   **an** egg

Read the sentences. Circle the articles. Underline the other adjectives.
1. A suspicious package was left on the porch.
2. The wooden steps creaked as I walked up them.
3. Renee saw an ugly crack in the stone wall.
4. Terrence walked into the empty room.

Writer's Companion ▪ UNIT 4
Lesson 18 *Vivid Words and Phrases*

114

SHARING AND DISCUSSING

After students have completed the items on the checklist, ask volunteers to share the results of their evaluations. Have students discuss how well they thought the writer created a sense of suspense. Encourage students to point to specific words and phrases to support their opinions. Then have students explain how well they thought the writer organized the plot to make the feeling of suspense grow. If students feel that the writer did not successfully create a feeling of suspense or make the suspense grow, encourage them to discuss specific things that the writer could have done better.

Revise: Adding Vivid Words and Phrases

OBJECTIVES
- To understand the purpose of revising
- To revise a suspense story by adding vivid words and phrases

Teach/Model Explain that students should view the revision process as a chance to develop the ideas that are already on paper. Tell them that one way to develop ideas is by adding vivid words and phrases.

Guided Practice Read aloud the introduction and the example. Explain to students that the example shows the steps writers should take when they think about how a sentence should be revised. Point out that the writer added the vivid verb *crept* to show exactly how Tina went out of the tent. Then point out how the writer added the adverb *nervously* to describe how Tina crept. Explain that these vivid words help add to the feeling of suspense. Read aloud the directions for Part A and guide students through Item 1. Suggest that students use the Word Bank for ideas.

Independent Writing Practice Have students complete Items 2–4 of Part A on their own. Then have them complete Part B independently. Ask volunteers to read aloud their revisions to the class.

LESSON 18: VIVID WORDS AND PHRASES

Name _____

Revising the Student Model

Revise: Adding Vivid Words and Phrases

One thing the writer could have done better was to use vivid words and phrases. These would have helped develop the feeling of suspense. She could have done this by asking *who, what, where, when, why,* and *how.* Here is an example of how a sentence from the Student Model could be improved.

Example

Read: Tina went out of the tent.

Ask Yourself: *How* did she go out of the tent?

Ask Yourself: *What* did she feel *when* she was going outside?

Improve the Sentence: *Tina nervously crept out of the tent.*

A. Read the following sentences. Then improve them by adding vivid words and phrases and by using adjectives to add details. Use the Word Bank to help you.   Possible responses are given.

1. John went into the room and told his brother to do something.

   John marched confidently into the living room and demanded that his

   brother turn off the television.

2. Helena opened the door and saw the box.

   Helena swung open the closet door and discovered the ancient wooden box.

3. Mr. Phelps filled the hole in the lawn.

   Mr. Phelps carefully shoveled the fresh, black dirt back into the hole at the

   edge of the lawn.

4. The little cat walked across the room.

   The kitten silently padded across the tile floor toward the open canary cage.

Word Bank

ancient
closet
confidently
demand
discover
edge
fresh
carefully
living room
open
silently

B. Revise the draft of the suspense story that you wrote on page 112. Be sure that you have used vivid words and phrases to bring the characters and events to life. Write your revision on another sheet of paper.

115

Writer's Companion • UNIT 4
Lesson 18 *Vivid Words and Phrases*

WRITER'S STRATEGY: REVISING THE LEAD SENTENCE

Suggest that students experiment with revising their lead sentences by adding new vivid words and phrases, even if they are satisfied with the ones they used in the first draft. Explain that sometimes writers find that if they begin a piece of writing with a different lead, the whole tone or feeling of the piece of writing can change with it. Students might discover that a different lead will make it easier to make other revisions to the entire draft.

© Harcourt

Review Writer's Craft

OBJECTIVES

- To review the terms *sensory details* and *vivid words and phrases*
- To identify *sensory details* and *vivid words and phrases* in literature

Standard: LA.5.3.1.1 generate ideas

Teach/Model Tell students that, in this lesson, they will review how writers use sensory details to breathe life into their writing. They also will review how writers choose vivid words and phrases to develop their ideas and make them more clear. Read aloud the introduction and the Literature Model, asking students to listen for sensory details and vivid words and phrases.

Guided Practice Read aloud the directions to Part B and Item 1. Guide students in completing Item 1 by asking them to identify the words that tell readers how to turn on and off the current. Then guide students in completing Item 2 by asking them to identify specific nouns.

Independent Writing Practice After reading aloud the directions, have students complete Part C independently.

Use a Literature Model

LESSON 19: REVIEW WRITER'S CRAFT

Name _____

Writer's Craft in Literature

Review Writer's Craft

In this unit you have learned how sensory details can be used to make writing come alive for readers. You have also learned how to use vivid words and phrases to make writing more lively and more entertaining.

A. Read the following passage. Notice how the writer used sensory details and vivid words and phrases.

Literature Model

(1) Telegraph wires reached from coast to coast by this time. (2) Invented by Samuel Morse in 1837, the telegraph was a sort of electric switch. (3) Current passing through it could be turned on and off with the tap of a finger. (4) Messages were created by sending long or short pulses of current through a telegraph at one end of a wire to another telegraph at the other end of the wire. (5) At the receiving end of the wire, marks were indented on a roll of paper tape moving around a cylinder, a device called a Morse register. (6) Long pulses made dashes, short pulses made dots. (7) Morse created a code in which the dots and dashes represented the letters of the alphabet. (8) Telegraph operators receiving a message translated the code into letters and wrote them down.

—from *Inventing the Future: A Photobiography of Thomas Alva Edison*
by Marfé Ferguson Delano

B. Identify how the writer used sensory details.
1. Underline the words in the third sentence that appeal to the sense of touch.
2. Circle the specific nouns used in the sixth sentence.

C. Write two sentences that describe how the telegraph works. Use sensory details and vivid words and phrases to make your description come alive.

Possible response: Pulses of electricity indented marks on a roll of paper. They

formed a code made up of dots and dashes that the telegraph operators could read.

_____

_____

Writer's Companion • UNIT 4
Lesson 19 *Review Writer's Craft*

116

SHARING AND DISCUSSING

After students have completed Part C, have students read their sentences to a partner. Ask partners to listen for the sensory details and vivid words. Then, have partners discuss the words they heard that made the description come alive. Next have students brainstorm a short list of sensory details and vivid words to describe how to use a telephone. Have partners collaborate to write a sentence, using the words from their list. Invite partners to share their sentences with the class.

© Harcourt

Review Writer's Craft

OBJECTIVES
- To review the terms *sensory details* and *vivid words and phrases*
- To identify *sensory details* and *vivid words and phrases*

Standard: LA.5.3.1.1 generate ideas

Teach/Model Read aloud the introduction and use the graphic organizer to remind students that writers can use sensory details to create a personal voice. Also point out that word choice, such as selecting vivid words and phrases, can make their writing more interesting and entertaining.

Guided Practice Read aloud the directions and the example for Part A. Point out the underlined words and explain that they give readers a specific idea of how the truck sounded. Guide students in completing Item 1. Ask students which words tell how the sand felt to Amanda. Then guide students in completing Items 2–5. Next read aloud the directions and passage for Part B. Guide students in completing Item 1. Point out the vivid verb *promoted* and explain how it gives readers a clear understanding of why the man built the tower.

Independent Writing Practice Have students complete Items 2–3 independently.

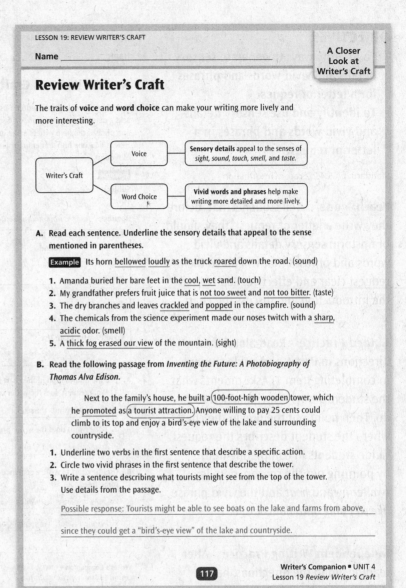

EXTENDING THE CONCEPT: CREATING A PERSONAL VOICE

Remind students that they can use sensory details to create a personal voice in their own writing. Explain that a personal voice will give the readers the sense that they are hearing the words of a real person who cares deeply about the subject. Point out to students that they also can use sensory details to create specific voices for the different characters who appear in their writing. Explain that these can be real people or fictional characters. Tell students that they can use sensory details to show the readers what the characters are like or how the characters feel about a topic.

© Harcourt

Review Writer's Craft

OBJECTIVES
- To identify ways to generate sensory details and vivid words and phrases for a letter of request
- To identify and use sensory details and vivid words and phrases in a letter of request

Standard: LA.5.4.2.2 record information

Teach/Model   Tell students that, before they write a letter of request, they should brainstorm sensory details and vivid words and phrases that will make their request clear and effective. Read aloud the introduction and discuss the chart.

Guided Practice   Read aloud the directions to Part A and guide students in completing Item 1. Ask students what the student wants Principal Chen to do. Then point out the line in the chart where the student describes the request. Guide students in completing Item 2 by pointing out the sensory details *sweltering* and *heat* and the vivid phrase *like stepping onto hot coals*.

Independent Writing Practice   After reading aloud the directions, have students complete Part B independently.

LESSON 19: REVIEW WRITER'S CRAFT

Name _____

Practice with Writer's Craft

Review Writer's Craft

In a **letter of request**, the writer asks for information, orders something, or asks a person or organization to do something. Sensory details and vivid words and phrases can help writers make sure that a request is accurate and clear. Here is how one fifth grader brainstormed words and phrases to use in a letter of request.

Example

Subject: *Playground*
To: *Principal Chen*
Request: *Plant some trees and grass in the school playground.*

Sensory Details I Can Use				
Sight	**Sound**	**Touch**	**Smell**	**Taste**
shade		*sweltering*	*pine*	
trees		*heat*		

Vivid Words I Can Use
propose
welcomed

Vivid Phrases I Can Use
like stepping onto hot coals

A. Use the information in the chart to answer these questions.
  1. What request does the writer make?
     The writer wants the school to plant trees and grass in the playground.

  2. What words does the writer plan on using to appeal to the sense of touch?
     "sweltering," "heat," "like stepping onto hot coals"

B. Use the chart to write a sentence that tells why the writer wants the school to plant some trees.
  Possible response: They will provide shade from the heat so that playing on the

  playground is not "like stepping onto hot coals."

Writer's Companion • UNIT 4
Lesson 19 *Review Writer's Craft*   118

Reaching All Learners

BELOW LEVEL
For Part B, have students work with a partner or aide. Before students write, have them discuss what the sensory words and vivid phrases tell them about the playground when it is hot.

ADVANCED
Encourage students to write an additional sentence to explain why planting trees in the playground is a good idea. Tell students to use sensory details and vivid words and phrases.

ENGLISH-LANGUAGE LEARNERS
Have students work in small groups. Ask them to discuss the meaning of the vivid phrase *like stepping onto hot coals* and how planting trees would help the situation.

© Harcourt

The Parts of a Letter of Request

OBJECTIVES
- To understand the parts of a letter of request.
- To analyze a Student Model

Teach/Model Read aloud the introduction. Before reading aloud the call-outs, tell students that the call-outs show how a letter of request should be organized. Point out that the return and inside addresses usually appear at the top of the letter. Explain that they could not fit on this page and were not included in the Student Model. Then read aloud the Student Model. Ask students to listen for how the writer uses sensory details and vivid words to develop the request.

Guided Practice Point out the questions below the Student Model. Then guide students in completing Item 1. Explain that the writer uses the greeting to address the person who will receive the letter. Point out that the closing appears above the writer's name. Guide student in completing Item 2 by pointing out that the writer makes her request clear by beginning the sentence with "I am writing to request...."

Independent Writing Practice Have students complete Items 3 and 4 independently.

© Harcourt

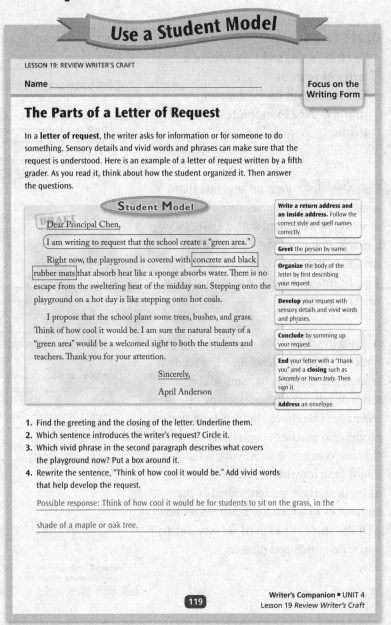

Use a Student Model

LESSON 19: REVIEW WRITER'S CRAFT

Name _____

Focus on the Writing Form

The Parts of a Letter of Request

In a **letter of request**, the writer asks for information or for someone to do something. Sensory details and vivid words and phrases can make sure that the request is understood. Here is an example of a letter of request written by a fifth grader. As you read it, think about how the student organized it. Then answer the questions.

Student Model

DRAFT

Dear Principal Chen,

I am writing to request that the school create a "green area."

Right now, the playground is covered with concrete and black rubber mats that absorb heat like a sponge absorbs water. There is no escape from the sweltering heat of the midday sun. Stepping onto the playground on a hot day is like stepping onto hot coals.

I propose that the school plant some trees, bushes, and grass. Think of how cool it would be. I am sure the natural beauty of a "green area" would be a welcomed sight to both the students and teachers. Thank you for your attention.

Sincerely,

April Anderson

- **Write a return address and an inside address.** Follow the correct style and spell names correctly.
- **Greet** the person by name.
- **Organize** the body of the letter by first describing your request.
- **Develop** your request with sensory details and vivid words and phrases.
- **Conclude** by summing up your request.
- **End** your letter with a "thank you" and a **closing** such as *Sincerely* or *Yours truly.* Then sign it.
- **Address** an envelope.

1. Find the greeting and the closing of the letter. Underline them.
2. Which sentence introduces the writer's request? Circle it.
3. Which vivid phrase in the second paragraph describes what covers the playground now? Put a box around it.
4. Rewrite the sentence, "Think of how cool it would be." Add vivid words that help develop the request.

   Possible response: Think of how cool it would be for students to sit on the grass, in the

   shade of a maple or oak tree.

119

Writer's Companion • UNIT 4
Lesson 19 *Review Writer's Craft*

EXTENDING THE CONCEPT: SENSORY DETAILS AND VIVID WORDS AND PHRASES

Point out that the writer of the Student Model uses sensory details and vivid words and phrases to express her viewpoint. She also uses them to convince the principal to fulfill her request. Have students discuss how sensory details, such as *sweltering heat,* and vivid phrases, such as *like stepping onto hot coals,* might convince the principal that the school needs a "green area." Ask students to identify other words and phrases in the letter that they think will help convince the principal.

Evaluate a Letter of Request

OBJECTIVES

- To understand how to evaluate a letter of request
- To understand how a 4–point rubric is used to evaluate a piece of writing

Teach/Model Remind students that some of the writing they do on tests and in school is evaluated with a chart called a *rubric*. Point out the 4-point rubric on the following page. Explain that on a 4-point rubric, a 4 is the highest score a writer can earn.

Guided Practice Read aloud the directions to Part A and then the Student Model. Ask students to listen to the letter of request without looking at the page. Then have students read the model and teacher's comments. Explain that the comments show what a teacher might look for when evaluating a letter of request. Have students identify the comments in which the teacher says how well the student has used sensory details and vivid words and phrases.

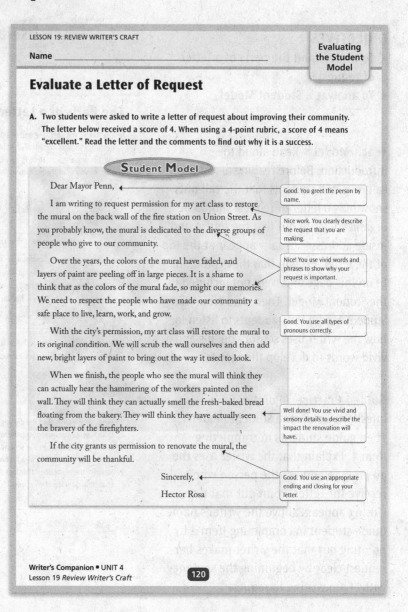

LESSON 19: REVIEW WRITER'S CRAFT

Name _____

Evaluating the Student Model

Evaluate a Letter of Request

A. Two students were asked to write a letter of request about improving their community. The letter below received a score of 4. When using a 4-point rubric, a score of 4 means "excellent." Read the letter and the comments to find out why it is a success.

Student Model

Dear Mayor Penn,

I am writing to request permission for my art class to restore the mural on the back wall of the fire station on Union Street. As you probably know, the mural is dedicated to the diverse groups of people who give to our community.

Over the years, the colors of the mural have faded, and layers of paint are peeling off in large pieces. It is a shame to think that as the colors of the mural fade, so might our memories. We need to respect the people who have made our community a safe place to live, learn, work, and grow.

With the city's permission, my art class will restore the mural to its original condition. We will scrub the wall ourselves and then add new, bright layers of paint to bring out the way it used to look.

When we finish, the people who see the mural will think they can actually hear the hammering of the workers painted on the wall. They will think they can actually smell the fresh-baked bread floating from the bakery. They will think they have actually seen the bravery of the firefighters.

If the city grants us permission to renovate the mural, the community will be thankful.

Sincerely,

Hector Rosa

Comments:
- Good. You greet the person by name.
- Nice work. You clearly describe the request that you are making.
- Nice! You use vivid words and phrases to show why your request is important.
- Good. You use all types of pronouns correctly.
- Well done! You use vivid and sensory details to describe the impact the renovation will have.
- Good. You use an appropriate ending and closing for your letter.

Writer's Companion • UNIT 4
Lesson 19 *Review Writer's Craft*   120

WRITER'S STRATEGY: CHOOSING THE RIGHT WORDS FOR YOUR AUDIENCE

Point out that a letter of request gives the writer an opportunity to choose vivid words and phrases that will appeal to a particular audience. Explain that when people write letters, they know exactly who their audience will be. Point out that the writer of the Student Model uses words and phrases that he knows will affect his audience, Mayor Penn. Point out the phrase *diverse groups of people who give to our community*. Explain that this phrase works well because it will have an impact on someone who cares about the community, such as the mayor.

© Harcourt

Evaluate a Letter of Request

OBJECTIVES

- To understand why a letter of request received a low score on a rubric
- To understand how a 4–point rubric is used to evaluate a letter of request

Teach/Model   Tell students that they now will read a letter of request that received a score of 2 on a 4-point rubric. Read aloud the Student Model. Have students listen to the letter without reading along. As they listen, have them think about how the letter could be improved.

Guided Practice   Invite students to discuss the strengths and weaknesses they noticed while listening to the Student Model. Then have students read the Student Model and the teacher's comments. Guide students in identifying the areas in which the letter of request needs improvement.

Independent Writing Practice   Explain to students how to use the 4-point rubric at the bottom of the page. Have students use it to evaluate the Student Model on page 119.

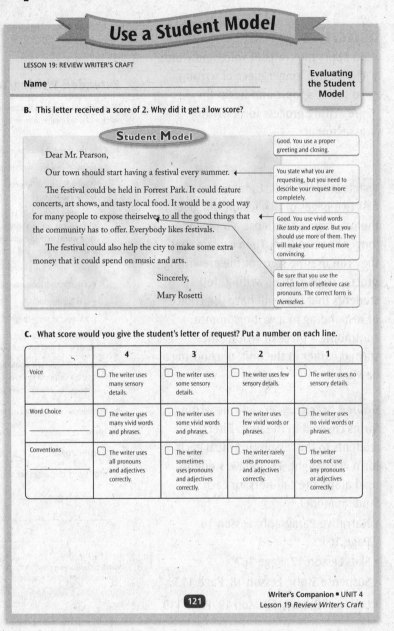

Use a Student Model

LESSON 19: REVIEW WRITER'S CRAFT

Name _____

Evaluating the Student Model

B. This letter received a score of 2. Why did it get a low score?

Student Model

Dear Mr. Pearson,

Our town should start having a festival every summer.

The festival could be held in Forrest Park. It could feature concerts, art shows, and tasty local food. It would be a good way for many people to expose theirselves to all the good things that the community has to offer. Everybody likes festivals.

The festival could also help the city to make some extra money that it could spend on music and arts.

Sincerely,

Mary Rosetti

Good. You use a proper greeting and closing.

You state what you are requesting, but you need to describe your request more completely.

Good. You use vivid words like tasty and expose. But you should use more of them. They will make your request more convincing.

Be sure that you use the correct form of reflexive case pronouns. The correct form is themselves.

C. What score would you give the student's letter of request? Put a number on each line.

	4	3	2	1
Voice _____	☐ The writer uses many sensory details.	☐ The writer uses some sensory details.	☐ The writer uses few sensory details.	☐ The writer uses no sensory details.
Word Choice _____	☐ The writer uses many vivid words and phrases.	☐ The writer uses some vivid words and phrases.	☐ The writer uses few vivid words or phrases.	☐ The writer uses no vivid words or phrases.
Conventions _____	☐ The writer uses all pronouns and adjectives correctly.	☐ The writer sometimes uses pronouns and adjectives correctly.	☐ The writer rarely uses pronouns and adjectives correctly.	☐ The writer does not use any pronouns or adjectives correctly.

121

Writer's Companion • UNIT 4
Lesson 19 *Review Writer's Craft*

SHARING AND DISCUSSING

After students have completed Part C, have them work in pairs to share and discuss their evaluations. As partners share each score they gave the letter of request, have them explain the process they used for determining it. Encourage students to support their reasons with examples from the Student Model. Also encourage students to discuss how they interpreted the words in the rubric, such as *many, some,* and *few,* and how these interpretations might affect the score.

© Harcourt

Extended Writing/Test Prep

OBJECTIVES
- To apply the crafts of voice and word choice in a longer piece of writing
- To select a topic and begin the prewriting process for a writing assessment

Teach/Model   Tell students that the first two pages of this lesson will give them a chance to choose a topic for a longer composition. Then explain that they can use the steps of the prewriting process to plan their writing. Tell students that they will have the choice of responding to a writing prompt, continuing a piece of writing they started earlier in the unit, or choosing a new topic.

Guided Practice   Review the writing forms covered in the unit. Direct students to the lessons in which each form was taught. Then have students read aloud the call-outs for each Student Model.
- Narrative Paragraph: Lesson 16, Page 101
- Skit: Lesson 17, Page 107
- Suspense Story: Lesson 18, Page 113
- Letter of Request: Lesson 19, Page 119

Have students begin the prewriting process by completing Part B independently.

Extended Writing/Test Prep

On the first two pages of this lesson, you will use what you have learned about voice and word choice to write a longer written work.

A. Read the three choices below. Put a star by the writing activity you would like to do.

1. Respond to a Writing Prompt

   Writing Situation: Sometimes communities can do things that help make life better for everyone.

   Directions for Writing: Think of something your community could do to make life better for its residents. Write a letter of request to your community leaders. Use sensory details and vivid words to help explain your request. Be sure to use a return address, an inside address, a greeting, a body, and a closing.

2. Choose one of the pieces of writing you started in this unit:
   - a narrative paragraph (page 100)
   - a skit (page 106)
   - a suspense story (page 112)

   Revise and expand your draft into a complete piece of writing. Use what you have learned about voice and word choice.

3. Choose a topic you would like to write about. You may write a narrative paragraph, a skit, a suspense story, or a letter of request. Use sensory details and vivid words and phrases. Be sure to create specific voices for different characters.

B. Use the space below and on the next page to plan your writing.

TOPIC: _____

WRITING FORM: _____

HOW I WILL ORGANIZE MY WRITING: _____

_____

_____

_____

SHARING AND DISCUSSING

After students have completed Part B, have partners share the topics and writing forms that they have chosen. Then ask partners to discuss the best way to organize ideas for each of their writing forms. Tell students that, on the next page, they will be asked to choose a graphic organizer to help them plan their writing. Have partners select the kinds of graphic organizers they could use to best help them organize their ideas.

© Harcourt

Extended Writing/Test Prep

OBJECTIVES
- To use a graphic organizer to plan a piece of writing
- To use the steps of the writing process to complete a longer piece of writing

Standard: LA.5.3.2.1 use a pre-writing plan

Teach/Model   Read aloud the introduction to Part C. Tell students they will use the graphic organizer to generate and organize ideas. Explain that they can use an organizer from the lessons in the unit, or they can pick a new one. Have students review the chart on page 106. Ask volunteers to model how they might use the chart to generate ideas.

Guided Practice   Have students copy the organizer they have chosen into the space provided in Part C. Explain to students that the goal of prewriting is to generate ideas. Tell students that they should jot down whatever comes to mind. Later they can cross out the details that are off topic.

Independent Writing   Draft, Revise, and Publish   After students have finished their drafts, remind them to revise by adding sensory details and vivid words. Copy the students' revised drafts for a class publication. Have students work in groups to design and create covers.

LESSON 20: WRITING TEST PRACTICE

Name _____

C. In the space below, draw a graphic organizer that will help you plan your writing. Fill in the graphic organizer. Write additional notes on the lines below.

Notes

_____

_____

_____

_____

_____

_____

_____

D. Do your writing on another sheet of paper.

123

Writer's Companion • UNIT 4
Lesson 20 *Writing Test Practice*

Reaching All Learners

BELOW LEVEL
Have students work with a partner or aide to generate ideas. Then have them use the notes section to build sentences using the ideas from the organizer.

ADVANCED
Encourage students to consider their audience as they write their drafts. Remind them that they will want to use different language depending on who is going to read their piece.

ENGLISH-LANGUAGE LEARNERS
Remind less fluent English speakers that the prewriting stage is not evaluated for spelling and grammar.

© Harcourt

Answering Multiple-Choice Questions

Name _____

OBJECTIVES
- To become familiar with test items that require interpreting a graphic organizer
- To learn how to read the answer choices and identify the correct one

Standard: LA.5.3.1.1 generate ideas

Teach/Model   Read aloud the directions for Part A. Explain that the questions will help them learn how to interpret and use information on a graphic organizer. Read aloud Item 1. Model answering it by pointing out the row on the chart that lists the personality traits. Then read aloud the answer choices. Explain that students should choose C because that trait best fits the details on the chart. Point out that the other answers show personality traits that would not fit someone who is quiet, serious, and nice.

Guided Practice   Guide students in completing Item 2 by reading aloud the Test Tip. Tell them to choose the answer with the words that would not likely be spoken by a serious but nice detective.

Independent Writing Practice   Have students complete Item 3 independently.

Answering Multiple-Choice Questions

For questions on pages 124–127, fill in the bubble next to the correct answer.

A. Gabriella made the chart below to organize ideas for a paper. Use her chart to answer questions 1–3.

Gabriella's Writing Plan

Setting: art museum

Name of Character	Detective Rita Gomez
Personality	• very serious • nice, but rarely smiles • never raises her voice
Words that Character Might Use	• interesting • evidence • I presume

1. Which personality trait fits the character and should be added to the chart?
   - Ⓐ She often yells at people.
   - Ⓑ She is always joking around with her friends.
   - Ⓒ She quietly and calmly does her job.
   - Ⓓ She isn't very nice to people she doesn't know.

2. Which word or phrase does not fit the character's voice and should not be added to the chart?
   - Ⓐ "I hate that!"
   - Ⓑ "Be careful when you move that."
   - Ⓒ "Let's think about the facts."
   - Ⓓ "May I look at that package, please?"

Test Tip: A character's voice is the unique way that he or she speaks. For Question 2, choose the word or phrase that sounds most different from those in the chart.

3. Based on the information in Gabriella's Writing Plan, what kind of paper is Gabriella planning to write?
   - Ⓐ a newspaper story about the art museum
   - Ⓑ a paper that tells a story about Detective Gomez
   - Ⓒ a paper that tells the story of Gabriella's life
   - Ⓓ a letter of request to Detective Gomez

Writer's Companion • UNIT 4
Lesson 20 *Writing Test Practice*   124

ASSESSING STUDENT RESPONSES

Students who have answered Items 1 and 2 incorrectly might misunderstand the important terms *personality trait* and *character's voice*. Have these students look back at Lesson 17, Pages 104–105 and 109, to review how to identify a character's voice and traits. Students might also have difficulty understanding how to use the graphic organizer to answer the questions. Have students describe the process they used to answer Items 1 and 2. Encourage students to look back at Pages 106–107 to review how the writer used the chart to organize ideas for a skit.

© Harcourt

Answering Multiple-Choice Questions (cont.)

OBJECTIVES
- To become familiar with a multiple-choice format that involves reading a passage
- To develop a strategy of answering questions that relate to a passage

Teach/Model Read aloud the directions to Part B. Tell students that this page will help them learn how to answer multiple-choice questions about a story. Then read the story to them. Model how to answer Item 1 by reading each answer choice. For each sentence, ask: **Does this dialogue include vivid words and phrases that create a specific voice and make the character seem real?** Point out that the phrase *stinky old steel pipe* creates a specific voice for Jake, by showing that he doesn't think they will find any buried treasure.

Guided Practice Guide students in choosing the correct answer for Item 2 by explaining that they should choose the sentence that uses sensory details and vivid words to add to the feeling of suspense in the story.

Independent Writing Practice Read the Test Tip aloud and have students complete Item 3 independently.

LESSON 20: WRITING TEST PRACTICE

Name _____

Writing Test Practice

B. The story below is a first draft that Billy wrote. The story contains mistakes. Read the story to answer questions 1–3.

Buried Treasure
(1) The metal detector made a noise. (2) "Something is down there," Tim said. (3) "Naw, it's probably just a stinky old steel pipe," said Jake. (4) Tim started digging. (5) He hoped it was a chest of gold coins like in the pirate movies. (6) As he dug, he thought about all the things he could buy with the gold. (7) On his last dig into the dirt, the shovel hit something. (8) Tim got down and looked. (9) He pulled the jar out and scraped off the dirt. (10) "What's in it?" Jake asked. (11) "Coins," Tim said. (12) He held the jar up to the light, so they both could see. (13) "Pennies!" they said.

1. Which sentence contains dialogue that best creates a specific voice for one of the characters?
   - (A) sentence (2)
   - (B) sentence (3)
   - (C) sentence (11)
   - (D) sentence (13)

2. Which sentence below could be added after sentence (7) to give a more vivid description of the events in the paragraph?
   - (A) His pants were already dirty.
   - (B) Jake shuffled his feet in the dirt and waited.
   - (C) His glasses slid to the end of his nose.
   - (D) He saw a jar, sunken in the dirt and protected by flat stones.

3. Which sentence below best shows how sentence (8) could be revised to give sensory details?
   - (A) Tim walked around and looked.
   - (B) Tim examined things closely and carefully.
   - (C) Tim knelt in the damp hole and brushed away clumps of soil.
   - (D) Tim thought about what could be there.

Test Tip:
A sensory detail appeals to the senses of *sight, sound, taste, touch,* or *smell.* For Question 3, choose the sentence that uses these types of details most effectively.

Writer's Companion • UNIT 4
Lesson 20 *Writing Test Practice*
125

USING ACADEMIC LANGUAGE

Tell students that most tests contain academic language that is written in a way they might not fully understand. Explain to students that they might understand what a word in a question means, but they might not understand exactly how that word affects their answer choice. Point out the word *best* in Item 1. Explain that all of the answer choices tell what characters say, but one sentence creates a specific voice. This sentence is the *best* choice.

© Harcourt

Answering Multiple-Choice Questions (cont.)

OBJECTIVES
- To become familiar with a multiple-choice format that involves reading a passage
- To develop a strategy of choosing the word that best completes a sentence

Standard: LA.5.3.3.3 add supporting details/modify word choice

Teach/Model Read aloud the directions to Part C. Tell students that this page will allow them to practice choosing words that correctly complete sentences in a passage. Read aloud Item 1. Tell students to look for the pronoun that completes the sentence in a way that makes sense. Model how to complete Item 1 by substituting each answer choice for the first blank. Explain that the correct answer is B, since the possessive pronoun *our* is used before a noun.

Guided Practice Guide students in completing Item 2 by telling them to choose the only article that should go before *ruins*.

Independent Writing Practice Read the Test Tip aloud and have students complete Items 3–5 independently.

LESSON 20: WRITING TEST PRACTICE

Name _____

Writing Test Practice

C. Read the story, "The Search." Choose the word or words that correctly complete questions 1–5.

The Search

Mr. Franks and I set off on _____(1)_____ mission to find _____(2)_____ ruins of the mining camp. I brought extra water for _____(3)_____, because I knew it was going to be an especially hot and humid day. As we walked deeper into the woods, _____(4)_____ pushed through the thick vines. Mr. Franks was only five feet ahead of me, but I could barely see _____(5)_____! The briers stuck to our pants, as if to hold us back from discovering the secret they hid. Finally, after two hours, I stumbled over a clue that we were close—a rusty wheel of a coal car!

1. Which answer should go in blank (1)?
   - Ⓐ we
   - **Ⓑ our**
   - Ⓒ ours

2. Which answer should go in blank (2)?
   - **Ⓐ the**
   - Ⓑ a
   - Ⓒ an

3. Which answer should go in blank (3)?
   - Ⓐ me
   - Ⓑ mine
   - **Ⓒ myself**

4. Which answer should go in blank (4)?
   - **Ⓐ we**
   - Ⓑ us
   - Ⓒ ourselves

5. Which answer should go in blank (5)?
   - Ⓐ he
   - Ⓑ himself
   - **Ⓒ him**

Test Tip:
A pronoun that comes after an action verb or preposition is an object pronoun.

Singular object pronouns: *me, you, him, her, it*

Plural object pronouns: *us, you, them*

Writer's Companion • UNIT 4
Lesson 20 *Writing Test Practice*

126

Reaching All Learners

BELOW LEVEL
Help students understand their answer choices by reading aloud the sentence with each answer choice. Have students mark the correct answer as they listen.

ADVANCED
Challenge students writing above grade level to use context clues to fill in the blanks as they read the passage. Explain that context clues are the words in the sentences that tell them which pronouns will work in the blanks.

ENGLISH-LANGUAGE LEARNERS
Encourage less fluent English speakers to look back at the grammar lessons in the unit to help them choose the correct pronoun. Provide enough time for them to complete all of the questions.

© Harcourt

Answering Multiple-Choice Questions (cont.)

OBJECTIVES
- To become familiar with test items that require putting ideas together to build sentences
- To identify a sentence that has been put together in a way that makes sense

Standard: LA.5.3.3.2 create clarity using sentence structures

Teach/Model Tell students that some multiple-choice questions will ask them to choose the sentence that has been built correctly from a list of words and phrases. Read aloud Item 1 and model completing it by pointing out that the adjective *famous* is placed differently in each answer. Tell students that Answer B is incorrect because adjectives usually appear before the word they modify. Then point out that Answer C is incorrect because *famous* does not modify the word *saw*. Finally explain that Answer A is correct because *famous* is correctly placed before the noun that it modifies.

Guided Practice Read aloud Item 2, and then guide students in completing it by reading aloud the Test Tip. Tell students that they should immediately rule out Answer C, since the sentence does not make sense. Then explain to students that they should choose Answer B in which the articles are used correctly.

Independent Writing Practice Have students complete Item 3 independently.

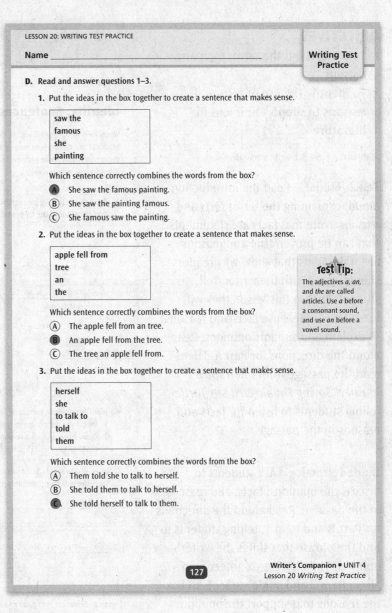

LESSON 20: WRITING TEST PRACTICE

Name _____

Writing Test Practice

D. Read and answer questions 1–3.

1. Put the ideas in the box together to create a sentence that makes sense.

> saw the
> famous
> she
> painting

Which sentence correctly combines the words from the box?

(A) She saw the famous painting.
(B) She saw the painting famous.
(C) She famous saw the painting.

2. Put the ideas in the box together to create a sentence that makes sense.

> apple fell from
> tree
> an
> the

Which sentence correctly combines the words from the box?

(A) The apple fell from an tree.
(B) An apple fell from the tree.
(C) The tree an apple fell from.

Test Tip:
The adjectives *a*, *an*, and *the* are called articles. Use *a* before a consonant sound, and use *an* before a vowel sound.

3. Put the ideas in the box together to create a sentence that makes sense.

> herself
> she
> to talk to
> told
> them

Which sentence correctly combines the words from the box?

(A) Them told she to talk to herself.
(B) She told them to talk to herself.
(C) She told herself to talk to them.

127

Writer's Companion ■ UNIT 4
Lesson 20 *Writing Test Practice*

© Harcourt

SHARING AND DISCUSSING

Have students work in pairs and compare their responses to Items 1–3. Ask students to model the steps they used to answer each item. Students should explain to each other why they chose their answers and give specific reasons why they did not choose the others. Encourage students to adopt their partners' process if they think it will help them answer the questions more easily.

Identify: Sentences with Facts and Reasons

OBJECTIVES

- To understand the terms *facts* and *reasons*
- To identify the use of facts and reasons to support opinions in literature

Standard: LA.5.4.3.1 write persuasive text

Teach/Model Read the introduction aloud, explaining the terms *facts* and *reasons*. Note that facts are statements that can be proven true and reasons are statements that show why readers should agree with the writer. Tell students that in this lesson they will learn how writers use facts and reasons to explain and support opinions. Read aloud the directions for Part A. Then read the passage from *Interrupted Journey: Saving Endangered Sea Turtles*, telling students to listen for facts and reasons in the passage.

Guided Practice Ask students to discuss the opinions, facts, and reasons in the passage. Read aloud the directions for Part B and Item 1, telling students to find the phrase that states the writer's opinion. Then have a volunteer read aloud Item 2 and guide students to box the reasons that support the opinion.

Independent Writing Practice Have students complete Part C independently.

Use a Literature Model

LESSON 21: SENTENCES WITH FACTS AND REASONS

Name _____

Writer's Craft in Literature

Identify: Sentences with Facts and Reasons

When they write to persuade, writers voice their opinions. They develop and support their opinions by writing sentences with facts and reasons. **Facts** are statements that can be proven. **Reasons** are statements that explain why readers should agree with the writer.

A. Read the following passage from *Interrupted Journey: Saving Endangered Sea Turtles*. Pay attention to the facts and reasons the writer gives to support her opinion.

Literature Model

Max and his mother and the other volunteers work for a vital cause. All sea turtles are threatened or endangered; Kemp's ridleys are the most endangered of all. Right now on our planet there are fewer than eight thousand Kemp's ridley turtles left. They are a vanishing species.

—from *Interrupted Journey: Saving Endangered Sea Turtles*
by Kathryn Lasky

B. Identify opinions, facts, and reasons in the passage. Possible responses are given.
1. Underline the phrase in the first sentence that shows an opinion.
2. Draw a box around a reason that supports this opinion.
3. Circle a statement that is a fact and can be proven.

C. In your own words, summarize the passage. Tell the writer's opinion and the reasons and facts she gives for her opinion.

Possible response: Since all sea turtles are threatened or endangered, volunteers who work to save them are doing a very important job. With fewer than 8,000 left in the world, the Kemp's ridley turtles are especially at risk.

SHARING AND DISCUSSING

Before students complete their summaries for Part C, remind them that a summary should tell the main idea and most important details of the passage in their own words. Invite students to share their summaries. As students take turns reading their completed summaries aloud, have the class discuss what makes each similar to, and different from, the others.

© Harcourt

Explore: Sentences with Facts and Reasons

OBJECTIVES

- To understand how facts and reasons are used to support opinions
- To identify facts, reasons, and opinions

Standard: LA.5.4.3.1 write persuasive text

Teach/Model Review the terms *facts, reasons,* and *opinions.* Then use the introductory text and the graphic organizer to help students understand how facts and reasons are used to explain and support opinions. Review the graphic organizer and provide students with examples of statistics, examples, expert opinions, and emotional appeals. Ask students to discuss the differences between each type of statement.

Guided Practice Read aloud the directions for Part A. Then model the example as an opinion. Ask volunteers to read aloud each of the remaining sentences. Work with students to complete the activity. Read the directions to Part B aloud and guide students to find the facts and reasons in the paragraph.

Independent Writing Practice Have students complete Part C independently. For additional instruction, *see Extending the Concept.*

LESSON 21: SENTENCES WITH FACTS AND REASONS

Name _____

> A Closer Look at Writer's Craft

Explore: Sentences with Facts and Reasons

Opinions are a matter of personal belief. They cannot be proven right or wrong. When you write to persuade someone of your opinion, you must use **facts** and **reasons** to support your point of view.

> **Support Opinions With:**
>
> **Facts**—statistics and other statements that can be proven true
>
> **Reasons**—examples, expert opinions, and emotional appeals

A. Read each sentence. Tell whether the sentence states a fact, reason, or opinion.

Example   *A Tree Grows in Brooklyn* is a wonderful book. *opinion*

1. Betty Smith's first novel, *A Tree Grows in Brooklyn,* is considered an American classic.

   reason

2. The book sold 300,000 copies in the first six weeks after it was published.

   fact

3. The main character, Francie, is more interesting than any other character in the book.

   opinion

B. Read these sentences from *Interrupted Journey: Saving Endangered Sea Turtles.* Then underline the words that tell facts and draw boxes around the words that tell reasons.

> Richie Moretti is the owner, director, and founder of the hospital. He is not a veterinarian. He is not a marine biologist. He is a man who loves turtles, and his calling in life is to help injured animals.

C. Write a sentence with an opinion that could be supported by the facts and reasons above.

Possible response: Richie Moretti is a person with a big heart.

_____

EXTENDING THE CONCEPT: IDENTIFYING PURPOSE

Remind students that an important part of reading critically is thinking about *why* the writer is writing. After students read the passage from Part B, ask them what they think the writer wants to convey about Richie Moretti. What kind of characterization is she developing? What does this say about her opinion of this person? Have pairs of students discuss these questions. Then ask students to work independently to write a sentence with an opinion that is supported by the facts and reasons in the paragraph. Invite students to share their work.

© Harcourt

Use: Sentences with Facts and Reasons

OBJECTIVES
- To prepare to write by stating an opinion and listing facts and reasons that support it
- To write a persuasive letter with opinions, facts, and reasons

Standard: LA.5.3.2.1 use a pre-writing plan

Teach/Model Before reading the introduction, discuss the term *persuasive* with students. Explain that when people write to persuade they write to convince someone of something. Read the introduction and discuss the text in the graphic organizer. Then have students summarize what the information in the organizer tells them about the persuasive letter the student is planning to write.

Guided Practice Read aloud the directions for Part A. Ask students to think about where they would like to go on a field trip. Guide students as they complete their graphic organizers.

Independent Writing Practice Read the directions for Part B. Have students complete the activity independently.

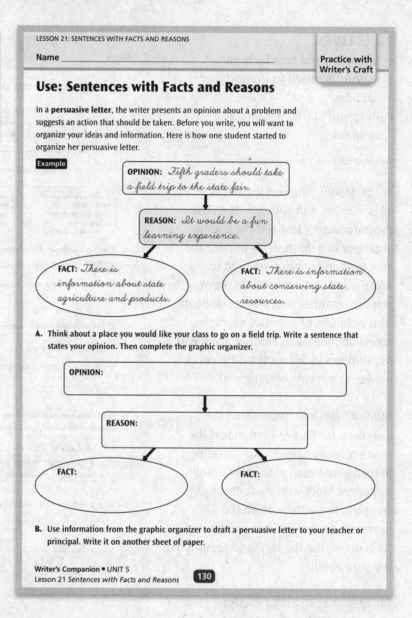

LESSON 21: SENTENCES WITH FACTS AND REASONS

Name _____

Practice with Writer's Craft

Use: Sentences with Facts and Reasons

In a **persuasive letter**, the writer presents an opinion about a problem and suggests an action that should be taken. Before you write, you will want to organize your ideas and information. Here is how one student started to organize her persuasive letter.

Example

OPINION: Fifth graders should take a field trip to the state fair.

REASON: It would be a fun learning experience.

FACT: There is information about state agriculture and products.

FACT: There is information about conserving state resources.

A. Think about a place you would like your class to go on a field trip. Write a sentence that states your opinion. Then complete the graphic organizer.

OPINION:

REASON:

FACT:

FACT:

B. Use information from the graphic organizer to draft a persuasive letter to your teacher or principal. Write it on another sheet of paper.

Writer's Companion • UNIT 5
Lesson 21 *Sentences with Facts and Reasons*   130

Reaching All Learners

BELOW LEVEL
Once students have chosen the place they would like to go, help them think about reasons and facts to support this opinion. Prompt them with questions such as: *What reasons might you give your school officials to convince them that this field trip is a good idea?*

ADVANCED
Encourage students to consider what concerns their principal or teacher may have about the proposed trip. Ask them how they can address these concerns in their letter. What can they say to reassure school officials who may hesitate to give permission?

ENGLISH-LANGUAGE LEARNERS
Work with students in small groups. Ask students to discuss their ideas for a place to go on a field trip. Then have them help each other to identify appropriate words and phrases to use to complete their graphic organizers.

© Harcourt

The Parts of a Persuasive Letter

OBJECTIVES
- To understand the parts of a persuasive letter
- To analyze a Student Model

Standard: LA.5.3.3.1 evaluate for writing traits

Teach/Model   Explain to students that the Student Model is a first draft of a fifth-grade student's persuasive letter. Read students the introduction and boxed call-outs. Then read aloud the model and ask students to pay careful attention to how the writer uses facts and reasons to support her argument. After you have read the model, ask students whether they think the letter was convincing and why or why not.

Guided Practice   Call students' attention to the items below the model. Read aloud Item 1, and guide them to find the sentence that states the purpose of the letter. Then read Item 2 aloud and guide students to identify facts and reasons the writer gives in her letter to support her opinion.

Independent Writing Practice   Have students complete Item 3 on their own. After they have finished, invite them to share and discuss their responses.

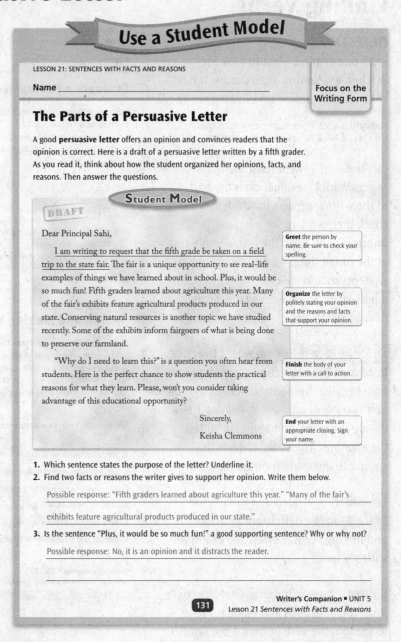

Use a Student Model

LESSON 21: SENTENCES WITH FACTS AND REASONS

Name _____

Focus on the Writing Form

The Parts of a Persuasive Letter

A good **persuasive letter** offers an opinion and convinces readers that the opinion is correct. Here is a draft of a persuasive letter written by a fifth grader. As you read it, think about how the student organized her opinions, facts, and reasons. Then answer the questions.

Student Model

DRAFT

Dear Principal Sahi,

   I am writing to request that the fifth grade be taken on a field trip to the state fair. The fair is a unique opportunity to see real-life examples of things we have learned about in school. Plus, it would be so much fun! Fifth graders learned about agriculture this year. Many of the fair's exhibits feature agricultural products produced in our state. Conserving natural resources is another topic we have studied recently. Some of the exhibits inform fairgoers of what is being done to preserve our farmland.

   "Why do I need to learn this?" is a question you often hear from students. Here is the perfect chance to show students the practical reasons for what they learn. Please, won't you consider taking advantage of this educational opportunity?

                                          Sincerely,

                                          Keisha Clemmons

Greet the person by name. Be sure to check your spelling.

Organize the letter by politely stating your opinion and the reasons and facts that support your opinion.

Finish the body of your letter with a call to action.

End your letter with an appropriate closing. Sign your name.

1. Which sentence states the purpose of the letter? Underline it.
2. Find two facts or reasons the writer gives to support her opinion. Write them below.

   Possible response: "Fifth graders learned about agriculture this year." "Many of the fair's

   exhibits feature agricultural products produced in our state."

3. Is the sentence "Plus, it would be so much fun!" a good supporting sentence? Why or why not?

   Possible response: No, it is an opinion and it distracts the reader.

131   **Writer's Companion** ▪ UNIT 5
Lesson 21 *Sentences with Facts and Reasons*

EXTENDING THE CONCEPT: EVERYDAY PERSUASION

Discuss how people use persuasion in everyday communication. Ask students to think of occasions in which they have tried to convince someone of something. Invite volunteers to describe what they said, and ask the class to decide if the statements were facts, reasons, expert opinions, emotional appeals, or statistics. Ask students to tell whether their persuasion worked and why they think it was successful or not.

© Harcourt

Evaluate a Persuasive Letter/Grammar: Action and Linking Verbs

OBJECTIVES

- To understand what to look for when evaluating a persuasive letter
- To identify action and linking verbs

Standard: LA.5.3.3.1 evaluate for writing traits
LA.5.3.3.4 use parts of speech correctly

Evaluate Teach/Model Remind students that evaluation is the part of the writing process in which they check their work to see what needs improvement. Read the introductory text at the top of the page and discuss what students should look for when evaluating a persuasive letter. Review the terms *opinion, facts,* and *reasons* with students.

Guided Practice/Independent Practice

Read aloud the directions for completing the checklist. Guide students through the first two items on the list, helping them decide if the Student Model included these points. Then ask students to complete the evaluation on their own.

Grammar Teach/Model Read and discuss the definitions of action and linking verbs. Review the examples with students.

Guided Practice/Independent Practice

Read the directions and guide students to see that the verb in Item 1 does not describe an action. It links *telephone* with the words that tell its position. Then have students complete Items 2–6 independently.

LESSON 21: SENTENCES WITH FACTS AND REASONS

Name _____

Evaluating the Student Model

Evaluate a Persuasive Letter

When you evaluate a persuasive letter, ask yourself if the writer's opinions, facts, and reasons are convincing.

Now evaluate the Student Model. Put a check in the box next to each thing the writer did well. If you do not think the writer did a good job, do not check the box.

- ☐ The writer wrote a greeting.
- ☐ The writer stated her opinion clearly and politely.
- ☐ The writer organized the letter by stating an opinion and giving facts and reasons to support it.
- ☐ The writer used persuasive details.
- ☐ The writer concluded with a call to action and signed the letter.

Writer's Grammar
Action and Linking Verbs

Action verbs describe an action. The action may be physical or mental. *Jump* and *consider* are examples of action verbs.
Linking verbs do not describe an action. They link, or connect, a noun or pronoun with another word. The verb *to be* is often used as a linking verb. *Are* and *seem* are examples of linking verbs.

Underline the verb in each sentence. Then write *action* or *linking* to tell what kind of verb it is.

1. The telephone <u>is</u> on the table in the hall.   linking
2. Eric <u>felt</u> upset yesterday after school.   linking
3. They <u>hurry</u> to the park for a game of baseball.   action
4. I <u>ran</u> up the stairs with the letter in my hand.   action
5. Zora <u>asked</u> Juliet the question.   action
6. Enrique and Elvia <u>are</u> from Venezuela.   linking

Writer's Companion • UNIT 5
Lesson 21 *Sentences with Facts and Reasons*   132

WRITER'S STRATEGY: READING THE WRITING OF OTHERS

Tell students that reading the writing of other writers is helpful in thinking critically about what works and what does not work for a particular writing form. Point out that it is often easier to think and talk objectively about writing we have not done ourselves. By evaluating others' writing for strengths and weaknesses, students can see which writing habits to imitate and which to avoid.

© Harcourt

Revise: Adding Persuasive Details

OBJECTIVES
- To revise sentences by adding persuasive details
- To revise their own writing by adding persuasive details

Standard: LA.5.3.3.3 add supporting details/modify word choices

Teach/Model   Tell students that revising their writing gives them an opportunity to make changes and improvements. Explain that during the revision process they might add, delete, or change words, sentences, or ideas.

Guided Practice   Read aloud the introduction and example revision. Ask students to identify the details that were added to the sentence, explaining that these details strengthened the writer's argument. Read the directions for Part A and model rewriting the first sentence to add persuasive details. Then ask students to suggest other revisions. Call students' attention to the Word Bank and remind them to use it as they revise the sentences.

Independent Writing Practice   Have students complete Items 2 and 3 independently. Then read the directions for Part B and ask students to revise their persuasive letters on their own.

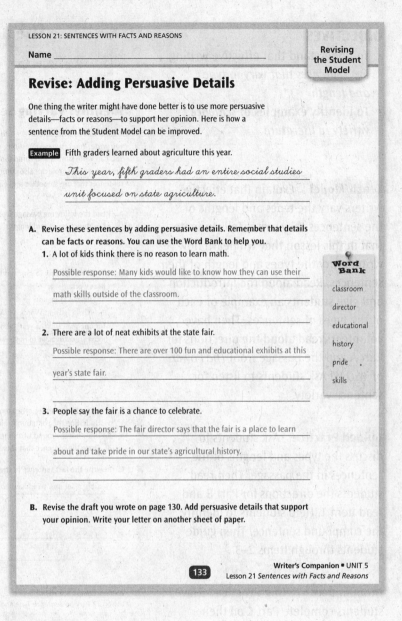

LESSON 21: SENTENCES WITH FACTS AND REASONS

Name _____

Revising the Student Model

Revise: Adding Persuasive Details

One thing the writer might have done better is to use more persuasive details—facts or reasons—to support her opinion. Here is how a sentence from the Student Model can be improved.

Example   Fifth graders learned about agriculture this year.

This year, fifth graders had an entire social studies unit focused on state agriculture.

A. Revise these sentences by adding persuasive details. Remember that details can be facts or reasons. You can use the Word Bank to help you.

1. A lot of kids think there is no reason to learn math.

Possible response: Many kids would like to know how they can use their

math skills outside of the classroom.

2. There are a lot of neat exhibits at the state fair.

Possible response: There are over 100 fun and educational exhibits at this

year's state fair.

3. People say the fair is a chance to celebrate.

Possible response: The fair director says that the fair is a place to learn

about and take pride in our state's agricultural history.

B. Revise the draft you wrote on page 130. Add persuasive details that support your opinion. Write your letter on another sheet of paper.

Word Bank

classroom
director
educational
history
pride
skills

133

Writer's Companion • UNIT 5
Lesson 21 *Sentences with Facts and Reasons*

SHARING AND DISCUSSING

Before students begin revising their persuasive letters, have them summarize the main points of their letter for a partner. Have them ask the partner to respond to the letter and tell whether they find it convincing and why or why not. Then have partners talk about reasons or facts that they might add to the letter. Suggest that students use what they learn from the discussion to help them as they work on a final draft of their letter.

© Harcourt

Identify: Varying Sentence Type and Length

OBJECTIVES
- To understand that effective writing has *sentences that vary in type and length*
- To identify examples of *sentence variety in literature*

Teach/Model Explain that effective writers vary the types and lengths of the sentences they write. Tell students that in this lesson they will learn how writers vary the types and length of their sentences. Read aloud the introduction and give students an example of each of the types of sentences. Then have volunteers read aloud the directions for Part A and the passage from *The Power of W.O.W!* Ask students to listen for sentence variety.

Guided Practice Ask students to discuss the types and lengths of the sentences in the passage. Then read students the directions for Part B and read Item 1. Help students to identify the compound sentence. Then guide students through Items 2–3.

Independent Writing Practice Have students complete Part C on their own. Invite volunteers to share their sentences with the class.

Use a Literature Model

LESSON 22: VARYING SENTENCE TYPE AND LENGTH

Name _____

Writer's Craft in Literature

Identify: Varying Sentence Type and Length

A good way to write effectively is to vary the type and length of the sentences you write. You can have questions, statements, commands, and exclamations. You can write simple and compound sentences as well as sentences that contain items in a series. You can also combine short, choppy sentences into longer sentences that are smoother and easier to read.

A. Read the following passage from *The Power of W.O.W!* Notice how the writer uses a variety of sentence types and lengths.

Literature Model

Mrs. Nguyen: (Sighs, and her shoulders slump) Words on Wheels won't be back after next week.

Ileana: Why not?

Mrs. Nguyen: Words on Wheels is just a pilot program. The library funded W.O.W. for one year, and the year's almost up. There's no more money to pay for gas and repairs, to pay the driver, or to buy new books. I'll have to go back to the library downtown.

—from *The Power of W.O.W!* by Crystal Hubbard

B. Identify the examples of sentence variety in the passage.
1. Underline the compound sentence.
2. Draw boxes around two simple sentences. Possible responses are given.
3. Circle the sentence that lists items in a series.

C. Rewrite the last sentence in the passage as a question.

Possible response: Will I have to go back to the library downtown?

_____
_____
_____

Writer's Companion • UNIT 5
Lesson 22 *Varying Sentence Type and Length*   **134**

EXTENDING THE CONCEPT: ANALYZING VARIETY

Ask students to work in small groups to analyze the effect of sentence variety on writing. Suggest that students select a passage from a piece of writing (for example, the selection on this page) and work as a group to rewrite the passage so that the sentences are all about the same length and/or same type. Ask each group to read both versions of the chosen passage aloud. Using the passages as their model, ask them to explain why sentence variety makes writing more interesting to read.

© Harcourt

Explore: Varying Sentence Type and Length

OBJECTIVES

- To understand ways to introduce sentence variety in writing
- To practice writing sentences of various types and lengths

Standard: LA.5.4.3.1 write persuasive text

Teach/Model Use the introduction and the graphic organizer to introduce and discuss strategies for creating variation in sentences. Ask students to discuss the strategies you name, and encourage them to identify other possible strategies for varying sentence type and length. List all of these strategies on the board and suggest that students use the list as a resource as they work through the lesson.

Guided Practice Read aloud the directions for Part A, and then read the sentences in the example. Ask students how the sentence was changed. Discuss other ways the sentence could have been rewritten. Then guide students through the rest of the activity.

Independent Writing Practice Read the directions for Part B aloud. Ask students to complete the exercise on their own.

LESSON 22: VARYING SENTENCE TYPE AND LENGTH

Name _____

A Closer Look at Writer's Craft

Explore: Varying Sentence Type and Length

Varying sentence type and length is a great way to make sentences more enjoyable for readers. You can also emphasize information this way. When you write, review your sentences. Consider how you might change your sentences in length or form to make the writing both interesting and clear.

Strategies for Variation

Vary sentence type.
- Write simple and compound sentences.
- Write sentences with items in a series.
- Write statements, questions, commands, and exclamations.

Vary sentence length.
- Alternate short and long sentences.
- Combine short sentences into longer sentences.

A. Write a new sentence that includes the information from each item below. You can use any strategy to change the sentence.

Example Al went to the store and bought some peanuts.

Did Al buy some peanuts when he went to the store?

1. I ran all the way home. I did my homework in a flash.

   Possible response: I ran all the way home and did my homework in a flash.

2. We caught eleven fireflies last night. Then we let them go.

   Possible response: We caught eleven fireflies last night, but we let them go.

3. Jorge speaks French. He also speaks some Spanish and Portuguese.

   Possible response: Jorge speaks French, Spanish, and Portuguese.

B. Read these sentences from *The Power of W.O.W.!*. Underline the compound sentence.

   Ileana: I wish I had King Midas's golden touch. I could turn this picnic table into gold, and then we could sell it to pay for W.O.W..

Writer's Companion • UNIT 5
Lesson 22 *Varying Sentence Type and Length*

135

Reaching All Learners

BELOW LEVEL

Help students by reminding them that a compound sentence uses a comma and the word *and, or,* or *but* to join two or more simple sentences. Encourage students to look for a comma followed by one of those words as they do Part B.

ADVANCED

Encourage students to write an example of each of the following:

- compound sentence
- question
- command
- statement

ENGLISH-LANGUAGE LEARNERS

Students might have difficulty with more technical terms of grammar. Have them begin a personal glossary of grammar terms and definitions (*compound sentence, exclamation*, etc.). Tell them to keep it handy for easy reference.

© Harcourt

Use: Varying Sentence Type and Length

OBJECTIVES
- To prepare to write by stating an opinion and listing facts and reasons that support it
- To write a persuasive letter with opinions, facts, and reasons

Standard: LA.5.3.2.1 use a pre-writing plan

Teach/Model Ask students to discuss what they have learned about persuasive writing. Review that writing persuasively means writing to convince readers to believe or act a certain way. Read the introduction and discuss the graphic organizer, making sure students see how each reason relates to its heading.

Guided Practice Read aloud the directions for Part A. Then guide students as they complete a graphic organizer for their own ideas. If they need to review the differences between opinions, facts, and reasons, suggest they go back to the preceding lesson to review the meaning of these terms.

Independent Writing Practice Read the directions for Part B. Have students complete the activity independently.

LESSON 22: VARYING SENTENCE TYPE AND LENGTH

Name _____

Practice with Writer's Craft

Use: Varying Sentence Type and Length

In a **persuasive paragraph**, the writer's purpose is to convince readers to believe, or act, in a certain way. Before you write to persuade, you will want to think about how to include persuasive language and sentence variety in your paragraph. Here is how one student started to organize a paragraph about her favorite city.

Example

My Opinion	Facts and Reasons	Persuasive Language	Ways to Vary Sentences
Boulder, Colorado, is a great place to live.	Rocky Mountains Arts and cultural activities Won awards	Natural beauty Special place	Combine short, choppy sentences. Write simple and compound sentences.

A. What is a place you think is special? Think about how you would persuade someone of your opinion. Then complete the graphic organizer.

My Opinion	Facts and Reasons	Persuasive Language	Ways to Vary Sentences

B. Use information from the graphic organizer to draft a paragraph that would persuade people to agree with you. Make sure that you create sentence variety by using different types and lengths of sentences. Write it on another sheet of paper.

Writer's Companion • UNIT 5
Lesson 22 *Varying Sentence Type and Length*   136

WRITER'S STRATEGY: FOCUSING ON TOPIC, PURPOSE, AND AUDIENCE

Tell students that effective persuasive writing focuses on a specific topic. It also is written for a particular audience and with a specific purpose in mind. Ask students to write down their focus (their opinion statement) and purpose (to persuade). Instruct them to think about the readers for whom they are writing. Invite students to share their ideas. Then have students review their graphic organizers. Suggest they make adjustments to their writing plan and work to improve their focus on their topic, purpose, and audience.

© Harcourt

The Parts of a Persuasive Paragraph

OBJECTIVES
- To understand the parts of a persuasive paragraph
- To analyze a Student Model

Standard: LA.5.3.1.3 organize ideas

Teach/Model　Tell students that, on this page, they will read a first draft of a fifth-grade student's persuasive paragraph. Read aloud the introduction and boxed call-outs. Then read the model, asking students to listen to how the paragraph is organized. After you have read the model, ask students whether they were persuaded by the paragraph and why or why not. Encourage students to cite examples from the text to support their reasoning.

Guided Practice　Point out the items below the model. Guide students to find the sentence that states the writer's opinion. Also help them find examples of simple and compound sentences.

Independent Writing Practice　Read Item 3 aloud and ask students to answer the question on their own. After they have finished, invite them to share and discuss their responses.

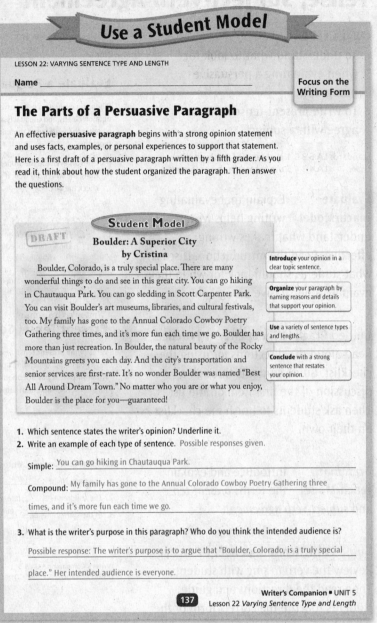

Use a Student Model

LESSON 22: VARYING SENTENCE TYPE AND LENGTH

Name _____

Focus on the Writing Form

The Parts of a Persuasive Paragraph

An effective **persuasive paragraph** begins with a strong opinion statement and uses facts, examples, or personal experiences to support that statement. Here is a first draft of a persuasive paragraph written by a fifth grader. As you read it, think about how the student organized the paragraph. Then answer the questions.

Student Model

DRAFT

Boulder: A Superior City
by Cristina

Boulder, Colorado, is a truly special place. There are many wonderful things to do and see in this great city. You can go hiking in Chautauqua Park. You can go sledding in Scott Carpenter Park. You can visit Boulder's art museums, libraries, and cultural festivals, too. My family has gone to the Annual Colorado Cowboy Poetry Gathering three times, and it's more fun each time we go. Boulder has more than just recreation. In Boulder, the natural beauty of the Rocky Mountains greets you each day. And the city's transportation and senior services are first-rate. It's no wonder Boulder was named "Best All Around Dream Town." No matter who you are or what you enjoy, Boulder is the place for you—guaranteed!

Introduce your opinion in a clear topic sentence.

Organize your paragraph by naming reasons and details that support your opinion.

Use a variety of sentence types and lengths.

Conclude with a strong sentence that restates your opinion.

1. Which sentence states the writer's opinion? Underline it.
2. Write an example of each type of sentence. Possible responses given.

   Simple: You can go hiking in Chautauqua Park.

   Compound: My family has gone to the Annual Colorado Cowboy Poetry Gathering three times, and it's more fun each time we go.

3. What is the writer's purpose in this paragraph? Who do you think the intended audience is?

   Possible response: The writer's purpose is to argue that "Boulder, Colorado, is a truly special place." Her intended audience is everyone.

Writer's Companion • UNIT 5
137
Lesson 22 *Varying Sentence Type and Length*

SHARING AND DISCUSSING

Tell students that the word *tone* refers to the way someone says something. In writing, the word refers to the effect of the words the writer uses. The tone of a piece of writing could be critical, upbeat, regretful, angry, or a host of other options. Have students discuss the tone of the Student Model. Ask them to respond to the following questions: *How would you describe the tone of the paragraph? Do you think the tone is appropriate? Why or why not? What would an inappropriate tone be? Why?*

© Harcourt

Evaluate a Persuasive Paragraph/Grammar: Present Tense, Subject-Verb Agreement

OBJECTIVES

- To understand what to look for when evaluating a persuasive paragraph
- To write present-tense verbs to agree with a subject

Standard: LA.5.3.3.1 evaluate for writing traits
LA.4.3.4.5 use subject/verb agreement

Evaluate
Teach/Model Explain that evaluating writing helps writers understand what makes writing effective. Read the introduction. Discuss what students should look for when they evaluate a persuasive paragraph.

Guided Practice/Independent Practice
Read aloud the directions for using the checklist. Guide students through a discussion of the first item on the list. Then ask students to finish the checklist on their own.

Grammar
Teach/Model Introduce and explain the terms *present tense* and *subject-verb agreement*.

Guided Practice/Independent Practice
Review the verb *to sing* with students. Then read the directions and guide students to write the correct form of the verb for Item 1. Have students complete Items 2–4 on their own.

LESSON 22: VARYING SENTENCE TYPE AND LENGTH

Name _____

Evaluating the Student Model

Evaluate a Persuasive Paragraph

When you evaluate a persuasive paragraph, ask yourself if the writer stated an opinion clearly and used facts and reasons to support it. You should also ask whether the writer used sentence variety to keep the writing from becoming repetitive.

Now evaluate the Student Model. Put a check in the box next to each thing the writer did well. If you do not think the writer did a good job, do not check the box.

- ☐ The writer stated an opinion in a clear topic sentence.
- ☐ The writer included reasons and details to support the opinion.
- ☐ The writer used persuasive language.
- ☐ The writer used a variety of sentence types and lengths.
- ☐ The writer concluded with a strong restatement of her opinion.

Writer's Grammar
Present Tense; Subject-Verb Agreement

Verbs in the **present tense** describe actions that are happening now. They end in *–s* or *–es* or have no ending, depending upon whose action they are expressing.

When you write, pay attention to **subject-verb agreement**. Singular subjects should have singular verbs, and plural subjects should have plural verbs.

Singular	Plural
I sing	we sing
you sing	you sing
she/he sings	they sing

Complete each sentence. Write the correct present-tense form of the verb in parentheses.

1. The traffic light ___changes___ from red to green every two minutes. (to change)

2. The children ___arrive___ late to the party. (to arrive)

3. In the springtime, bees ___pollinate___ flowers. (to pollinate)

4. He ___studies___ both karate and jujitsu. (to study)

Writer's Companion • UNIT 5
Lesson 22 *Varying Sentence Type and Length*   **138**

EXTENDING THE CONCEPT: EVALUATING PERSUASION IN DAILY LIFE

Explain the many different ways in which people experience persuasion in their daily lives. Discuss the various forms of media—print, radio, television, and the Internet—and how each strives to reach particular audiences and convince them to act or think a certain way. Ask students to discuss which forms of persuasion they think are more effective than others. Encourage them to discuss how they can be aware of and think critically about the forms of persuasion around them.

Revise: Varying Sentences

OBJECTIVES

- To revise sentences by varying their type and/or length
- To revise their own writing by varying sentence type and length

Standard: LA.5.3.3.2 create clarity using sentence structures

Teach/Model Tell students that revising is an important part of the writing process. When they revise, they can correct errors, strengthen word choice, and make their organization more logical. Explain that, in this activity, students will revise by varying sentences. Remind students that sentence variety adds interest for the reader.

Guided Practice Read the introduction and example aloud. Ask students to compare the first version and the revised version. Ask students to suggest other ways to revise the sentences. Then read the directions for Part A and model how to revise the sentences by changing their length or type. Remind students that there are many ways to revise sentences in order to create effective writing.

Independent Writing Practice Have students complete Items 2–4 on their own. Then read the directions for Part B and ask students to work independently to revise their writing.

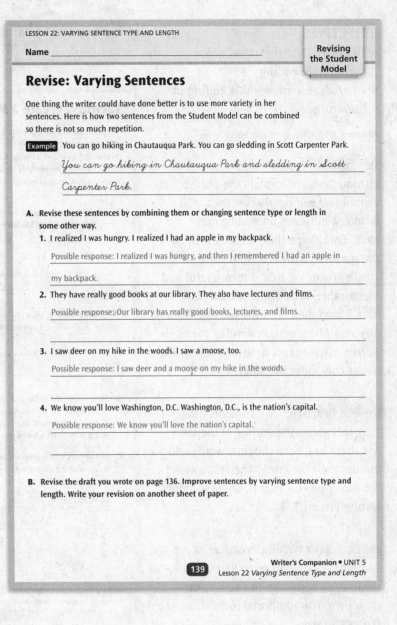

LESSON 22: VARYING SENTENCE TYPE AND LENGTH

Name _____

Revising the Student Model

Revise: Varying Sentences

One thing the writer could have done better is to use more variety in her sentences. Here is how two sentences from the Student Model can be combined so there is not so much repetition.

Example You can go hiking in Chautauqua Park. You can go sledding in Scott Carpenter Park.

You can go hiking in Chautauqua Park and sledding in Scott Carpenter Park.

A. Revise these sentences by combining them or changing sentence type or length in some other way.

1. I realized I was hungry. I realized I had an apple in my backpack.

Possible response: I realized I was hungry, and then I remembered I had an apple in my backpack.

2. They have really good books at our library. They also have lectures and films.

Possible response: Our library has really good books, lectures, and films.

3. I saw deer on my hike in the woods. I saw a moose, too.

Possible response: I saw deer and a moose on my hike in the woods.

4. We know you'll love Washington, D.C. Washington, D.C., is the nation's capital.

Possible response: We know you'll love the nation's capital.

B. Revise the draft you wrote on page 136. Improve sentences by varying sentence type and length. Write your revision on another sheet of paper.

139

Writer's Companion • UNIT 5
Lesson 22 *Varying Sentence Type and Length*

WRITER'S STRATEGY: CHOOSING THE BEST SUPPORT

Tell students that the revision stage is the time to analyze their writing and make sure they have conveyed their ideas clearly and effectively. Before students begin their revisions, suggest they jot down some notes about what forms of support they have used to persuade readers. Are there other forms they could incorporate as well? For example, what kind of expert opinions could they use? Are there facts or statistics that would strengthen their argument? Is there an emotional appeal they might try? Suggest that students add specific details to make their paragraphs as persuasive as possible.

© Harcourt

Identify: Create a Memorable Ending

OBJECTIVES

- To understand the effect of a memorable ending
- To analyze a memorable ending in literature

Standard: LA.5.4.1.2 write expressive forms

Teach/Model Read aloud the introduction and explain the phrase *memorable ending*. Discuss the different purposes an ending may have. Emphasize that, regardless of the purpose, writers should strive to create an ending that is meaningful and memorable. Read the directions for Part A, and then read the passage from *Any Small Goodness: A Novel of the Barrio*. Ask students to listen for how the writer concludes the story.

Guided Practice Ask students how they feel about the ending of the story. Ask them to reread the final words and discuss their meaning. Then read aloud the directions for Part B. Guide students through Items 1–3.

Independent Writing Practice Read students the directions to Part C. Ask students to complete the activity on their own. For additional instruction, see *Writer's Strategy*.

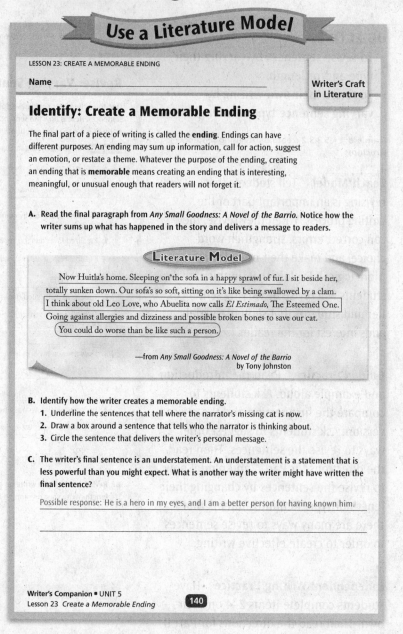

WRITER'S STRATEGY: USING UNDERSTATEMENT

Tell students that an understatement is a statement that shows restraint on the part of the speaker. Explain that understatement is often used for effect. Provide students with a few examples of the use of understatement. First express a sentiment literally (*I won a million dollars yesterday!*) and then as an understatement (*I won a bit of money yesterday,*). Invite volunteers to share their own examples. Ask students to discuss when writers might use understatement and why it might be effective.

© Harcourt

Explore: Create a Memorable Ending

OBJECTIVES
- To understand how to create a memorable ending
- To practice writing a memorable ending

Standard: LA.5.4.1.2 write expressive forms

Teach/Model Use the introduction and the graphic organizer to introduce and discuss how to create a memorable ending. Guide students to see that a memorable ending depends on the writing form and the effect a writer wants to have on readers.

Guided Practice Read students the directions for Part A, and then read the sentence in the left column of the example. Read each of the answer choices A–C and model matching the appropriate one to the sentence. Ask students to explain why that is the correct match. Then guide students through completing Items 1–2.

Independent Writing Practice Read Part B aloud. Have students complete the exercise independently.

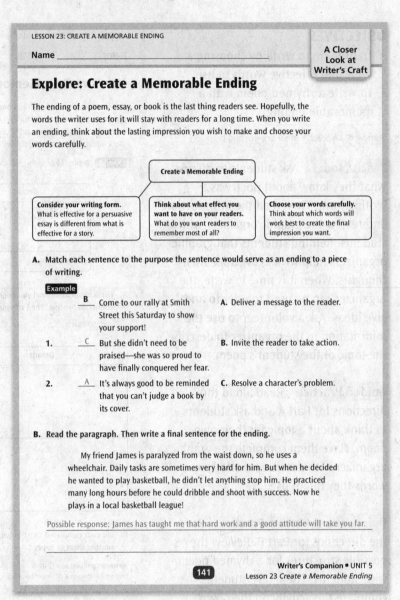

EXTENDING THE CONCEPT: UNDERSTANDING STRUCTURE

Explain that understanding the organizational structure of a piece of writing is an important part of creating an effective ending for it. Divide students into groups and assign each group a writing form—persuasive paragraph, journal entry, narrative paragraph, and so on. Ask each group to discuss how their writing form is organized. Have them consider how each part of the writing form works to support the other parts, and in particular, how the ending fits in. Invite groups to share their ideas. After every group has presented its findings, challenge the class to come up with some generalizations about how the ending fits into the organization of that particular writing form.

© Harcourt

Use: Create a Memorable Ending

OBJECTIVES
- To prepare to write by choosing a topic and effective words to use
- To write a rhymed poem with a memorable ending

Standard: LA.5.3.2.1 use a pre-writing plan

Teach/Model   Ask students to discuss what they know about poetry as a writing form. Then read the introduction and review the graphic organizer with students. Remind students that graphic organizers help writers organize their thoughts. When it is time to write, the organizer can be used to refer to and give ideas. Ask a volunteer to use the information in the organizer to describe the topic of the student's poem.

Guided Practice   Read aloud the directions for Part A and ask students to think about a topic for their own poem. Have them complete the graphic organizer with details and effective words they might use.

Independent Writing Practice   Read the directions for Part B. Review the possible structures for a rhymed poem with students. Then have students complete the activity on their own.

LESSON 23: CREATE A MEMORABLE ENDING

Name _____

Practice with
Writer's Craft

Use: Create a Memorable Ending

In a short piece of writing, like a **poem**, every word counts. Before you write a poem, you will want to think about how you can use language most effectively—especially to create a memorable ending. Here is how one student started to think about word choice before writing a poem.

Example Topic: *Watching a Butterfly*

Details	Ideas for Effective Words
Butterfly flying	Flutters Dances Beating wings
Sky above	Milky blue

A. Think about an animal you might choose as the topic for a poem. Write the name of the animal on the line. Then complete the chart

Topic: _____

Details	Ideas for Effective Words

B. Use your completed chart to help you write a draft of a rhymed poem. Write your poem on another sheet of paper.

Writer's Companion ▪ UNIT 5
Lesson 23 Create a Memorable Ending   142

Reaching All Learners

BELOW LEVEL
Once students have selected an animal for the topic of their poem, encourage them to close their eyes and imagine the animal in front of them. Tell them to ask themselves these questions: *What details do I see? What words can I use to describe this animal to others?*

ADVANCED
Encourage students to think about how they might use literary devices they have already learned. Have them ask themselves: *What device— imagery, simile, metaphor— would help me write my poem?*

ENGLISH-LANGUAGE LEARNERS
Help students choose a rhyme scheme and select words that fit that scheme. Pair less proficient speakers with more proficient speakers and ask them to work together to make their rhymes and develop their poems.

© Harcourt

The Parts of a Poem

OBJECTIVES
- To understand the parts of a poem
- To analyze a Student Model

Standard: LA.5.3.1.3 organize ideas

Teach/Model   Tell students that on this page they will read a first draft of a fifth-grade student's rhymed poem. Read students the introduction and boxed call-outs. Review the terms *lines, stanzas,* and *rhyme schemes* with students. Discuss each of the rhyme schemes mentioned (*aabb, abab, abcb*) and provide an example of each. Then read the Student Model, asking students to pay attention to how the poem is organized.

Guided Practice   Point out the questions below the model. Guide students to identify the experience described by the poem and write a sentence that summarizes it.

Independent Writing Practice   Have students complete Items 2 and 3 independently. After they have finished, invite them to share and discuss their answers.

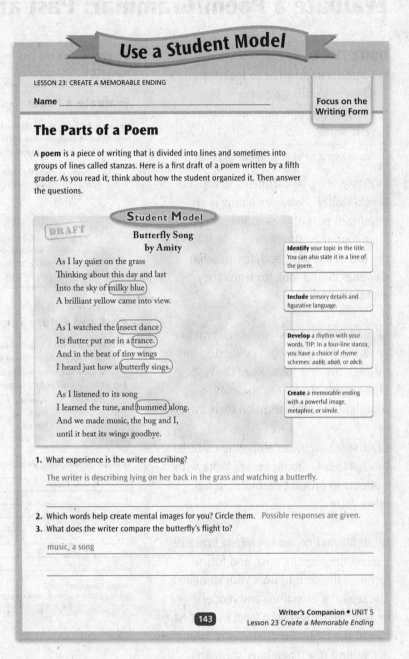

Use a Student Model

LESSON 23: CREATE A MEMORABLE ENDING

Name _____

Focus on the Writing Form

The Parts of a Poem

A **poem** is a piece of writing that is divided into lines and sometimes into groups of lines called stanzas. Here is a first draft of a poem written by a fifth grader. As you read it, think about how the student organized it. Then answer the questions.

Student Model

DRAFT

Butterfly Song
by Amity

As I lay quiet on the grass
Thinking about this day and last
Into the sky of milky blue
A brilliant yellow came into view.

As I watched the insect dance
Its flutter put me in a trance.
And in the beat of tiny wings
I heard just how a butterfly sings.

As I listened to its song
I learned the tune, and hummed along.
And we made music, the bug and I,
until it beat its wings goodbye.

Identify your topic in the title. You can also state it in a line of the poem.

Include sensory details and figurative language.

Develop a rhythm with your words. TIP: In a four-line stanza, you have a choice of rhyme schemes: *aabb, abab,* or *abcb.*

Create a memorable ending with a powerful image, metaphor, or simile.

1. What experience is the writer describing?

   The writer is describing lying on her back in the grass and watching a butterfly.

2. Which words help create mental images for you? Circle them.   Possible responses are given.
3. What does the writer compare the butterfly's flight to?

   music, a song

_____

143

Writer's Companion ■ UNIT 5
Lesson 23 *Create a Memorable Ending*

WRITER'S STRATEGY: FIGURATIVE LANGUAGE

Explain that writers often use simile, metaphor, and personification in poetry. Emphasize that this creates language that is different from what we speak every day. Review the meaning of each of the following terms: *simile, metaphor,* *personification,* and *analogy.* Ask students to identify examples of figurative language in the Student Model. Discuss how the writer's use of figurative, rather than literal, language affects the mood and tone of the poem.

© Harcourt

Evaluate a Poem/Grammar: Past and Future Tenses

OBJECTIVES
- To understand what to look for when evaluating a poem
- To write present, past, and future verb tenses

Standard: LA.5.3.3.1 evaluate for writing traits

Evaluate Teach/Model Ask students to explain why evaluating is an important part of the writing process. Then read the introductory text at the top of the page and discuss what students should look for when they evaluate a poem.

Guided Practice/Independent Practice
Read the directions and guide students through the first item. Read the rest of the items aloud. Ask students to complete the evaluation on their own.

Grammar Teach/Model Read aloud the material about tenses. Work with students to provide examples using other verbs.

Guided Practice/Independent Practice
Review the present, past, and future forms of the verb to *walk* with students. The read the directions and model writing the correct verb form in the first row of the table. Guide students through the second row. Then have students complete rows 3–6 independently.

LESSON 23: CREATE A MEMORABLE ENDING

Name _____

Evaluating the Student Model

Evaluate a Poem

When you evaluate a poem, ask yourself if the writer introduced a focus and used figurative language and sensory details to develop it. You should also ask whether the writer created a memorable ending.

Now evaluate the Student Model. Put a check in the box next to each thing the writer did well. If you do not think the writer did a good job, do not check the box.

- ☐ The writer identified the focus of the poem.
- ☐ The writer included sensory details and figurative language.
- ☐ There is a clear rhythm in the poem.
- ☐ The writer created a memorable ending.

Writer's Grammar
Past and Future Tenses

Verbs in the **past tense** describe actions that have already happened. Most past tense verbs end in –*ed*. Irregular verbs have special forms that must be memorized.

Verbs in the **future tense** describe what will happen in the future. Most future tense verbs are formed by using *will* and the simple form of the verb.

Present	Past	Future
I walk	I walked	I will walk
it plays	it played	it will play
they grow	they grew	they will grow

Complete the table. Write the correct form for each missing verb.

Present Tense	Past Tense	Future Tense
push	pushed	will push
know	knew	will know
joke	joked	will joke
study	studied	will study
think	thought	will think
grin	grinned	will grin

Writer's Companion • UNIT 5
Lesson 23 *Create a Memorable Ending*   **144**

SHARING AND DISCUSSING

Have students work in pairs to discuss their evaluations of the Student Model. Ask pairs to discuss how they evaluated each item on the checklist. Encourage partners to justify their responses with examples from the Student Model.

Then have pairs discuss their personal responses to the poem. Discussion should involve why they liked or did not like the poem. Ask pairs to report their discussion and conclusions to the class.

© Harcourt

Revise: Creating a More Specific Ending

OBJECTIVES

- To revise writing to create a more specific ending
- To revise their own writing by using exact words and creating a specific ending

Standard: LA.5.3.3.2 create clarity using sentence structures

Teach/Model   Discuss why revising is important to the writing process. Remind students that when they revise they can correct mistakes, improve organization, and clarify ideas. Explain that in this activity students will also focus on creating a more specific ending. Remind students that the ending is a writer's last chance to make an impression on readers.

Guided Practice   Read the introduction and example revision aloud. Ask students to discuss what changes were made and what the effects of those changes might be. Invite students to suggest other ways the ending could be revised. Then read students the directions for Part A and guide them to revise the lines of poetry. Point out the Word Bank and suggest students use it as they revise.

Independent Writing Practice   Read the directions for Part B. Ask students to revise their poems on their own. Invite students to share their revised versions by reading them aloud.

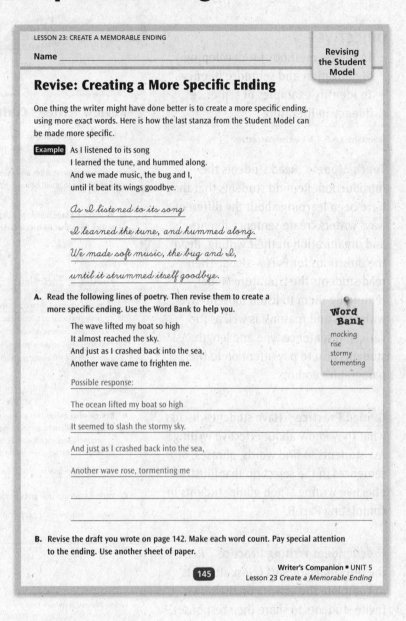

LESSON 23: CREATE A MEMORABLE ENDING

Name _____

Revising the Student Model

Revise: Creating a More Specific Ending

One thing the writer might have done better is to create a more specific ending, using more exact words. Here is how the last stanza from the Student Model can be made more specific.

Example   As I listened to its song
I learned the tune, and hummed along.
And we made music, the bug and I,
until it beat its wings goodbye.

As I listened to its song

I learned the tune, and hummed along.

We made soft music, the bug and I,

until it strummed itself goodbye.

A. Read the following lines of poetry. Then revise them to create a more specific ending. Use the Word Bank to help you.

Word Bank
mocking
rise
stormy
tormenting

The wave lifted my boat so high
It almost reached the sky.
And just as I crashed back into the sea,
Another wave came to frighten me.

Possible response:

The ocean lifted my boat so high

It seemed to slash the stormy sky.

And just as I crashed back into the sea,

Another wave rose, tormenting me

B. Revise the draft you wrote on page 142. Make each word count. Pay special attention to the ending. Use another sheet of paper.

145

Writer's Companion • UNIT 5
Lesson 23 *Create a Memorable Ending*

WRITER'S STRATEGY: PRESENTING AND PUBLISHING

Tell students that there are many ways they can present and publish their poems. Discuss different presentation options with students. Suggest that students make a neat, final copy using their best handwriting, or type their poem on a computer. Encourage students to draw an illustration to accompany their work. Invite students to read their poems to the class. When students read, instruct them to speak clearly and look at the audience at appropriate points in their reading. Encourage them to try to convey the poem's rhythm as they read.

Review Writer's Craft

OBJECTIVES

- To review methods for developing organization and sentence fluency
- To identify examples of sentence fluency in literature

Standard: LA.5.4.1.1 write narratives

Teach/Model Read students the introduction. Remind students that they have been learning about the different ways writers create sentence fluency and organization in their writing. Read the directions for Part A aloud. Then read students the Literature Model, reminding them to listen for sentences with facts and reasons as well as for variety in sentence type and length. Ask students also to pay attention to the paragraph's ending.

Guided Practice Have students discuss what they know about effective writing. Ask students to find words, phrases, or sentences in the selection that illustrate effective writing. Then guide students in completing Part B.

Independent Writing Practice Read the directions for Part C. Ask students to complete the activity on their own. Invite students to share their responses.

Use a Literature Model

LESSON 24: REVIEW WRITER'S CRAFT

Name _____

Writer's Craft in Literature

Review Writer's Craft

By concentrating on sentence fluency and organization, your writing can become clearer, easier to understand, and more memorable. Successful writers use facts and reasons to develop their ideas, and they vary sentence type and length to hold readers' interest. They also think about the purpose of their writing and write an ending that will be remembered by their audience.

A. Read the passage below. Notice how the writer includes facts and reasons in his narrative. Notice, also, that he uses a variety of sentence types and lengths.

Literature Model

And now Chester had another thrill. For there weren't only sycamore trees in the park. The cricket could smell birches, beeches, and maples—elms, oaks—almost as many kinds of trees as Connecticut itself had to offer. And there was the moon!—the crescent moon—reflected in a little lake. Sounds, too, rose up to him: the shooshing of leaves, the nighttime countryside whispering of insects and little animals, and—best of all—a brook that was arguing with itself, as it splashed over rocks. The miracle of Central Park, a sheltered wilderness in the midst of the city, pierced Chester Cricket's heart with joy.

—from *Chester Cricket's Pigeon Ride*
by George Selden

B. Review what makes this writing clear, easy to understand, and memorable.
1. Look for different sentence types and lengths. Underline a simple sentence. Draw a box around a sentence that lists items in a series. Possible responses are given.
2. What is one fact given in the passage?

Possible response: Central Park has a lake and a brook.

C. Write a sentence that gives a reason for Chester's happiness.

Possible response: He has found a bit of the countryside in the big city.

_____

SHARING AND DISCUSSING

Instruct students to reread the passage from *Chester Cricket's Pigeon Ride*. Ask them to focus on the ending of the paragraph and think about what effect the writer wanted to produce. Have students discuss their thoughts with a partner. Record these questions on the board and ask students to answer them in their discussion:

- What is Chester Cricket's reaction to the park?
- What do you think the writer wants readers to feel when they read this sentence?
- Do you think this is an effective ending for the paragraph? Why or why not?

Review Writer's Craft

OBJECTIVES
- To deepen students' understanding of sentence fluency and organization
- To rewrite sentences to vary their type and length

Teach/Model Use the graphic organizer to review how to use sentence fluency and organization to develop effective writing. Remind students that effective writing is both clear and interesting to the reader.

Guided Practice Read students the directions for Part A. Tell students that the passage is an example of effective writing. Then read the passage aloud. Invite students to discuss the paragraph, asking them to read aloud portions of the passage that they think clearly illustrate effective writing.

Independent Writing Practice Read aloud the directions for Part B and model changing the sentence in Item 1. Ask students to suggest other ways the sentence might be changed. Then ask students to complete Item 2 on their own.

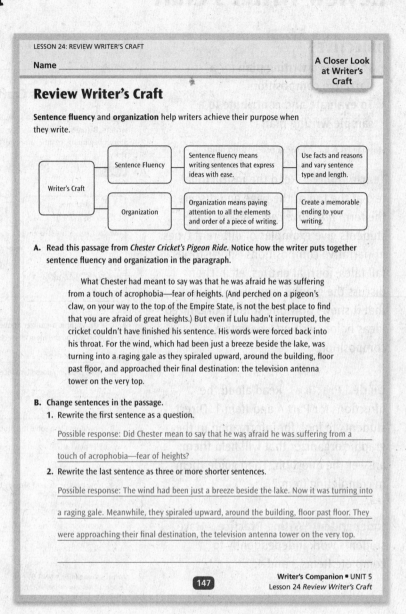

EXTENDING THE CONCEPT: COMBINING AND BREAKING APART SENTENCES

Review the different ways students have learned to change sentence type and length. Explain that one way to determine whether sentences need to be combined or broken apart is to read them aloud. Tell students that, as they read, they should listen to how the sentences sound. If they think several sentences sound too clipped and short, they may want to combine them and make them longer. If they think sentences go on and on with no pause, they may want to break them into shorter sentences. Remind students to read their changed sentences aloud, too. In this way, they can check that their changes have improved sentence fluency.

© Harcourt

Review Writer's Craft

OBJECTIVES

- To review a writing plan for a narrative composition
- To evaluate and contribute to a sample writing plan

Standard: LA.5.3.2.1 use a pre-writing plan

Teach/Model   Read the instructonal text at the top of the page and discuss the term *narrative composition*. Have students give examples of different types of narrative compositions (short stories, tall tales, journal entries, etc.). Then discuss the graphic organizer. Explain that it shows how one student organized ideas before writing a narrative composition.

Guided Practice   Read aloud the directions for Part A and Item 1. Direct students to look for information in the graphic organizer that will help them answer the question. Then guide them in completing Item 2.

Independent Writing Practice   Have students work independently to complete Items 3 and 4.

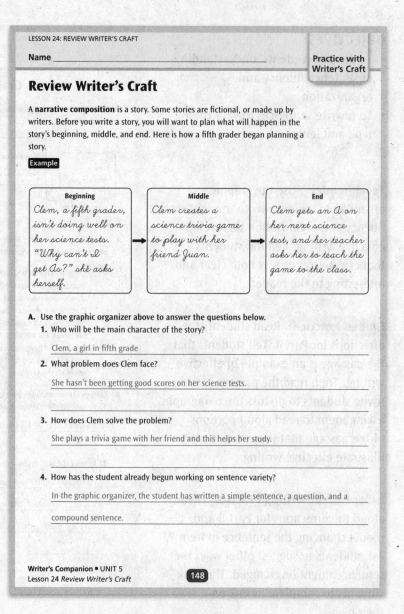

LESSON 24: REVIEW WRITER'S CRAFT

Name _____

Practice with Writer's Craft

Review Writer's Craft

A **narrative composition** is a story. Some stories are fictional, or made up by writers. Before you write a story, you will want to plan what will happen in the story's beginning, middle, and end. Here is how a fifth grader began planning a story.

Example

Beginning	Middle	End
Clem, a fifth grader, isn't doing well on her science tests. "Why can't I get A's?" she asks herself.	Clem creates a science trivia game to play with her friend Juan.	Clem gets an A on her next science test, and her teacher asks her to teach the game to the class.

A. Use the graphic organizer above to answer the questions below.

1. Who will be the main character of the story?

   Clem, a girl in fifth grade

2. What problem does Clem face?

   She hasn't been getting good scores on her science tests.

3. How does Clem solve the problem?

   She plays a trivia game with her friend and this helps her study.

4. How has the student already begun working on sentence variety?

   In the graphic organizer, the student has written a simple sentence, a question, and a

   compound sentence.

Writer's Companion ▪ UNIT 5
Lesson 24 *Review Writer's Craft*   148

EXTENDING THE CONCEPT: ORGANIZING A NARRATIVE

Tell students that narrative compositions can be organized in several different ways. However, any organizational strategy must allow readers to follow the narrative's central ideas. A narrative composition should begin meaningfully. It also must develop logically. And it must end with a definite conclusion. Ask students to review the graphic organizer on page 148. Have them tell whether they think the student's writing plan demonstrates an organizational plan that makes sense, given the student's topic. Encourage students to explain their reasoning.

© Harcourt

The Parts of a Narrative Composition

OBJECTIVES

- To understand how the elements of a narrative composition are organized
- To analyze a Student Model

Standard: LA.5.3.1.3 organize ideas

Teach/Model Explain that the writing model on this page is a draft of a narrative composition written by a student. Read aloud the introduction, and define and discuss the terms *characters, setting,* and *plot.* Then read the boxed call-outs that describe the organization of the narrative. Finally read the model aloud and ask students to pay careful attention to how the story begins, develops, and ends.

Guided Practice Point out the questions below the Student Model. Read the first question aloud. Guide students to find the topic sentence of the paragraph.

Independent Writing Practice
Direct students to answer Items 1–3 on their own.

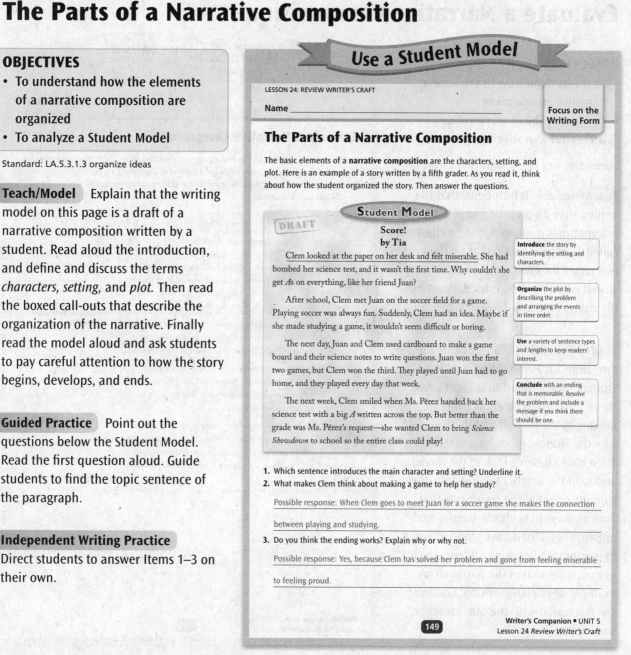

Use a Student Model

LESSON 24: REVIEW WRITER'S CRAFT

Name _____

Focus on the Writing Form

The Parts of a Narrative Composition

The basic elements of a **narrative composition** are the characters, setting, and plot. Here is an example of a story written by a fifth grader. As you read it, think about how the student organized the story. Then answer the questions.

Student Model

DRAFT

Score!
by Tia

Clem looked at the paper on her desk and felt miserable. She had bombed her science test, and it wasn't the first time. Why couldn't she get *A*s on everything, like her friend Juan?

After school, Clem met Juan on the soccer field for a game. Playing soccer was always fun. Suddenly, Clem had an idea. Maybe if she made studying a game, it wouldn't seem difficult or boring.

The next day, Juan and Clem used cardboard to make a game board and their science notes to write questions. Juan won the first two games, but Clem won the third. They played until Juan had to go home, and they played every day that week.

The next week, Clem smiled when Ms. Pérez handed back her science test with a big *A* written across the top. But better than the grade was Ms. Pérez's request—she wanted Clem to bring *Science Showdown* to school so the entire class could play!

> **Introduce** the story by identifying the setting and characters.

> **Organize** the plot by describing the problem and arranging the events in time order.

> **Use** a variety of sentence types and lengths to keep readers' interest.

> **Conclude** with an ending that is memorable. Resolve the problem and include a message if you think there should be one.

1. Which sentence introduces the main character and setting? Underline it.
2. What makes Clem think about making a game to help her study?

Possible response: When Clem goes to meet Juan for a soccer game she makes the connection

between playing and studying.

3. Do you think the ending works? Explain why or why not.

Possible response: Yes, because Clem has solved her problem and gone from feeling miserable

to feeling proud.

149

Writer's Companion • UNIT 5
Lesson 24 *Review Writer's Craft*

EXTENDING THE CONCEPT: SENTENCE FLUENCY

Tell students that sentence fluency is the rhythm of a writer's language. This is the way the words sound to the ear, not look to the eye. The best test of sentence fluency is to read a piece of writing aloud. Fluent writing does not have awkward word patterns that slow the reader down. Instead, sentences vary in length and style so that the reader moves through the ideas easily. Invite students to take turns reading the Student Model to a partner. Remind students to speak clearly and read with expression. Have partners discuss the model. Ask them to find specific examples of sentence fluency and discuss what makes the sentence effective.

© Harcourt

Evaluate a Narrative Composition

OBJECTIVES

- To understand how to evaluate a narrative composition
- To identify the characteristics of a successful narrative composition

Standard: LA.5.3.3.1 evaluate for writing traits

Teach/Model Tell students that the writing they do on tests and in school is sometimes evaluated using a chart called a *rubric*. Explain that on the next two pages they will review how writing is scored when a rubric is used. Point out the rubric on the following page.

Guided Practice Read students the directions for Part A. Then read the Student Model aloud to students. Ask students to listen carefully (without looking at the model) and think about why the Student Model is a success. Then have students look at the model and read the teacher's comments. Have students identify the comments that have to do with sentence fluency and organization. Then have students work in groups (see *Reaching All Learners*) to discuss what makes the narrative an example of effective writing. Continue the discussion with the other teacher comments.

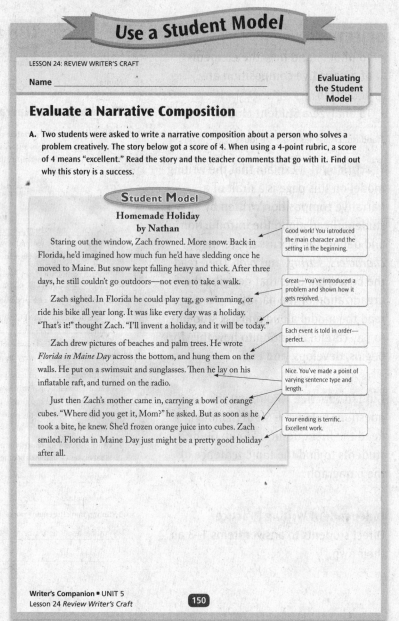

Use a Student Model

LESSON 24: REVIEW WRITER'S CRAFT

Name _____

Evaluating the Student Model

Evaluate a Narrative Composition

A. Two students were asked to write a narrative composition about a person who solves a problem creatively. The story below got a score of 4. When using a 4-point rubric, a score of 4 means "excellent." Read the story and the teacher comments that go with it. Find out why this story is a success.

Student Model

Homemade Holiday
by Nathan

Staring out the window, Zach frowned. More snow. Back in Florida, he'd imagined how much fun he'd have sledding once he moved to Maine. But snow kept falling heavy and thick. After three days, he still couldn't go outdoors—not even to take a walk.

Zach sighed. In Florida he could play tag, go swimming, or ride his bike all year long. It was like every day was a holiday. "That's it!" thought Zach. "I'll invent a holiday, and it will be today."

Zach drew pictures of beaches and palm trees. He wrote *Florida in Maine Day* across the bottom, and hung them on the walls. He put on a swimsuit and sunglasses. Then he lay on his inflatable raft, and turned on the radio.

Just then Zach's mother came in, carrying a bowl of orange cubes. "Where did you get it, Mom?" he asked. But as soon as he took a bite, he knew. She'd frozen orange juice into cubes. Zach smiled. Florida in Maine Day just might be a pretty good holiday after all.

Good work! You introduced the main character and the setting in the beginning.

Great—You've introduced a problem and shown how it gets resolved.

Each event is told in order—perfect.

Nice. You've made a point of varying sentence type and length.

Your ending is terrific. Excellent work.

Writer's Companion • UNIT 5
Lesson 24 *Review Writer's Craft*   150

Reaching All Learners

BELOW LEVEL	**ADVANCED**	**ENGLISH-LANGUAGE LEARNERS**
Give students simple questions to discuss. For example, ask them: *What happens in the beginning of the story?* Model answering each question: "In the beginning of the story …"	Ask students to discuss the writer's viewpoint, the use of dialogue, and the importance of the setting to the story's conflict.	Ask students to answer simple questions and give them sentence starters to help them respond, such as: "The main character is …" and "The conflict is …"

Evaluate a Narrative Composition

OBJECTIVES

- To understand a narrative composition
- To use a rubric to evaluate a narrative composition

Standard: LA.5.3.3.1 evaluate for writing traits

Teach/Model Tell students that they will read a narrative composition that received a score of 2 on a 4-point rubric. Read the Student Model aloud. Ask students to listen (without looking at the narrative) and think about how the composition could be improved.

Guided Practice Have students reread the Student Model to themselves. Then ask them to comment on any strengths or weaknesses they noticed in the narrative composition. Read the teacher's comments aloud, and ask students to summarize how the narrative composition could be improved.

Independent Writing Practice Present and discuss how to use the 4-point rubric at the bottom of the page. Ask students to complete the rubric to show what score they would give the narrative composition on page 149.

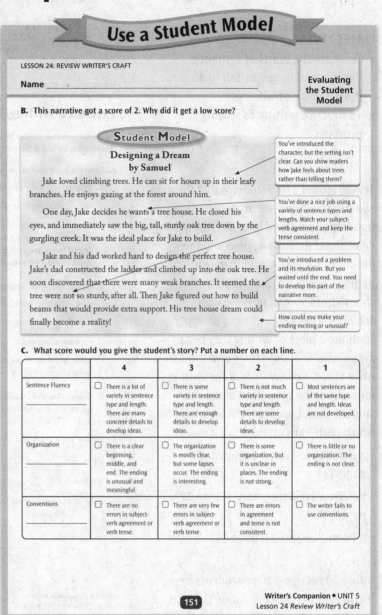

Use a Student Model

LESSON 24: REVIEW WRITER'S CRAFT

Name _____

Evaluating the Student Model

B. This narrative got a score of 2. Why did it get a low score?

Student Model

Designing a Dream
by Samuel

Jake loved climbing trees. He can sit for hours up in their leafy branches. He enjoys gazing at the forest around him.

> You've introduced the character, but the setting isn't clear. Can you show readers how Jake feels about trees rather than telling them?

One day, Jake decides he wants a tree house. He closed his eyes, and immediately saw the big, tall, sturdy oak tree down by the gurgling creek. It was the ideal place for Jake to build.

> You've done a nice job using a variety of sentence types and lengths. Watch your subject-verb agreement and keep the tense consistent.

Jake and his dad worked hard to design the perfect tree house. Jake's dad constructed the ladder and climbed up into the oak tree. He soon discovered that there were many weak branches. It seemed the tree were not so sturdy, after all. Then Jake figured out how to build beams that would provide extra support. His tree house dream could finally become a reality!

> You've introduced a problem and its resolution. But you waited until the end. You need to develop this part of the narrative more.

> How could you make your ending exciting or unusual?

C. What score would you give the student's story? Put a number on each line.

	4	3	2	1
Sentence Fluency _____	☐ There is a lot of variety in sentence type and length. There are many concrete details to develop ideas.	☐ There is some variety in sentence type and length. There are enough details to develop ideas.	☐ There is not much variety in sentence type and length. There are some details to develop ideas.	☐ Most sentences are of the same type and length. Ideas are not developed.
Organization _____	☐ There is a clear beginning, middle, and end. The ending is unusual and meaningful.	☐ The organization is mostly clear, but some lapses occur. The ending is interesting.	☐ There is some organization, but it is unclear in places. The ending is not strong.	☐ There is little or no organization. The ending is not clear.
Conventions _____	☐ There are no errors in subject-verb agreement or verb tense.	☐ There are very few errors in subject-verb agreement or verb tense.	☐ There are errors in agreement and tense is not consistent.	☐ The writer fails to use conventions.

Writer's Companion • UNIT 5
Lesson 24 *Review Writer's Craft*

SHARING AND DISCUSSING

Ask students to work in pairs to discuss the Student Model on this page. Have students focus their discussion on sentence fluency and organization. Ask one partner to read the composition aloud while the other partner listens for sentence variety, story development, and correct grammar. Then have partners switch roles and repeat. After each partner has had a chance to read and listen, ask students to work independently to score the composition. Afterwards, ask partners to share and discuss the scores they gave the composition. Have students explain their scoring by pointing out examples from the text.

© Harcourt

Extended Writing/Test Prep

OBJECTIVES

- To apply the crafts of sentence fluency and organization to a longer piece of writing
- To practice writing to writing prompts

Teach/Model Tell students that the next two pages will give them an opportunity to select a topic for a long piece of writing. Read aloud the introduction and the directions for Part A, and then read Items 1–3. Explain that students can choose from several possible writing activities. They can write to a prompt, continue a piece of writing they began in the unit, or choose their own topic to write about. Review each of the writing forms from the unit. Read aloud the Student Model tips from the lesson in which each form appears:

- a Persuasive Letter: Lesson 21, page 131
- a Persuasive Paragraph: Lesson 22, page 137
- a Poem: Lesson 23, page 143

Guided Practice Have students begin the prewriting process. Guide them as they select a topic and complete Part B.

Use a Literature Model

LESSON 25: WRITING TEST PRACTICE

Name _____

Extended Writing/Test Prep

Extended Writing/Test Prep

On the first two pages of this lesson, you will use what you have learned about sentence fluency and organization to write a longer written work.

A. Read the three choices below. Put a star by the writing activity you would like to do.

1. Respond to a Writing Prompt

   Writing Situation: Your teacher is considering getting a pet for your classroom.

   Directions for Writing: Think about what kind of an animal you would like to have in the classroom. Now, write a letter to convince your teacher that the animal you want is the best animal to get. You can also write to convince your teacher that an animal in the classroom is not a good idea. Remember to use different facts and reasons to support your opinion.

2. Choose one of the pieces of writing you started in this unit:

   - a persuasive letter (page 130)
   - a persuasive paragraph (page 136)
   - a poem (page 142)

   Revise and expand your draft into a complete piece of writing. Use what you have learned about sentence fluency and organization to write effectively.

3. Choose a topic you would like to write about. Write a narrative composition. Your narrative can be fiction or nonfiction.

B. Use the space below and on the next page to plan your writing.

TOPIC: _____

WRITING FORM: _____

HOW I WILL ORGANIZE MY WRITING: _____

_____

_____

Writer's Companion ▪ UNIT 5
Lesson 25 *Writing Test Practice*

152

SHARING AND DISCUSSING

Divide students into groups based on their choice of writing topic. Have each group review the parts of their chosen writing form—persuasive letter, persuasive paragraph, or poem. Ask them to read the model for the chosen form, and then discuss the role of sentence fluency and organization in their writing. After their review session, direct students to work independently to complete their writing assignment.

© Harcourt

Extended Writing/Test Prep

OBJECTIVES
- To use a graphic organizer to plan a piece of writing
- To use the writing process to complete a longer written work

Standard: LA.5.3.2.1 use a pre-writing plan

Teach/Model   Tell students that they will select a graphic organizer and use it to help them develop a writing plan for their chosen topic and writing form. Review the graphic organizers found in this and previous units. Tell students they can pick a new organizer or reuse one from the lessons they have reviewed. Model how to complete one of the graphic organizers.

Guided Practice   Help students complete their graphic organizers and develop a writing plan. For additional prewriting help, see *Reaching All Learners*.

Independent Writing
Draft, Revise, Publish Have students write their drafts on a separate sheet of paper. Review with students the different ways they have learned to revise their work: adding persuasive details, varying sentences, and creating a more specific ending. Ask students how they might present and publish their writing.

LESSON 25: WRITING TEST PRACTICE

Name _____

Extended Writing/Test Prep

C. In the space below, draw a graphic organizer that will help you plan your writing. Fill in the graphic organizer. Write additional notes on the lines below.

Notes

_____

_____

_____

_____

_____

_____

_____

D. Do your writing on another sheet of paper.

153

Writer's Companion • UNIT 5
Lesson 25 *Writing Test Practice*

Reaching All Learners

BELOW LEVEL	ADVANCED	ENGLISH-LANGUAGE LEARNERS
Help students choose an appropriate graphic organizer for their chosen topic. Remind them that organizers can help them plan the major parts of a writing piece. Guide them to complete the organizer.	Ask students to use more than one organizer to develop their writing plan. For example, they might use a flow chart to organize a persuasive letter and a word web to record persuasive language they want to use.	Ask students to use their own words to explain why writing is easier when they have prepared by completing a graphic organizer. Then have students work in pairs to complete their writing plans.

Answering Multiple-Choice Questions

OBJECTIVES

- To answer questions that involve reading and evaluating a writing plan
- To use knowledge of the Venn diagram structure to answer test questions

Teach/Model   Tell students that many writing tests include multiple-choice questions. Explain that the questions on this page require them to read and evaluate a writing plan. Read aloud the directions, the Test Tip, and Question 1. Model using the tip to find the correct answer. Explain that the statement *Using pay phones isn't very cool* cannot be proven true. It is a personal belief or opinion of the writer. Have students mark answer choice C.

Guided Practice   Ask a volunteer to read Question 2 aloud and ask students to read the answer choices silently to themselves. Remind students to think about what information the graphic organizer gives them as they select their answer. Have students mark the correct answer.

Independent Practice   Ask students to answer the last item independently.

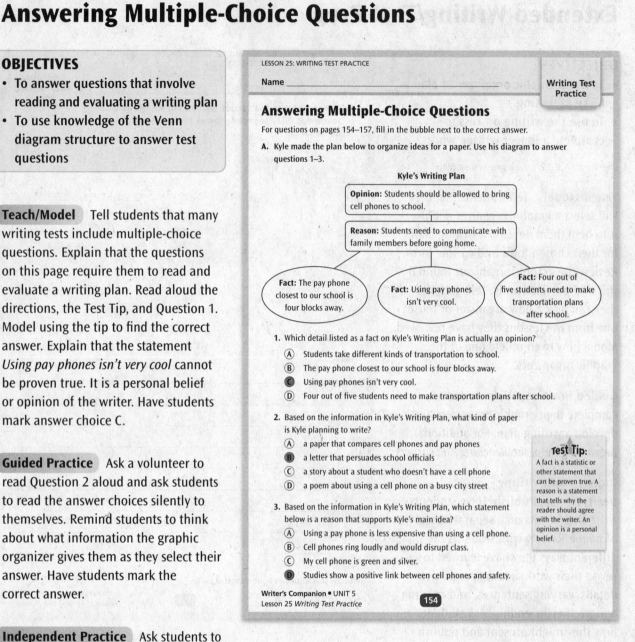

LESSON 25: WRITING TEST PRACTICE

Name _____

Writing Test Practice

Answering Multiple-Choice Questions

For questions on pages 154–157, fill in the bubble next to the correct answer.

A. Kyle made the plan below to organize ideas for a paper. Use his diagram to answer questions 1–3.

Kyle's Writing Plan

Opinion: Students should be allowed to bring cell phones to school.

Reason: Students need to communicate with family members before going home.

Fact: The pay phone closest to our school is four blocks away.

Fact: Using pay phones isn't very cool.

Fact: Four out of five students need to make transportation plans after school.

1. Which detail listed as a fact on Kyle's Writing Plan is actually an opinion?
   - (A) Students take different kinds of transportation to school.
   - (B) The pay phone closest to our school is four blocks away.
   - (C) Using pay phones isn't very cool.
   - (D) Four out of five students need to make transportation plans after school.

2. Based on the information in Kyle's Writing Plan, what kind of paper is Kyle planning to write?
   - (A) a paper that compares cell phones and pay phones
   - (B) a letter that persuades school officials
   - (C) a story about a student who doesn't have a cell phone
   - (D) a poem about using a cell phone on a busy city street

3. Based on the information in Kyle's Writing Plan, which statement below is a reason that supports Kyle's main idea?
   - (A) Using a pay phone is less expensive than using a cell phone.
   - (B) Cell phones ring loudly and would disrupt class.
   - (C) My cell phone is green and silver.
   - (D) Studies show a positive link between cell phones and safety.

Test Tip:
A fact is a statistic or other statement that can be proven true. A reason is a statement that tells why the reader should agree with the writer. An opinion is a personal belief.

Writer's Companion • UNIT 5
Lesson 25 *Writing Test Practice*   154

USING ACADEMIC LANGUAGE

Tell students that many tests contain academic language. Academic language includes words and phrases they may not see in their regular reading. Before students complete the test items on this page, review the academic words and phrases this page contains. Introduce and explain words and phrases such as *Use the diagram to answer questions*, and *based on*. Ask students to restate each direction line or question in their own words to demonstrate their understanding of the language being used.

Answering Multiple-Choice Questions (cont.)

OBJECTIVES
- To answer questions that involve reading a passage
- To learn how to distinguish between fact and opinion in a reading passage

Standard: LA.5.3.2.2 organize information in logical sequence

Teach/Model Tell students that some multiple-choice questions require them to read a passage and answer questions about it. Explain that the sentences are numbered because on many tests the items deal with specific sentences. Read aloud the directions for Part B and the Test Tip. Ask students to read the passage silently. Read aloud the first test item, and model reading each sentence in the passage to determine whether it is or is not related to the main idea. Model marking the correct answer choice.

Guided Practice Read Question 2 aloud. Point out that students are being asked to find the best answer. Guide students to choose the correct answer.

Independent Practice Have students complete Question 3 independently. Remind them to consider what they know about effective persuasive writing before choosing their answer.

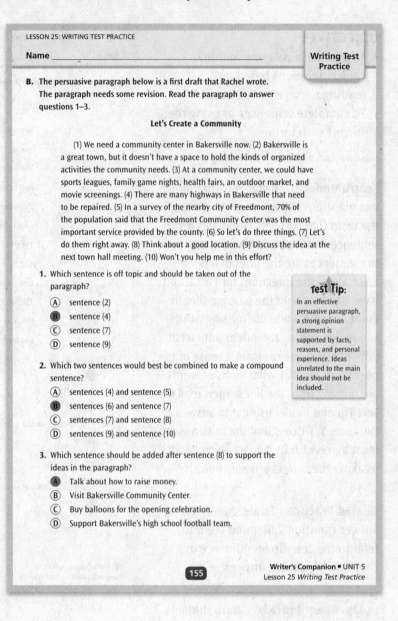

LESSON 25: WRITING TEST PRACTICE

Name _____

Writing Test Practice

B. The persuasive paragraph below is a first draft that Rachel wrote. The paragraph needs some revision. Read the paragraph to answer questions 1–3.

Let's Create a Community

(1) We need a community center in Bakersville now. (2) Bakersville is a great town, but it doesn't have a space to hold the kinds of organized activities the community needs. (3) At a community center, we could have sports leagues, family game nights, health fairs, an outdoor market, and movie screenings. (4) There are many highways in Bakersville that need to be repaired. (5) In a survey of the nearby city of Freedmont, 70% of the population said that the Freedmont Community Center was the most important service provided by the county. (6) So let's do three things. (7) Let's do them right away. (8) Think about a good location. (9) Discuss the idea at the next town hall meeting. (10) Won't you help me in this effort?

1. Which sentence is off topic and should be taken out of the paragraph?
   - Ⓐ sentence (2)
   - Ⓑ sentence (4)
   - Ⓒ sentence (7)
   - Ⓓ sentence (9)

2. Which two sentences would best be combined to make a compound sentence?
   - Ⓐ sentences (4) and sentence (5)
   - Ⓑ sentences (6) and sentence (7)
   - Ⓒ sentences (7) and sentence (8)
   - Ⓓ sentences (9) and sentence (10)

3. Which sentence should be added after sentence (8) to support the ideas in the paragraph?
   - Ⓐ Talk about how to raise money.
   - Ⓑ Visit Bakersville Community Center.
   - Ⓒ Buy balloons for the opening celebration.
   - Ⓓ Support Bakersville's high school football team.

Test Tip:
In an effective persuasive paragraph, a strong opinion statement is supported by facts, reasons, and personal experience. Ideas unrelated to the main idea should not be included.

155

Writer's Companion • UNIT 5
Lesson 25 *Writing Test Practice*

ASSESSING STUDENT RESPONSES

If a student answers a test item incorrectly, try to find out why. The student may be selecting an answer before reading all of the answer choices. Review with students how to answer a multiple-choice question. Read the item and reread the passage. Then read each answer choice, pausing to discuss why it is or is not correct. Emphasize that the correct answer may be any of the choices, not just the first one.

Answering Multiple-Choice Questions (cont.)

OBJECTIVES
- To practice answering multiple-choice questions based on a reading passage
- To complete sentences by using the correct verb form

Standard: LA.5.3.4.5 use subject/verb agreement

Teach/Model Tell students that some test questions will ask them to choose the word that correctly completes a sentence. Point out that on this test page the sentences are the lines of a poem. Read aloud the directions for Part C and have students read the passage silently. Point out that while the missing words will make reading the poem somewhat difficult, students can gain a sense of the poem and identify what kinds of words are missing from the lines. Then read the Test Tip and model using it to answer Question 1. Discuss that the missing verb must agree with its subject—*you*. Model marking the correct answer choice.

Guided Practice Guide students to answer Question 2. Remind them to refer to the Test Tip for guidance in choosing the correct answer.

Independent Practice Have students complete Question 3 on their own.

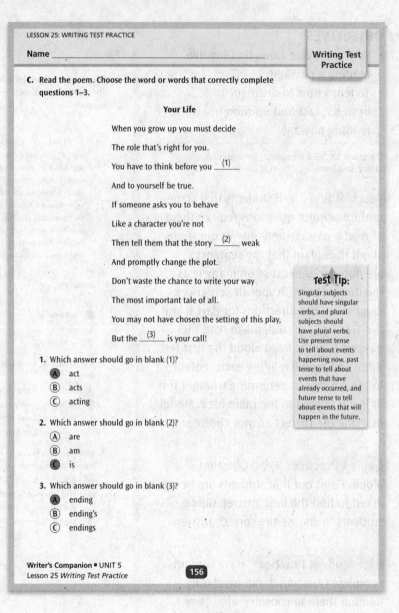

SHARING AND DISCUSSING

Have students work in pairs to share and compare their answers to Question 3. Have students explain how they chose the answer to the item.

Ask students to identify the subject the verb must agree with, and how they know when the present, past, or future tense should be used.

© Harcourt

Answering Multiple-Choice Questions (cont.)

OBJECTIVES
- To answer questions that require choosing a correctly written sentence
- To use knowledge of different types of sentences to answer test questions

Standard: LA.5.3.3.2 create clarity using sentence structures

Teach/Model Tell students that some multiple-choice formats require them to read several sentences and decide which is correctly written. Read the directions and Test Tip to students. Then read Question 1 and each of the answer choices. Model using the information from the boxed tip to choose the correct answer. Explain that neither choice A nor choice C combines all of the information from the original pair of sentences. Help students conclude that choice B shows the correct way to combine the two sentences.

Guided Practice Ask a volunteer to read Question 2 aloud and have students read the three answer choices to themselves. Remind them to look carefully to see which sentence correctly combines all of the information from all three original sentences. Have students mark the correct answer.

Independent Practice Have students complete Question 3 independently.

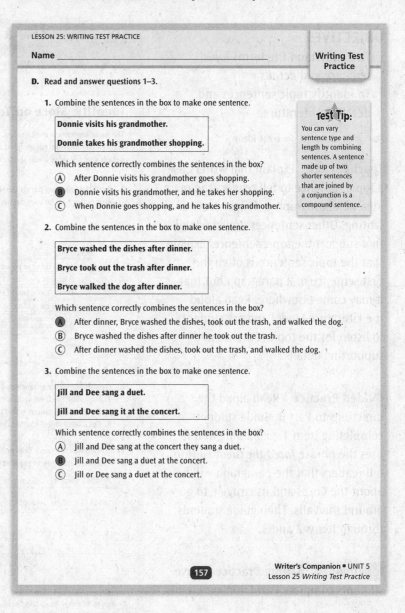

LESSON 25: WRITING TEST PRACTICE

Name _____

Writing Test Practice

D. Read and answer questions 1–3.

1. Combine the sentences in the box to make one sentence.

> Donnie visits his grandmother.
>
> Donnie takes his grandmother shopping.

Which sentence correctly combines the sentences in the box?
- (A) After Donnie visits his grandmother goes shopping.
- (B) Donnie visits his grandmother, and he takes her shopping.
- (C) When Donnie goes shopping, and he takes his grandmother.

2. Combine the sentences in the box to make one sentence.

> Bryce washed the dishes after dinner.
>
> Bryce took out the trash after dinner.
>
> Bryce walked the dog after dinner.

Which sentence correctly combines the sentences in the box?
- (A) After dinner, Bryce washed the dishes, took out the trash, and walked the dog.
- (B) Bryce washed the dishes after dinner he took out the trash.
- (C) After dinner washed the dishes, took out the trash, and walked the dog.

3. Combine the sentences in the box to make one sentence.

> Jill and Dee sang a duet.
>
> Jill and Dee sang it at the concert.

Which sentence correctly combines the sentences in the box?
- (A) Jill and Dee sang at the concert they sang a duet.
- (B) Jill and Dee sang a duet at the concert.
- (C) Jill or Dee sang a duet at the concert.

Test Tip:
You can vary sentence type and length by combining sentences. A sentence made up of two shorter sentences that are joined by a conjunction is a compound sentence.

157

Writer's Companion • UNIT 5
Lesson 25 *Writing Test Practice*

ASSESSING STUDENT RESPONSES

If students are consistently answering questions incorrectly, explore why they are struggling. Students may not be reading all of the directions. Point out that the first part of the direction for Question 1 is above the boxed sentences. Then point out that the rest of the directions follow after the box. These directions tell students *which kind* of sentence the answer should be. Help students read through each answer choice, eliminating those sentences that are not compound. Review the rest of the test items in the same way.

© Harcourt

Identify: More on Topics and Details

OBJECTIVES

- To understand the terms *topic sentence* and *details*
- To identify topic sentences and details in literature

Standard: LA.5.3.1.1 generate ideas

Teach/Model   Explain that writers use a topic sentence to tell readers the main idea of a paragraph or longer piece of writing. Other sentences provide details that support the topic sentence. Explain that the topic sentence is often the first sentence of a paragraph but that it may come elsewhere. Read aloud the Literature Model and ask students to listen for the topic sentence and supporting details.

Guided Practice   Read aloud the directions to Part B. Guide students in completing Item 1, explaining that it uses the phrase *faced the Great Falls* to tell readers that the paragraph will be about the Corps and its struggle to go around the Falls. Then guide students through Items 2 and 3.

Independent Writing Practice   Have students complete Part C independently.

Use a Literature Model

LESSON 26: MORE ON TOPICS AND DETAILS

Name _____

Writer's Craft in Literature

Identify: More on Topics and Details

The **topic sentence** is the broadest, most general statement in a paragraph. It tells readers what the paragraph is about. Other sentences in the paragraph give **details** that tell more about the topic.

A. Read the following paragraph. Notice how the writer uses a general topic sentence. Also notice how he uses details to tell more about that topic.

> ### Literature Model
>
> Before they could cross the Rockies, the Corps of Discovery faced the Great Falls of the Missouri River in present-day Montana. Here the river tumbled down a bluff that was as high as a modern six-story building. The roar of the water was deafening. Lewis called it, "the grandest sight I ever beheld." But the waterfall meant that the explorers had to carry their boats and supplies up steep cliffs before they could set out again on quieter waters upstream. Traveling around the falls took the party twenty-four days, and left everyone exhausted.
>
> —from *Lewis and Clark* by R. Conrad Stein

B. Identify the topic sentence and details in the paragraph.
1. Underline the topic sentence of the paragraph.
2. Circle a detail sentence that tells Lewis's impression of the falls.
3. Put a box around another detail sentence that tells about the falls.

Possible responses are given.

C. Explain why the Great Falls presented a challenge to the Corps of Discovery. Use information from the paragraph to support your ideas.

Possible response: The Corps of Discovery had to travel around the Great Falls, which was as

tall as "a modern six-story building" and was the "grandest sight" Lewis ever saw.

_____

_____

SHARING AND DISCUSSING

After students have completed Part C, have them share their responses with a partner. Ask students to discuss how the details about the Great Falls are helpful for showing that the Corps of Discovery's challenge was a difficult one. Encourage students to try to find additional details in the passage that could support their ideas. Then have partners brainstorm a list of other details that the writer might use to describe how difficult the Great Falls were to pass. Ask volunteers to share the details with the class.

© Harcourt

Explore: More on Topics and Details

OBJECTIVES

- To deepen students' understanding of topic sentences and details
- To explore using a topic sentence and supporting details

Standard: LA.5.3.1.2 determine purpose/audience

Teach/Model   Read aloud the introduction at the top of the page. Discuss the diagram, explaining that it shows the kinds of details writers can use to support a topic sentence. Remind students that a fact is a statement that can be proven to be true by checking a reliable source.

Guided Practice   Read aloud the directions to Part A. Guide students through the example by reading aloud the topic sentence and then asking the following question about each detail sentence: **Does this detail support the topic by explaining why Veronica's singing voice is beautiful?** Follow the same procedure to guide students in completing Items 1–3 of Part A.

Independent Writing Practice   Have students complete Parts B and C independently. Direct students to share their writing from Part C with a partner.

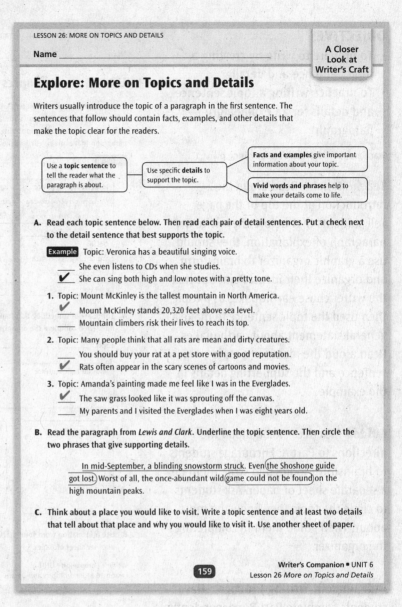

EXTENDING THE CONCEPT: TOPIC SENTENCES

Remind students that topic sentences are often, but not always, the first sentence of a paragraph. Explain that writers sometimes begin a paragraph with a lead sentence, such as a question or quotation, to spark the reader's imagination without actually telling what the paragraph is about. Explain that students should read the entire paragraph before trying to identify the topic sentence. They should then ask themselves: *What main idea is this paragraph trying to communicate? Which sentence tells me what the paragraph is about?*

Use: More on Topics and Details

OBJECTIVES
- To prepare to write by creating a topic sentence and details
- To practice writing a topic sentence and details for an explanatory paragraph

Standard: LA.5.3.2.1 use a pre-writing plan

Teach/Model   Read aloud the introduction at the top of the page. Tell students that before they write a paragraph of explanation, they should use a graphic organizer to brainstorm and organize their ideas. Point out that the writer chose earthquakes as a topic, then used the topic sentence to make a general statement about earthquakes. Read aloud the ideas for a topic sentence and the supporting details in the example.

Guided Practice   Read aloud the directions to Part A. Encourage students to brainstorm topics and write them on a separate sheet of paper. Ask students to circle the topic they know the most about. Then guide them in completing the organizer.

Independent Writing Practice   Have students complete Part B independently.

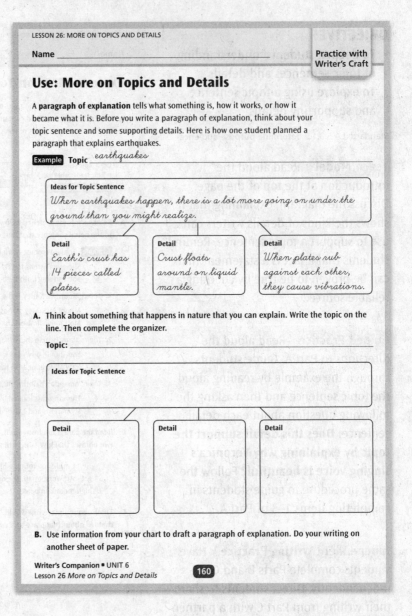

WRITER'S STRATEGY: BRAINSTORMING

Once students have chosen a topic for Part A, direct them to work with a partner to come up with ideas for topic sentences and supporting details. Explain that sometimes it helps writers generate ideas if they find out what other people want to know about the topic. Instruct students to discuss the topics they have chosen and explain why they find the topics interesting. Once students have shared and discussed their topics, ask them to write a list of three questions about their partners' topics. Encourage students to use their partners' questions to guide them in their prewriting.

© Harcourt

The Parts of a Paragraph of Explanation

OBJECTIVES

- To understand how a paragraph of explanation is organized
- To analyze a Student Model

Standard: LA.5.3.1.3 organize ideas

Teach/Model Explain that the model on this page is a first draft of a student's paragraph of explanation. Read aloud the introduction. Then point out the call-outs that show how a paragraph of explanation should be organized. Read aloud the call-outs and Student Model. As students listen, ask them to notice how the writer uses details to support the topic sentence.

Guided Practice Guide students in completing Item 1 by asking them to find the sentence that makes a broad statement about earthquakes. Then direct them to look back at page 160 to see how the writer used the organizer to write the topic sentence. Next, guide students in completing Item 2 by asking them to find the sentence that names the Earth's top layer.

Independent Writing Practice Have students complete Items 3 and 4 independently.

Use a Student Model

LESSON 26: MORE ON TOPICS AND DETAILS

Name _____

Focus on the Writing Form

The Parts of a Paragraph of Explanation

In a **paragraph of explanation** writers introduce a topic and use facts, examples, and other details to tell more about it. Here is an example of a paragraph of explanation written by a fifth grader. As you read, think about the writer's topic and the details that tell about it. Also think about how the student organized it. Then answer the questions.

Student Model

DRAFT

Earthquakes
by Terry

When earthquakes happen, there is a lot more going on under the ground than most people realize. The solid, top layer of Earth is called its crust. It is divided into fourteen huge plates, like a globe cut into fourteen jigsaw puzzle pieces. Right under the crust is a liquid layer called the mantle. The plates float around on the liquid mantle and sometimes rub up against each other. The vibrations make a low rumble. Then they shake the land near the edges of the plates that are being rubbed. Earthquakes only happen near fault lines. That is why there are more earthquakes in some parts of the world than others. An earthquake is simply the Earth readjusting itself.

> **Introduce the topic** with a clear statement.

> **Develop** the paragraph. Add details that support, illustrate, and explain the topic.

> **Organize** your ideas and details. Arrange them in a logical order.

> Be sure to use **irregular verbs** correctly.

> **Conclude** by restating or summing up the main idea.

1. Which sentence introduces the topic? Underline it.
2. Which sentence gives a detail that tells the name of the Earth's top layer? Circle it.
3. Which sentence provides more information about that detail? Put a box around it.
4. Why are there more earthquakes in some parts of the world than others? Use details from the paragraph to explain why.

Possible response: Earthquakes only happen near fault lines. Fault lines are where Earth's

fourteen plates of the crust are divided.

161   **Writer's Companion** • UNIT 6
Lesson 26 *More on Topics and Details*

EXTENDING THE CONCEPT: SUPPORTING DETAILS

Tell students that the writer does a good job of supporting the topic with specific details. Read aloud the third sentence of the paragraph. Point out that the writer uses facts as well as vivid words and phrases to support the topic. Explain that the writer presents the fact that Earth's crust is divided into fourteen plates. He then uses a vivid phrase to describe what the crust looks like. Ask students to identify other facts as well as vivid words and phrases in the Student Model.

© Harcourt

Evaluate a Paragraph of Explanation/ Grammar: Irregular Verbs

OBJECTIVES

- To understand how to evaluate a paragraph of explanation using a checklist
- To use the correct form of irregular verbs

Standard: LA.5.3.3.1 evaluate for writing traits

Evaluate Teach/Model Read aloud the introduction and discuss how evaluating others' writing can help students evaluate their own work.

Guided Practice/Independent Practice Read aloud the items on the checklist. Guide students in evaluating the first item. Have students complete the rest of the checklist independently.

Grammar Teach/Model Discuss the grammar material and model using irregular verbs.

Guided Practice/Independent Practice Guide students in completing Item 1. Have students complete Items 2–4 independently.

LESSON 26: MORE ON TOPICS AND DETAILS

Name _____

Evaluating the Student Model

Evaluate a Paragraph of Explanation

When you evaluate a paragraph of explanation, ask yourself how well the writer explained the topic. Also ask yourself how well the writer used details to support his or her ideas.

Now evaluate the Student Model. Put a check beside each thing the writer did well. If you do not think the writer did a good job, do not check the box.

- ☐ The writer introduced the topic with a clear statement.
- ☐ The writer organized the main details in a logical order.
- ☐ The writer developed the paragraph with details that support, illustrate, and explain the topic.
- ☐ The writer concluded the paragraph by restating or summing up the main idea.

Writer's Grammar
Irregular Verbs

Most verbs are regular. They form the past tense and past participle by adding –ed at the end of the verb (*I stop, I stopped, I have stopped*). **Irregular verbs** have special spellings for the past tense and past participle (*I see, I saw, I have seen*). The irregular verbs *be* and *have* also have special spellings for the present tense.

Example	Verb	Present	Past	Past Participle
	to be	am, are, is	were, was	(have, has, had) been
	to have	have, has	had	(have, has, had) had
	to see	see, sees	saw	(have, has, had) seen
	to do	do, does	did	(have, has, had) done
	to give	give, gives	gave	(have, has, had) given
	to teach	teach, teaches	taught	(have, has, had) taught

Complete each sentence with the correct past tense of the irregular verb in parentheses ( ).

1. We __saw__ a wonderful movie last night. (to see)

2. My father __taught__ math in high school and in college. (to teach)

3. He __was__ extremely happy that he could help. (to be)

4. We __gave__ them a framed copy of the photograph. (to give)

Writer's Companion ▪ UNIT 6
Lesson 26 *More on Topics and Details*   **162**

Reaching All Learners

BELOW LEVEL	ADVANCED	ENGLISH-LANGUAGE LEARNERS
Direct students to the third item on the checklist. Have them restate the topic to a partner or aide and then identify and discuss details the writer used to describe and explain the topic.	Instruct students to work with a partner to write additional items that would help them evaluate a paragraph of explanation. Encourage them to look back at previous lessons for ideas.	Work with students in small groups. Ask students to restate each item and describe the steps they will take to make their evaluations.

© Harcourt

Revise: Adding Details

OBJECTIVES
- To revise sentences by adding details
- To revise a paragraph of explanation by adding details

Teach/Model   Tell students that once they have evaluated their own writing, or have had their writing evaluated by a classmate, they can use the revision process to develop their writing.

Guided Practice   Read aloud the introduction. Then point out that the example models the steps for revising a sentence by adding details. Read the example aloud, pointing out that the writer added details that explain that fault lines are near the edges of the plates. Read aloud the introduction to Part A and guide students in completing Item 1. Explain that they should add details that help describe the squares on a checker board. Prompt students with the following questions: **Are the squares the same color? What color are they?** Guide students in completing Item 2 by asking them to add details to describe where the players put their checkers.

Independent Writing Practice   Have students complete Part A, Item 3 independently, before completing Part B.

LESSON 26: MORE ON TOPICS AND DETAILS

Name _____

Revising the Student Model

Revise a Paragraph of Explanation: Adding Details

The writer could have improved his paragraph by adding descriptive details to support the topic. Here is how a detail sentence from the Student Model could have been improved.

Example   **Read:** Earthquakes only happen near fault lines.

Ask Yourself: What are fault lines?

Improve the Sentence: *Earthquakes only happen near fault lines, or near the edges of the plates.*

A. Read this topic sentence from a paragraph of explanation a student wrote about checkers.

Checkers is a board game for two players.

Now read the following sentences. Rewrite them by adding details that support the main idea. Add other sentences as needed.   Possible responses are given.

1. There are squares on the board.

There are red and black squares on the board.

2. The players set up their checkers.

The players choose a color and set up their checkers, with red on one side of the board

and black on the other.

3. The object of the game is to take your opponent's checkers.

The object of the game is to take all of your opponent's checkers by hopping over them

as you move forward.

B. Revise the draft of the paragraph of explanation you wrote on page 160. Be sure to improve your topic sentence and supporting sentences by adding more details. Also make sure to correctly spell any irregular verbs. Do your writing on another sheet of paper.

163

Writer's Companion • UNIT 6
Lesson 26 *More on Topics and Details*

SHARING AND DISCUSSING

Direct students to read the first draft of their paragraph of explanation to a partner. Then ask them to read aloud their revisions. Their partners should listen carefully to each draft and identify which details the writer added in the revision.

Encourage students to discuss how the details help support the topic of the paragraph. Once partners have discussed each other's revisions, ask them to share their observations with the class.

© Harcourt

Identify: Facts Versus Opinion

OBJECTIVES

- To understand the terms *fact* and *opinion*
- To identify facts and opinion in literature

Standard: LA.5.3.1.1 generate ideas

Teach/Model Read aloud the introduction. Explain that facts can be proven to be true by checking an encyclopedia, textbook, or other reliable source of information. Explain that opinions are what someone thinks or feels about something. Then read the directions for Part A and the Literature Model aloud.

Guided Practice Read aloud the directions for Part B. Guide students in completing Item 1, prompting them to find where the writer describes how far Kate traveled each day. Then guide students in completing Item 2. Point out that the phrase that describes how far Glenora was up the river is a fact because it can be proven by checking a map. Next guide students in completing Item 3, telling students to look for a sentence that shows what someone thinks about Kate.

Independent Writing Practice Have students complete Part C independently.

Use a Literature Model

LESSON 27: FACTS VERSUS OPINION

Name _____

Writer's Craft in Literature

Identify: Facts Versus Opinion

A **fact** is a statement that can be proven to be true. An **opinion** is a statement that shows someone's feelings or thoughts.

A. Read the following passage. Notice how the writer included both facts and opinion.

Literature Model

Trudging behind her dogs, Kate traveled eight to ten grueling miles a day. When she finally pulled into the tiny settlement of Glenora, eighty miles up the river, the news spread fast: A white woman was in town! Not only that—she was as tall and strong as the men who were packing supplies into the North, and she wore a broad-brimmed cow driver's hat over her auburn curls. Jim Callbreath, a local resident who became Kate's friend, said, "Any woman who could make it up to the Stikine River on the ice should be treated as an equal to any packer in the territory."

—from *Klondike Kate*
by Liza Ketchum

B. Identify the facts and opinion in the passage.
1. Underline a sentence that includes a fact about Kate's journey. Possible response is given.
2. Circle the phrase that gives a fact about the location of Glenora.
3. Put a box around the opinion.

C. Using facts from the passage, explain why the people in Glenora found Kate unusual.

Possible responses: Kate had traveled up the river with her dogs, and she was white, tall, and

strong. She also wore a cow driver's hat.

_____

_____

Writer's Companion • UNIT 6
Lesson 27 *Facts Versus Opinion*

164

SHARING AND DISCUSSING

After students have completed Part B, Item 3, instruct volunteers to discuss how they identified the opinion. Ask students whose opinion it is. Point out that the writer uses the quotation to show that it is Jim Callbreath's opinion, not the writer's.

Then discuss what kinds of writing forms about historical subjects might contain many opinions and which might contain few. For example, historical fiction might contain many opinions, while an encyclopedia entry might contain none.

© Harcourt

Explore: Facts Versus Opinion

OBJECTIVES

- To deepen students' understanding of facts and opinions
- To identify and use facts and opinions

Standard: LA.5.4.2.2 record information

Teach/Model Read aloud the introduction and the definitions of fact and opinion in the graphic organizer. Discuss why opinions are not used in some writing forms. Read aloud the directions for Part A and model answering the example. Read aloud the first sentence. Tell students that this sentence is a fact, because it can be proven to be true by checking an encyclopedia. Explain that the second sentence is an opinion because it cannot be proven.

Guided Practice Guide students in completing Item 1. Tell students that even though they might agree with the second sentence, it is still an opinion because it expresses the writer's belief. Guide students in completing Items 2 and 3. After reading each sentence ask the following question: **Can you prove this statement is true?**

Independent Writing Practice Have students complete Parts B and C independently.

LESSON 27: FACTS VERSUS OPINION

Name _____

> A Closer Look at Writer's Craft

Explore: Facts Versus Opinion

Writers use facts to give the reader information about a topic. Writers use opinions to share feelings, thoughts, or beliefs about the topic.

> A **fact** is a statement that can be proven to be true by checking a reliable source.

> An **opinion** cannot be proven. It is a statement that expresses feelings, thoughts, or beliefs.

> **Opinions** are not used in some writing forms, such as newspaper stories and essays that give historical information.

A. Read each pair of sentences below. Write "F" next to the one that expresses a fact. Write "O" next to the one that expresses an opinion.

Example Rome is the capital of Italy, a country in southern Europe. _F_

Rome is the most beautiful city in the world. _O_

1. The first woman in space was Valentina Tereshkova, a Soviet cosmonaut. _F_
Valentina Tereshkova deserves respect for her hard work and dedication. _O_

2. My grandfather's accomplishments should be an inspiration to all. _O_
My grandfather emigrated from Mexico when he was twenty years old. _F_

3. John Coltrane was a jazz musician who played the saxophone. _F_
I believe that John Coltrane was the greatest saxophonist ever. _O_

B. Read the passage from *Klondike Kate*. Underline one fact. Then circle the opinion.

> Her friends were appalled. Had she lost her mind? Women shouldn't travel alone to that part of the world—and how would she get there? Boats could only navigate the Yukon River in summer, and there were no roads or trains.

C. Write one fact about something that happened today. Then write a sentence that gives your opinion about the event.

Fact: Answers will vary. _____

Opinion: Answers will vary. _____

_____

165

Writer's Companion • UNIT 6
Lesson 27 *Facts Versus Opinion*

EXTENDING THE CONCEPT: RELIABLE SOURCES

Remind students that facts can be proven by using reliable sources such as encyclopedias, textbooks, and dictionaries. Tell students that these sources are considered reliable because they have been written, evaluated, and revised by experts. Explain that some books and magazines are not written as carefully as others, and they may not be a reliable source of information. Tell students that they should ask you or a librarian if they need help finding a reliable source for a writing activity.

© Harcourt

Use: Facts Versus Opinion

OBJECTIVES
- To prepare to write by separating facts and opinions
- To practice writing a paragraph of historical information using facts

Teach/Model Read aloud the introduction at the top of the page, explaining that a paragraph of historical information should contain facts, not opinions. Read the example aloud.

Guided Practice Read aloud the directions to Part A and guide students in completing the chart. Tell students to ask themselves the following for each detail they write in their chart: **Can I prove this by checking a reliable source? Does this express my feeling or belief?** Once students have completed Part A, have them discuss their charts with a partner.

Independent Writing Practice Have students complete Part B independently. Ask volunteers to read their drafts to the class.

LESSON 27: FACTS VERSUS OPINION

Name _____

Practice with Writer's Craft

Use: Facts Versus Opinion

A **paragraph of historical information** tells about real events that happened in the past. The writer usually arranges the events in time order. When you write about historical information, try to separate facts from your personal opinions. Here is how one student started to organize information for a paragraph about a past event.

Example

Topic: the first person to be hit by a meteorite
Facts (can be proven to be true by checking an encyclopedia or textbook): The meteorite hit her while she was taking a nap. The meteorite was the size of a grapefruit.
Opinions (feelings or beliefs about the topic): a miracle I hope it never happens to me.

A. Think about a historical event that interests you. It can be an event that you have read about or one that you have heard about from a reliable source. Then fill out the chart.

Topic:
Facts (can be proven to be true by checking an encyclopedia or textbook):
Opinions (feelings or beliefs about the topic):

B. Now use only the facts from the chart to write a draft about a historical event. Describe the event in time order. Do your writing on another sheet of paper.

Writer's Companion • UNIT 6
Lesson 27 *Facts Versus Opinion*

166

Reaching All Learners

BELOW LEVEL	ADVANCED	ENGLISH-LANGUAGE LEARNERS
Have students work with a partner or aide. Ask students to describe the event while a partner takes notes. Have students use their partner's notes to help them fill in the chart.	If time permits, encourage students to use a reliable source to check the facts in their drafts. Remind students that if they use facts from a source, they should restate them in their own words.	Pair students with more-fluent English-speakers. Have students discuss the events and then help each other identify the appropriate English words to put in the chart.

© Harcourt

The Parts of a Paragraph of Historical Information

OBJECTIVES
- To understand how a paragraph of historical information is organized
- To analyze a Student Model

Teach/Model   Read aloud the introduction at the top of the page. Then read aloud the Student Model along with the call-outs that show how to organize the paragraph of historical information. As students listen, instruct them to pay attention to how the writer arranges the events in time order.

Guided Practice   Point out the questions beneath the Student Model and guide students in answering Item 1. Ask: **Which sentence is a broad statement that tells me what the paragraph is about?** Help students identify the first sentence, explaining that it tells the reader whom the paragraph is about and what happened. Guide students in answering Item 2, reminding them to look for the sentence that describes the meteorite hitting Mrs. Hodges.

Independent Writing Practice   Ask students to complete Item 3 independently.

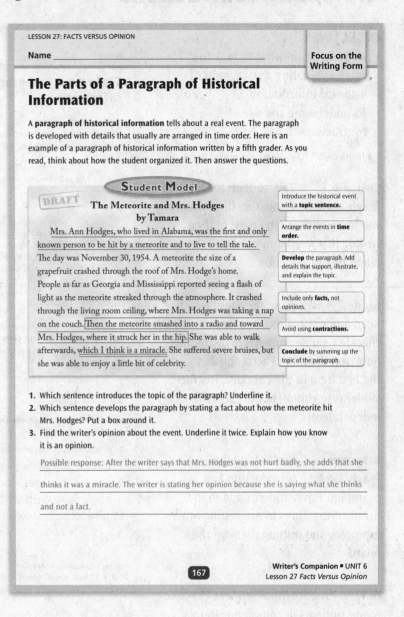

LESSON 27: FACTS VERSUS OPINION

Name _____

Focus on the Writing Form

The Parts of a Paragraph of Historical Information

A **paragraph of historical information** tells about a real event. The paragraph is developed with details that usually are arranged in time order. Here is an example of a paragraph of historical information written by a fifth grader. As you read, think about how the student organized it. Then answer the questions.

Student Model

DRAFT

The Meteorite and Mrs. Hodges
by Tamara

Mrs. Ann Hodges, who lived in Alabama, was the first and only known person to be hit by a meteorite and to live to tell the tale. The day was November 30, 1954. A meteorite the size of a grapefruit crashed through the roof of Mrs. Hodge's home. People as far as Georgia and Mississippi reported seeing a flash of light as the meteorite streaked through the atmosphere. It crashed through the living room ceiling, where Mrs. Hodges was taking a nap on the couch. Then the meteorite smashed into a radio and toward Mrs. Hodges, where it struck her in the hip. She was able to walk afterwards, which I think is a miracle. She suffered severe bruises, but she was able to enjoy a little bit of celebrity.

> Introduce the historical event with a **topic sentence**.

> Arrange the events in **time order**.

> **Develop** the paragraph. Add details that support, illustrate, and explain the topic.

> Include only **facts**, not opinions.

> Avoid using **contractions**.

> **Conclude** by summing up the topic of the paragraph.

1. Which sentence introduces the topic of the paragraph? Underline it.
2. Which sentence develops the paragraph by stating a fact about how the meteorite hit Mrs. Hodges? Put a box around it.
3. Find the writer's opinion about the event. Underline it twice. Explain how you know it is an opinion.

Possible response: After the writer says that Mrs. Hodges was not hurt badly, she adds that she thinks it was a miracle. The writer is stating her opinion because she is saying what she thinks and not a fact.

167

Writer's Companion • UNIT 6
Lesson 27 *Facts Versus Opinion*

EXTEND THE CONCEPT: WORD CHOICE

Tell students that the writing form influences the types of words they should use. Explain that for writing forms such as paragraphs of historical information they should choose words that will help create a more serious, formal tone. Point out the call-out for the Student Model that says to avoid contractions. Discuss how contractions can make writing sound less formal. Explain that students should only use contractions in less formal writing forms, such as ones that have dialogue, like narratives and plays.

© Harcourt

Evaluate a Paragraph of Historical Information/ Grammar: Contractions

OBJECTIVES
- To understand what to look for when evaluating a paragraph of hisorical information
- To understand the use of contractions

Standard: LA.5.3.3.1 evaluate for writing traits

Evaluate Teach/Model   Tell students that evaluating their writing will help them see the parts of their writing that need improvement. Read aloud the introduction.

Guided Practice/Independent Practice
Read aloud the directions for the checklist. Guide students in discussing how well the model accomplishes the first item in the checklist. Instruct students to complete the checklist independently.

Grammar Teach/Model   Read aloud the introduction and examples. Have students add to the list of contractions by suggesting other examples and putting them on the board.

Guided Practice/Independent Practice
Guide students in completing Item 1. Have students complete Items 2–5 independently.

LESSON 27: FACTS VERSUS OPINION

Name _____

Evaluating the Student Model

Evaluate a Paragraph of Historical Information

When you evaluate a paragraph of historical information, ask yourself how well the writer used facts to develop the topic. Also ask yourself if the writer avoided using personal opinions about the topic.

Now evaluate the Student Model. Put a check beside each thing the writer did well. If you do not think the writer did a good job, do not check the box.

- ☐ The writer introduced the historical event with a topic sentence.
- ☐ The writer arranged the events in time order.
- ☐ The writer used details to support, illustrate, and explain the topic.
- ☐ The writer used only facts and did not include opinions.
- ☐ The writer concluded by summing up the topic of the paragraph.

Writer's Grammar
Contractions
A **contraction** is the shortened form of two or more words. An apostrophe (') is used to replace the letter or letters that are taken out. The word *not* is often combined with a verb in a contraction. Contractions should not be used in formal writing.

you've = you + have	**you'll** = you + will
doesn't = does + not	**haven't** = have + not

Correct each sentence. Change the contraction in parentheses to the correct long form.

1. (It's) _It is_____ difficult to appreciate some art.

2. The Empire State Building (isn't) _is not_____ the tallest building in the United States.

3. I (can't) _cannot_____ believe that the Watts Towers were almost torn down.

4. Washington, D.C. (hasn't) _has not_____ always been the capital of the United States.

5. (You're) _You are_____ about to learn about the greatest athlete in the world.

Writer's Companion ▪ UNIT 6
Lesson 27 *Facts Versus Opinion*   **168**

SHARING AND DISCUSSING

Once students have completed evaluating the Student Model, ask them to share their results with a partner. For each item on the checklist, instruct students to describe, step by step, how they determined whether the writer did a good job.

Guide students to point out specific examples from the Student Model to support their opinions. If students think that the writer did not do something well, encourage them to discuss specific ways that the writer could have improved the paragraph.

© Harcourt

Revise: Deleting Opinions

OBJECTIVES
- To revise sentences by deleting opinions
- To revise a paragraph of historical information

Standard: LA.5.3.3.2 clarify by deleting/organizing

Teach/Model Remind students that when they revise their writing, they often add words, sentences, and new ideas. Explain that sometimes revision also involves deleting words, sentences, and ideas. Tell students that in this activity they will practice revising by deleting opinions. Read the introduction and example aloud, discussing how the example models revising a sentence.

Guided Practice Read the instructions to Part A aloud. Guide students in completing Item 1 by following the steps in the example. Point out that the writer expresses an opinion by saying that she felt surprised. Prompt students to see that they should delete the phrase "I was surprised that...."

Independent Writing Practice Instruct students to complete Part A, Items 2–4 independently. Then have them complete Part B independently. Tell students to share their revisions with a partner.

LESSON 27: FACTS VERSUS OPINION

Name _____

Revising the Student Model

Revise a Paragraph of Historical Information: Deleting Opinions

One way the writer could have improved the paragraph of historical information was by leaving out opinions. Here is how a sentence from the Student Model could be improved by deleting the opinion.

Example **Read:** "She was able to walk afterwards, which I think is a miracle."

Ask Yourself: How does the writer express an opinion in this sentence?

Think: The writer describes how she feels about the event. To avoid using her opinion, the writer should have only included the factual details.

Improve the Sentence: _She was able to walk afterwards._

A. Revise the following sentences by deleting the opinions and using only the facts.

1. I was surprised that Jessica Miller finished in first place and set a new school record.

   Jessica Miller finished in first place and set a new school record.

2. I think it was a bad idea for the explorers to build a fort in the middle of a mosquito-infested swamp.

   The explorers built a fort in the middle of a mosquito-infested swamp.

3. It is sad that the architect did not get to see the completed house she had designed for her husband.

   The architect did not get to see the completed house she had designed for her husband.

4. Last night the drama club performed *The Loon's Last Call*, which I thought was hilarious.

   Last night the drama club performed *The Loon's Last Call*.

B. Revise the draft of a paragraph of historical information that you wrote on page 166. Be sure to delete any opinions and change any contractions to the correct long form. Do your writing on another sheet of paper.

169

Writer's Companion ■ UNIT 6
Lesson 27 *Facts Versus Opinion*

Reaching All Learners

BELOW LEVEL
Have students work with a partner or aide to identify sentences in their first drafts that express opinions. Ask students to follow the steps in the example to delete any opinions they find.

ADVANCED
Encourage students to expand their first draft with facts they have found in a reliable reference source. Tell students to make sure that the facts they add support the topic sentences.

ENGLISH-LANGUAGE LEARNERS
Have students work with a partner to edit each other's first drafts and make suggestions for revisions. Tell students to note where the writer expresses an opinion.

© Harcourt

Identify: Putting Ideas in Sequence

OBJECTIVES

- To understand the term *putting ideas in sequence*
- To identify the sequence of ideas in literature

Standard: LA.5.3.2.2 sequence information

Teach/Model Read aloud the introduction and discuss how writers put ideas in sequence in order to describe, step by step, how something happens. Explain that transition words make it easier for the reader to understand the order of events. Read aloud Part A, instructing students to listen carefully to how the writer states the order of events.

Guided Practice Discuss the sequence of events in the passage, pointing out that the writer uses the times of day rather than transition words such as *first, next,* or *then*. Read aloud the directions to Part B and guide students in completing Item 1. Point out the second sentence. Ask students to find the part of the sentence that describes when the climbers leave for their climb. Then guide students to complete Items 2 and 3, explaining that different stages may occur in the same sentence.

Independent Writing Practice Have students complete Part C independently.

Use a Literature Model

LESSON 28: PUTTING IDEAS IN SEQUENCE

Name _____

Writer's Craft in Literature

Identify: Putting Ideas in Sequence

Putting ideas in sequence means organizing ideas in the order in which they happen. Good writers use transition words, such as *first, then, next,* and *finally,* to make the sequence of events clear.

A. Read the following passage. Notice how the writer puts his ideas in sequence.

> **Literature Model**
>
> It can take more than twelve hours to climb to the top from Camp 4. Since it's critical to make it back to camp before dark, climbers usually set out before midnight, and climb through the night by the light of a headlamp. With luck, these climbers will be on top the following noon.
>
> —from *The Top of the World: Climbing Mount Everest* by Steve Jenkins

B. Identify the sequence of ideas in the passage.
1. Underline the part of a sentence that describes the first stage of the climb to the top from Camp 4.
2. Circle the part of a sentence that describes the second stage of the climb.
3. Put a box around the sentence that describes the third stage of the climb.

C. In your own words, describe the sequence of steps that the climbers must take to climb to the top of the mountain from Camp 4. Use transition words, such as *first, then, next,* and *finally,* to make the sequence of events clear.

Possible response: First, the climbers set out before midnight. Then they climb at night using headlamps. Finally, they arrive at the top at noon.

EXTENDING THE CONCEPT: USING TRANSITION WORDS

Before students begin Part C, remind them that transition words should make the order of events clear. Tell students that good writers often use transition words as signals to guide the reader. Words such as *first* signal the beginning of the sequence of events. Words such as *then* and *next* signal that the first event has ended and the next event has begun, and so on. Explain that by using these transition words, the writer can make sure the reader fully understands the order of events.

Explore: Putting Ideas in Sequence

OBJECTIVES

- To deepen students' understanding of putting ideas in sequence
- To identify and use transition words and phrases

Teach/Model   Read aloud the introduction. Use the diagram to show students how they can use transition words to organize a series of events in time order. Tell students that they do not always have to put transition words at the beginning of a sentence. Demonsrate that they can also use transition words in the middle or end of a sentence, as long as the sequence of events is clear. Read aloud the directions to Part A. Model identifying the first transition word by telling students that the word *first* signals the first step in the process of making a pot of rice.

Guided Practice   Guide students in finding the other transition words. Ask: **Which transition word signals the next step in the process?** For each response, have students suggest other transition words that the writer could have used.

Independent Writing Practice   Have students complete Part B independently.

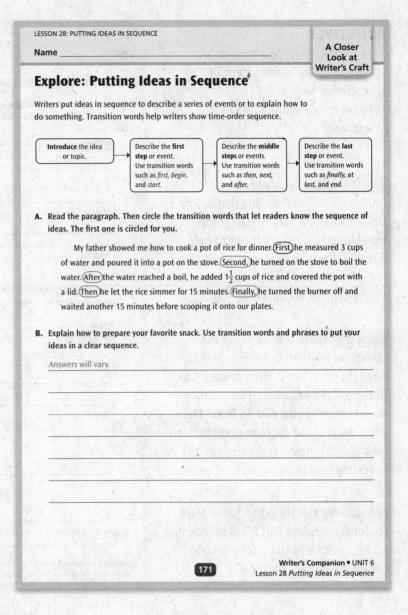

SHARING AND DISCUSSING

After students have completed Part B, encourage volunteers to share their descriptions in small groups. Ask students to listen carefully and raise their hands each time they hear a transition word. After each reading, have students discuss the transition words that the writer used.

Then challenge students to retell the steps in the process in their own words. Encourage students to use transition words correctly. To add a level of difficulty, ask students to use different transition words than were used in the original description.

Use: Putting Ideas in Sequence

OBJECTIVES
- To practice writing a how-to paragraph by putting steps in sequence
- To practice putting ideas in sequence

Teach/Model   Read aloud the introduction, emphasizing that before students write a how-to paragraph, they should use an organizer to help put their ideas in sequence. Read aloud the example and model what the writer might write in the space for Step 3.

Guided Practice   Read aloud the directions for Part A. Once students have chosen a topic, guide students in filling out the organizer. Prompt them by asking: **What do you do first? Then what do you do?** Encourage students to look back at the diagram on page 171 to review how to put ideas in sequence.

Independent Writing Practice   Have students complete Part B independently. Invite students to share their how-to paragraphs with a partner.

LESSON 28: PUTTING IDEAS IN SEQUENCE

Name _____

Practice with Writer's Craft

Use: Putting Ideas in Sequence

A **how-to paragraph** explains how to make or do something. The steps to follow are arranged in time order. Here is how one student planned to explain how to plant tomatoes.

Example How to *plant tomatoes*

Step 1: *picked a spot in the garden*

↓

Step 2: *dug a six-inch-deep hole*

↓

Step 3:

A. Think about something that you recently learned to do or make. Use the organizer below to put your ideas in sequence.

How to _____

Step 1:

↓

Step 2:

↓

Step 3:

B. Use the information from your chart to draft a how-to paragraph. Use transition words or phrases to help show the time order. Do your writing on another sheet of paper.

Writer's Companion ▪ UNIT 6
Lesson 28 *Putting Ideas in Sequence*   172

Reaching All Learners

BELOW LEVEL

Ask students to describe the steps to a partner. Tell students to begin each sentence with a transition word. Then have students work together to complete Part A.

ADVANCED

Challenge students to choose something that is easy to do but difficult to describe, such as tying a shoe or blowing a bubble. Tell students they may need another sheet of paper to include additional steps.

ENGLISH-LANGUAGE LEARNERS

Have students work in pairs to build sentences with the words and phrases on their organizers. Have students build three sentences that begin with the transition words *first, then*, and *next*.

© Harcourt

The Parts of a How-to Paragraph

OBJECTIVES
- To understand how to organize a how-to paragraph
- To analyze a Student Model

Standard: LA.5.3.1.3 organize ideas

Teach/Model   Have volunteers read aloud the introduction. Read aloud the call-outs and the Student Model. Explain that the model is a first draft of a student's writing and that the call-outs explain ways to organize a how-to paragraph. Point out how the writer organizes the paragraph by putting the ideas in sequence.

Guided Practice   Guide students to complete Item 1, helping them identify the first sentence as the one that tells what the paragraph is about. Point out that this sentence may not always state that instructions will be listed in the paragraph, but should still mention the topic of the how-to paragraph. Then guide students to complete Item 2, reminding them that they should read the entire paragraph before deciding what it is about.

Independent Writing Practice   Have students complete Items 3 and 4 independently.

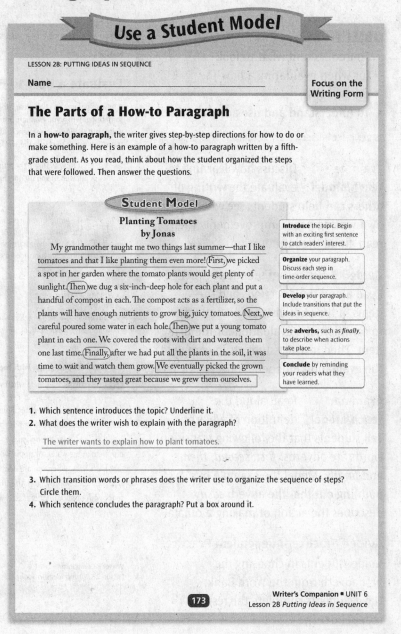

Use a Student Model

LESSON 28: PUTTING IDEAS IN SEQUENCE

Name _____

Focus on the Writing Form

The Parts of a How-to Paragraph

In a **how-to paragraph**, the writer gives step-by-step directions for how to do or make something. Here is an example of a how-to paragraph written by a fifth-grade student. As you read, think about how the student organized the steps that were followed. Then answer the questions.

Student Model

Planting Tomatoes
by Jonas

   My grandmother taught me two things last summer—that I like tomatoes and that I like planting them even more! First, we picked a spot in her garden where the tomato plants would get plenty of sunlight. Then we dug a six-inch-deep hole for each plant and put a handful of compost in each. The compost acts as a fertilizer, so the plants will have enough nutrients to grow big, juicy tomatoes. Next, we careful poured some water in each hole. Then we put a young tomato plant in each one. We covered the roots with dirt and watered them one last time. Finally, after we had put all the plants in the soil, it was time to wait and watch them grow. We eventually picked the grown tomatoes, and they tasted great because we grew them ourselves.

Introduce the topic. Begin with an exciting first sentence to catch readers' interest.

Organize your paragraph. Discuss each step in time-order sequence.

Develop your paragraph. Include transitions that put the ideas in sequence.

Use **adverbs**, such as *finally*, to describe when actions take place.

Conclude by reminding your readers what they have learned.

1. Which sentence introduces the topic? Underline it.
2. What does the writer wish to explain with the paragraph?

   The writer wants to explain how to plant tomatoes.

3. Which transition words or phrases does the writer use to organize the sequence of steps? Circle them.
4. Which sentence concludes the paragraph? Put a box around it.

173

Writer's Companion ■ UNIT 6
Lesson 28 *Putting Ideas in Sequence*

EXTEND THE CONCEPT: ADDING DETAILS

Tell students that the writer does a good job of explaining, step by step, how to plant tomatoes. Explain that the writer also does a good job of using vivid details to explain why each step is important. As an example, show that the writer explains why putting compost in each hole is important ("so each plant will have enough nutrients to grow big, juicy tomatoes"). Have students reread the Student Model and discuss other vivid details the writer uses to explain the steps.

© Harcourt

Evaluate a How-to Paragraph/Grammar: Adverbs

OBJECTIVES

- To understand what to look for when evaluating a how-to paragraph
- To understand and use adverbs

SS BENCHMARKS: LA.5.3.3.1 evaluate for writing traits

Evaluate Teach/Model   Discuss how learning to evaluate the writing of others can help students see where their own writing needs improvement. Then read aloud the introduction.

Guided Practice/Independent Practice

Read aloud the directions and the items in the checklist. Guide students to complete the evaluation for the first item. Then instruct students to complete the evaluation independently.

Grammar Teach/Model   Read aloud the definition of adverbs. Tell students that the following transition words are adverbs: *first, second, then,* and *finally*. Model the example by pointing out that the adverb *easily* describes the action of making a piñata.

Guided Practice/Independent Practice

Guide students in choosing the first adverb from the Word Bank. Have students complete the rest independently.

LESSON 28: PUTTING IDEAS IN SEQUENCE

Name _____

> Evaluating the Student Model

Evaluate a How-to Paragraph

A how-to paragraph gives clear, step-by-step directions for how to do or make something. When you evaluate a how-to paragraph, ask yourself how well the writer put the ideas in sequence. Also ask yourself whether the writer used transition words to clarify the sequence of steps or events.

Now evaluate the Student Model. Put a check beside each thing the writer did well. If you do not think the writer did a good job, do not check the box.

- ☐ The writer introduced the topic with a first sentence that caught readers' interest.
- ☐ The writer organized the paragraph in time-order sequence.
- ☐ The writer used transition words to help show the sequence of ideas.
- ☐ The writer concluded by reminding readers what they learned.

Writer's Grammar
Adverbs

An **adverb** is a word that tells about a verb, an adjective, or another adverb. Adverbs often tell *how* (happily), *when* (last), or *where* (inside). Transition words that describe *when* sometimes are adverbs.

Complete the paragraph with the correct adverb from the Word Bank.

Example   Why buy a piñata when you can ___easily___ make one at home?

To get started, you need water, flour, a bowl, newspaper, and a big balloon. ___First___, mix $\frac{1}{2}$ cup of flour and 2 cups of warm water in the bowl. ___Then___ tear the newspaper ___length-wise___ into long strips and dip them in the water. Wrap the wet strips around the balloon, covering it ___completely___. When you are done adding layers, place the balloon in a ___somewhat___ warm place. After the paper dries, pop the balloon and fill the space with candy. ___Finally___, you are ready to decorate your new piñata.

Word Bank

completely
easily
finally
first
length-wise
somewhat
then

SHARING AND DISCUSSING

Ask volunteers to read aloud the completed paragraph from the grammar activity. Have students point out which words the adverbs modify. Then have them identify whether the modified words are verbs, adjectives, or adverbs. Have the class brainstorm a new list of adverbs, and write the adverbs on the board. Challenge students to complete the paragraph using some of the new adverbs. Then ask volunteers to read aloud their completed paragraphs. Discuss how some of the adverbs may change the meaning of each sentence.

Revise: Proofreading

OBJECTIVES
- To understand the purpose of proofreading
- To revise a how-to paragraph by proofreading

Teach/Model   Tell students that revision gives writers the opportunity to make both large and small changes to their writing. Writers, however, should always use the revision process as an opportunity to proofread their writing.

Guided Practice   Read aloud the introduction and the example sentence. Point out the word *careful*. Explain that the word should be an adverb because it tells how the writer poured the water. Tell students that to make *careful* an adverb, *-ly* should be inserted at the end. Point out that the writer used the insert text symbol from the Proofreading Marks box. Read aloud the directions to Part A and guide students to complete Item 1. Point out that the word *extreme* describes the adjective *careful*, which means that it acts as an adverb. Ask students how they should change the word *extreme* to make it an adverb. Remind them to use the proofreading mark for inserting text.

Independent Writing Practice   Have students complete Part A, Items 2–5 on their own. Then have them complete the revision in Part B independently.

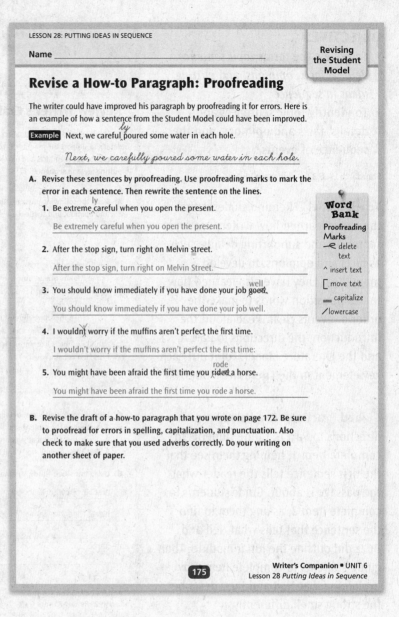

LESSON 28: PUTTING IDEAS IN SEQUENCE

Name _____

Revising the Student Model

Revise a How-to Paragraph: Proofreading

The writer could have improved his paragraph by proofreading it for errors. Here is an example of how a sentence from the Student Model could have been improved.

Example   Next, we careful poured some water in each hole.

Next, we carefully poured some water in each hole.

A. Revise these sentences by proofreading. Use proofreading marks to mark the error in each sentence. Then rewrite the sentence on the lines.

1. Be extreme careful when you open the present.

   Be extremely careful when you open the present.

2. After the stop sign, turn right on Melvin street.

   After the stop sign, turn right on Melvin Street.

3. You should know immediately if you have done your job good.

   You should know immediately if you have done your job well.

4. I wouldn't worry if the muffins aren't perfect the first time.

   I wouldn't worry if the muffins aren't perfect the first time.

5. You might have been afraid the first time you rided a horse.

   You might have been afraid the first time you rode a horse.

B. Revise the draft of a how-to paragraph that you wrote on page 172. Be sure to proofread for errors in spelling, capitalization, and punctuation. Also check to make sure that you used adverbs correctly. Do your writing on another sheet of paper.

Word Bank

Proofreading Marks
- ℛ delete text
- ^ insert text
- [move text
- ═ capitalize
- / lowercase

175   **Writer's Companion** • UNIT 6
Lesson 28 *Putting Ideas in Sequence*

WRITER'S STRATEGY: PROOFREADING

Tell students that even good writers overlook mistakes when they proofread their own work. Explain that they will be able to catch more mistakes if they also have someone else proofread their writing. After students have completed their revisions for Part B, have them trade paragraphs with a partner. Ask students to proofread their partners' paragraphs for errors in spelling, capitalization, and punctuation. Instruct the partners to discuss any errors they found.

© Harcourt

Review Writer's Craft

OBJECTIVES

- To review the terms *topic sentence*, *details*, *facts*, *opinions*, and *putting ideas in sequence*
- To identify topic sentences and details, facts and opinions, and the sequence of events

Standard: LA.5.3.1.1 generate ideas

Teach/Model Remind students that they have learned how writers use topic sentences and supporting details, such as facts and opinions, to develop a main idea. They have also learned how to use transition words to make the order of events clear. Read aloud the introduction, the directions to Part A, and the Literature Model. Point out each key element in the Literature Model.

Guided Practice Read aloud the directions to Part B. Guide students to complete Item 1, helping them see that the first sentence tells the reader what the passage is about. Guide students to complete Item 2, asking them to find the sentence that tells what Neil and Buzz did outside the lunar module. Then guide students to complete Item 3 by explaining that Neil and Buzz describe the strong smell differently.

Independent Writing Practice Have students complete Part C independently.

Use a Literature Model

LESSON 29: REVIEW WRITER'S CRAFT

Name _____

Writer's Craft in Literature

Review Writer's Craft

You have learned how to introduce a topic with a topic sentence and to use details to support the main idea. You have also learned to recognize the difference between facts and opinions and how to organize your writing by putting ideas in sequence.

A. Read the following passage. Notice how the writer uses a topic sentence and details, facts and opinion, and sequence.

Literature Model

Neil and Buzz stay on the moon for 21 hours and 36 minutes, but only a little more than 2 hours of that time is spent outside the lunar module. They perform three minor experiments and load two aluminum suitcases with 48 pounds (22 kilograms) of moon dust and rocks.

When they have climbed back into the lunar module and shut the hatch, they take their helmets off. They look at each other because they both sense a strong smell. Neil thinks it smells like wet ashes. Buzz says it smells like spent gunpowder. It is the moon. The moon has a smell.

—from *The Man Who Went to the Far Side of the Moon*
by Bea Uusma Schyffert

B. Identify topic sentences, details, facts, and opinions.
1. Underline the sentence in the first paragraph that introduces the topic.
2. Circle the detail that supports the topic sentence of the first paragraph.
3. Put a box around Neil's and Buzz's opinions about how the moon smells.

C. Using transition words, summarize the sequence of events in the second paragraph.

Possible response: First, Neil and Buzz climb back into the module. Second, they shut the

hatch. Third, they take off their helmets. Next, they smell something. Then they look at each

other. Finally, they say what they think the moon smells like.

_____

Writer's Companion • UNIT 6
Lesson 29 *Review Writer's Craft*   176

EXTENDING THE CONCEPT: PUTTING IDEAS IN SEQUENCE

Before students begin Part C, point out the first sentence of the second paragraph. Tell students that the writer uses one sentence to describe a sequence of three events. Then guide students to identify the events, asking them to suggest different transition words they could use to summarize them. After students have completed Part C, ask volunteers to share their responses.

Review Writer's Craft

OBJECTIVES

- To review the terms *topic sentence, details, facts, opinions, sequence,* and *transition words*
- To identify a topic sentence, supporting details, and transition words

Teach/Model   Use the diagram at the top of the page to review how students can use ideas and conventions to develop and organize their writing. Review the difference between facts and opinions. Remind students that they should not express their personal opinions in some forms of writing.

Guided Practice   Read aloud the directions and passage in Part A. Guide students to complete Part B, Item 1. Have them discuss how they know that the first sentence tells them what the paragraph is about. Then guide students to complete Items 2–3, explaining that students must clearly understand what the topic sentence is before deciding which details support it. Explain that extra information may be used to add interest to the story, but may not directly describe the topic sentence.

Independent Writing Practice   Instruct students to complete Part C independently.

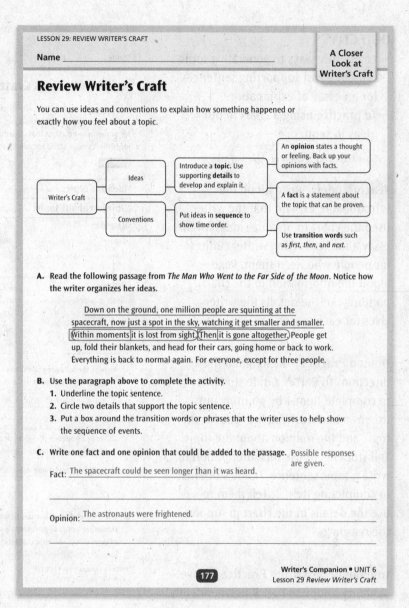

Reaching All Learners

BELOW LEVEL	ADVANCED	ENGLISH-LANGUAGE LEARNERS
Help students with Part C by prompting them with questions, such as **What did people do as the spacecraft disappeared?** and **How do you think people felt as they watched the spacecraft?**	Have students use Part C to add another paragraph to the passage. Ask them to use facts and opinions to describe what the astronauts did and how they may have felt as they headed toward the moon.	Before students complete Part C, have them work with a partner to develop ideas orally. Ask partners to brainstorm words to describe the spacecraft. Also ask them to describe how they would have felt to see it take off.

© Harcourt

Review Writer's Craft

OBJECTIVES

- To identify ways to generate a topic sentence and supporting sentences for an essay of explanation
- To practice using a chart to put ideas in sequence

Standard: LA.5.3.2.1 use a pre-writing plan

Teach/Model   Read aloud the introduction. Explain that the writer used the chart to organize ideas for an essay about collecting winter clothes for people who need them. Read aloud the information in the chart, pointing out the details the writer gives for each reason.

Guided Practice   Read aloud the directions to Part A. Guide students to complete Item 1 by pointing out the rows that describe the idea for the topic and the opinion about the topic. Tell students to use this information to write a topic sentence. Guide students in completing Item 2. Tell them to use the details in the chart to support the reason.

Independent Writing Practice   Have students complete Part B independently.

LESSON 29: REVIEW WRITER'S CRAFT

Name _____

Practice with Writer's Craft

Review Writer's Craft

In an **essay of explanation**, the writer explains what something is, how something happens, or how something is done. The writer also can use details to give reasons for his or her opinion about that something. Here is how one fifth grader organized her ideas for an essay about something that she is proud of doing recently.

Example

Idea for topic: *collecting winter clothes for the less fortunate*		
Opinion about topic: *everyone should help the community*		
Reason: *had fun decorating drop-off boxes*	**Reason:** *got to socialize with family friends at dinner*	**Reason:** *felt like I was doing something nice*
Details: *used creativity to decorate them*	**Details:** *asked permission to place boxes in front of family friends' businesses*	**Details:** *collected the donations and gave them to an organization*

A. Answer the following questions about the chart. Possible responses are given.

1. Using the information in the chart, write a topic sentence that the writer could use in this essay.

   Collecting winter clothes for the less fortunate is a great way to help the community.

2. Write a sentence that gives one reason why the writer thinks everyone should help the community. Use information from the chart to back up that opinion.

   I felt like I was doing something nice when I collected the donations and gave them to an

   organization.

B. Use the details in the chart to write two sentences about collecting winter clothes. Use transition words or phrases to put the ideas in sequence. Do your writing on another sheet of paper. Possible response: First, we decorated drop-off boxes. Then we placed the boxes in front of family friends' businesses.

Writer's Companion • UNIT 6
Lesson 29 *Review Writer's Craft*   178

SHARING AND DISCUSSING

Direct students to read their responses to Part B to a partner. Ask students to listen for transition words as their partners read. Encourage students to discuss how the transition words in their sentences help make the sequence of events clear. Instruct students to work together to write another pair of sentences about collecting winter clothes. Students may use information from the chart or generate new reasons and details that could be added to the chart.

© Harcourt

The Parts of an Essay of Explanation

OBJECTIVES
- To understand how an essay of explanation is organized
- To analyze a Student Model

Standard: LA.5.3.1.3 organize ideas

Teach/Model   Read aloud the introduction, explaining that the Student Model is an essay of explanation. Point out the call-outs and explain that they show how an essay of explanation should be organized. Then read aloud the Student Model along with the call-outs. Remind students to listen to how the writer organizes her ideas by putting them in sequence.

Guided Practice   Guide students to complete Item 1. Direct students to the first sentence and ask them if it states in an interesting way what the essay will be about. Then guide students to complete Item 2 by finding supporting details about making the boxes.

Independent Writing Practice   Have students complete Items 3 and 4 independently.

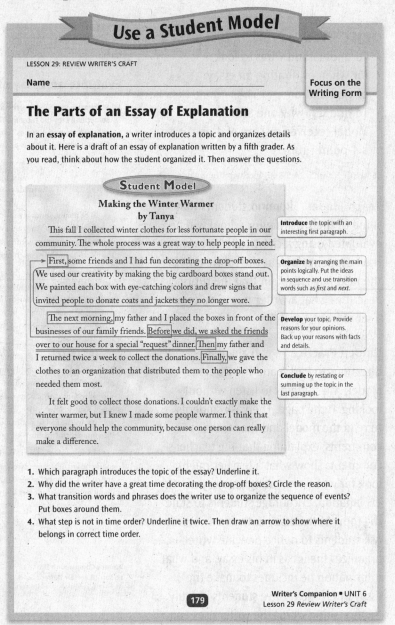

Use a Student Model

LESSON 29: REVIEW WRITER'S CRAFT

Name _____

Focus on the Writing Form

The Parts of an Essay of Explanation

In an **essay of explanation**, a writer introduces a topic and organizes details about it. Here is a draft of an essay of explanation written by a fifth grader. As you read, think about how the student organized it. Then answer the questions.

Student Model

Making the Winter Warmer
by Tanya

This fall I collected winter clothes for less fortunate people in our community. The whole process was a great way to help people in need.

First, some friends and I had fun decorating the drop-off boxes. We used our creativity by making the big cardboard boxes stand out. We painted each box with eye-catching colors and drew signs that invited people to donate coats and jackets they no longer wore.

The next morning, my father and I placed the boxes in front of the businesses of our family friends. Before we did, we asked the friends over to our house for a special "request" dinner. Then my father and I returned twice a week to collect the donations. Finally, we gave the clothes to an organization that distributed them to the people who needed them most.

It felt good to collect those donations. I couldn't exactly make the winter warmer, but I knew I made some people warmer. I think that everyone should help the community, because one person can really make a difference.

Introduce the topic with an interesting first paragraph.

Organize by arranging the main points logically. Put the ideas in sequence and use transition words such as *first* and *next*.

Develop your topic. Provide reasons for your opinions. Back up your reasons with facts and details.

Conclude by restating or summing up the topic in the last paragraph.

1. Which paragraph introduces the topic of the essay? Underline it.
2. Why did the writer have a great time decorating the drop-off boxes? Circle the reason.
3. What transition words and phrases does the writer use to organize the sequence of events? Put boxes around them.
4. What step is not in time order? Underline it twice. Then draw an arrow to show where it belongs in correct time order.

179

Writer's Companion • UNIT 6
Lesson 29 *Review Writer's Craft*

EXTENDING THE CONCEPT: FACTS AND OPINIONS

Tell students that the writer of the Student Model gives both facts and opinions about collecting winter clothes. Ask students to look back at the Student Model and identify the sentences in which the writer expresses her opinion. Then have students identify the details and facts that the writer uses to support her opinions. Encourage students to discuss why, in the concluding paragraph, the writer said it felt good to collect the donations.

© Harcourt

Evaluate an Essay of Explanation

OBJECTIVES
- To understand what to look for when evaluating an essay of explanation
- To find out why one Student Model received a score of 4 on a 4-point rubric

SS BENCHMARKS: LA.5.3.3.1 evaluate for writing traits

Teach/Model   Remind students that some of their writing for school will be evaluated using a chart called a *rubric*. Have students look at the rubric on the next page. Explain that the rubric describes what a writer has to do to earn a score from 1 to 4.

Guided Practice   Read aloud the directions to Part A and the Student Model. Ask students to listen without looking at the page. Then ask students to read the model and the teacher's comments, explaining that the teacher's comments show what a teacher might look for when evaluating an essay of explanation. Encourage students to state the topic of the essay in their own words. Ask students to notice how the writer organizes the ideas in his essay, and what information he includes to make the essay interesting. Have students identify the transition words the writer uses and determine if the writer clearly described the order of events.

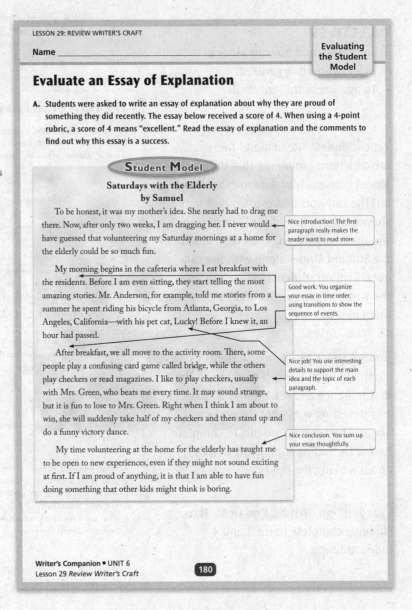

LESSON 29: REVIEW WRITER'S CRAFT

Name _____

Evaluating the Student Model

Evaluate an Essay of Explanation

A. Students were asked to write an essay of explanation about why they are proud of something they did recently. The essay below received a score of 4. When using a 4-point rubric, a score of 4 means "excellent." Read the essay of explanation and the comments to find out why this essay is a success.

Student Model

Saturdays with the Elderly
by Samuel

To be honest, it was my mother's idea. She nearly had to drag me there. Now, after only two weeks, I am dragging her. I never would have guessed that volunteering my Saturday mornings at a home for the elderly could be so much fun.

Nice introduction! The first paragraph really makes the reader want to read more.

My morning begins in the cafeteria where I eat breakfast with the residents. Before I am even sitting, they start telling the most amazing stories. Mr. Anderson, for example, told me stories from a summer he spent riding his bicycle from Atlanta, Georgia, to Los Angeles, California—with his pet cat, Lucky! Before I knew it, an hour had passed.

Good work. You organize your essay in time order, using transitions to show the sequence of events.

After breakfast, we all move to the activity room. There, some people play a confusing card game called bridge, while the others play checkers or read magazines. I like to play checkers, usually with Mrs. Green, who beats me every time. It may sound strange, but it is fun to lose to Mrs. Green. Right when I think I am about to win, she will suddenly take half of my checkers and then stand up and do a funny victory dance.

Nice job! You use interesting details to support the main idea and the topic of each paragraph.

My time volunteering at the home for the elderly has taught me to be open to new experiences, even if they might not sound exciting at first. If I am proud of anything, it is that I am able to have fun doing something that other kids might think is boring.

Nice conclusion. You sum up your essay thoughtfully.

Writer's Companion • UNIT 6
Lesson 29 *Review Writer's Craft*

180

WRITER'S STRATEGY: USING INTERESTING DETAILS

Point out the details the writer uses to support the main idea and the topic of each paragraph. Guide students in identifying the main idea of the essay by pointing out the topic sentence of the first paragraph. Then ask students to identify the details that show why the writer has so much fun. Point out that the writer makes these details interesting by making them vivid and humorous. Tell students that instead of just saying the residents told amazing stories, he adds details from the stories, such as the pet cat Lucky, to show how amazing the stories are.

© Harcourt

Evaluate an Essay of Explanation

OBJECTIVES
- To find out why one student model received a score of 2 on a 4-point rubric
- To use a rubric to evaluate an essay of explanation

Teach/Model Tell students that this Student Model received a score of 2 on a 4-point rubric. Read the Student Model aloud. As students listen, have them think about how the essay could be improved.

Guided Practice Ask students to discuss the strengths and weaknesses they noticed as they listened to the model. Then have students read the Student Model and the teacher's comments. Have students use the teacher's comments to identify the areas that need improvement. Guide students in discussing how the parts of the essay could be improved. For example, point to the introduction and ask students to discuss what details the writer could add to make the introduction complete. Suggest to students that the writer might add a detail that explains how she feels about learning to play the piano.

Independent Writing Practice Explain how to use the rubric at the bottom of the page. Then have students complete it independently to show what score they would have given the explanatory essay on page 179.

LESSON 29: REVIEW WRITER'S CRAFT

Name _____

Evaluating the Student Model

B. This essay received a score of 2. Why did it get a low score?

Student Model

The End, at Last
by Alexandra

I can play the piano.

At first, I had difficulty reading and playing the notes at the same time. I became familiar with the piece of music, and it actually sounded like my left hand and my right hand were playing from the same sheet of music!

When I am practicing, I sometimes get distracted and lose my concentration. To me it is easier to start at the beginning than to start from the middle. As a result, it was very difficult for me to reach the end of the piece.

It took a long time, but all the practice paid off.

Comments:
- You should include a whole paragraph that introduces your topic.
- You organized this paragraph by putting the events in time order but need more transition words to make the sequence of events more clear.
- These details do not support your topic very well. Find others to use.
- You conclude your essay, but you should use more details to sum up the topic.

C. What score would you give the essay? Put a number on each line.

	4	3	2	1
Ideas _____	☐ The writing is completely focused on a topic that is supported by strong, specific details.	☐ The writing is somewhat focused on a topic that is supported by details.	☐ The writing is related to the topic and has few supporting details.	☐ The writing is not related to the topic and has no supporting details.
Organization _____	☐ The ideas are in a logical sequence. Transition words make the relationships clear.	☐ The sequence is mostly clear. Some transition words are used.	☐ The sequence is unclear in some places. Few or no transition words are used.	☐ There is little or no sequence. No transition words are used.
Conventions _____	☐ All irregular verbs, contractions, and adverbs are used correctly.	☐ There are few errors in the use of irregular verbs, contractions, or adverbs.	☐ There are some errors in the use of irregular verbs, contractions, or adverbs.	☐ There are many errors in the use of irregular verbs, contractions, and adverbs.

SHARING AND DISCUSSING

After students have completed Part C, have them share their evaluations with a partner. For each row in the rubric, have students read the score and discuss how the writer could improve the essay. Encourage students to brainstorm specific supporting details and transition words that the writer could add. Challenge students to edit the Student Model so that it would earn a higher score if it were evaluated again using the same rubric.

© Harcourt

Extended Writing/Test Prep

OBJECTIVES
- To apply ideas and conventions in a long piece of writing
- To select a topic and begin the prewriting process for a writing assignment

Teach/Model Tell students that the first two pages of the lesson will give them an opportunity to select a topic for a long piece of writing. Explain that they should follow the steps of the writing process. Read aloud the introduction to Part A. Tell students they will have a choice of responding to a writing prompt, continuing a piece of writing they began earlier in the unit, or choosing a new topic.

Guided Practice Review the writing forms covered in the unit. Have students read the call-outs for each Student Model in the lesson where the form was taught:
- Paragraph of Explanation: Lesson 26, Page 161
- Paragraph of Historical Information: Lesson 27, Page 167
- How-to Paragraph: Lesson 28, Page 173
- An Essay of Explanation: Lesson 29, Page 179

Independent Writing Practice Have students begin the prewriting process by completing Part B independently.

Extended Writing/Test Prep

On the first two pages of this lesson, you will use what you have learned about topic sentences and details, fact and opinion, and sequence of ideas to write a longer work.

A. Read the three choices below. Put a star by the writing activity you would like to do.

1. Respond to a Writing Prompt

   Writing Situation: Everyone has succeeded at something.

   Directions for Writing: Think about something that you have done successfully. Now write an essay of explanation that explains how you succeeded. Tell your story in sequence and use details and examples.

2. Choose one of the pieces of writing you started in this unit:
   - a paragraph of explanation (page 160)
   - a paragraph of historical information (page 166)
   - a how-to paragraph (page 172)

   Revise and expand your draft into a complete piece of writing. Use what you have learned about ideas and conventions.

3. Choose a topic you would like to write about. You may write a paragraph or essay of explanation, a paragraph of historical information, or a how-to paragraph. Be sure to support your topic with details. Use facts and opinions when they are appropriate. Also remember to put your ideas in sequence.

B. Use the space below and on the next page to plan your writing.

TOPIC: _____

WRITING FORM: _____

HOW I WILL ORGANIZE MY WRITING: _____

_____

_____

_____

SHARING AND DISCUSSING

After students have completed Part B, have them share their responses in small groups. Encourage students to examine the ways that using different writing forms will change the way they organize their writing. Ask students to help each other plan their writing by discussing what they would like to learn about each other's topics. Then have students discuss which graphic organizers might be best for the writing forms. Allow students to make changes to their writing plans based on their discussions.

© Harcourt

Extended Writing/Test Prep

OBJECTIVES

- To use a graphic organizer to plan a piece of writing
- To complete a long piece of writing independently

Standard: LA.5.3.2.1 use a pre-writing plan

Teach/Model Have students choose a graphic organizer to help them plan their writing. Explain that they can use an organizer from the lessons in the unit, or they can choose a new one. Model using the organizer from Page 172 to put ideas in sequence for a how-to essay.

Guided Practice Ask students to copy the organizer they chose into the space provided in Part C. Tell students that they should not worry about spelling and grammar during the prewriting process. Explain that their primary goal is to brainstorm and organize ideas.

Independent Writing **Draft, Revise, Publish** Instruct students to work independently to build their first drafts using the ideas from their organizers. After they have completed their drafts, tell them to revise their work. Remind them to add details and to proofread.

LESSON 30: WRITING TEST PRACTICE

Name ______________________

Extended Writing/Test Prep

C. In the space below, draw a graphic organizer that will help you plan your writing. Fill in the graphic organizer. Write additional notes on the lines below.

Notes

____

____

____

____

____

____

____

D. Do your writing on another sheet of paper.

183 Writer's Companion ▪ UNIT 6
Lesson 30 *Writing Test Practice*

Reaching All Learners

BELOW LEVEL

Encourage students to use a graphic organizer from the unit when they plan their writing. Students who expand a previous draft may choose to build on the organizer they used earlier in the unit.

ADVANCED

Challenge students writing how-to essays to suppose that they are writing for a younger audience. Have them make sure they use details that a younger brother or sister would understand.

ENGLISH-LANGUAGE LEARNERS

Meet with students in small groups. Have students work together to build sentences using the words and phrases from their organizers.

Answering Multiple-Choice Questions

OBJECTIVES
- To become familiar with test items that require interpreting a graphic organizer
- To demonstrate understanding of sequence

Teach/Model Read aloud the directions for Part A. Explain that this page will help students practice for tests that ask about prewriting plans. Read aloud the question for Item 1. Model answering Item 1 by asking, for each answer choice: **Does this detail describe what to do immediately after applying glue to the pictures?**

Guided Practice Guide students to complete Item 2 by first reviewing Monica's topic. Tell students that a good strategy for this question is to read each answer choice and see if it matches the topic.

Independent Practice Have students complete Item 3 independently. Ask volunteers to share their answers and explain the strategies they used.

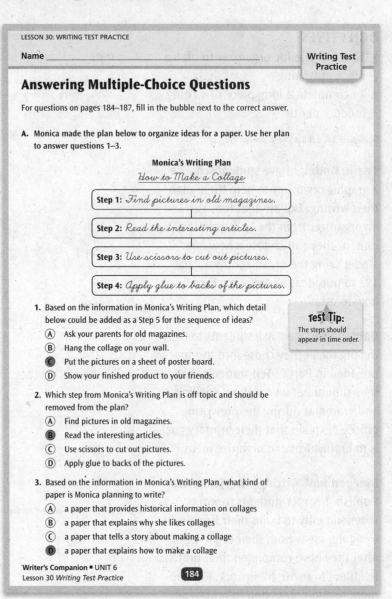

USING ACADEMIC LANGUAGE

Explain to students that most tests contain academic language. These are words and phrases they might not see in everyday reading. Before asking students to complete the test items above, review the term *writing plan*. Explain that a graphic organizer is a kind of writing plan that people use very often. Explain that the writing plans on tests show how other students have organized their writing. Remind students that the questions on the test will ask them to think about how another student planned his or her writing.

© Harcourt

Answering Multiple-Choice Questions (cont.)

OBJECTIVES
- To become familiar with a multiple-choice format that involves reading a passage
- To distinguish fact and opinion

Teach/Model Read aloud the directions to Part B. Tell students that this page will help them practice answering multiple-choice questions about a passage. Read aloud the passage and Item 1. Model answering the item by rereading each sentence aloud. Use the Test Tip to come up with the following question: **Does this sentence tell how the writer feels about shoveling snow?**

Guided Practice Guide students in completing Item 2. Point out that the ideas in the paragraph are organized in time order. Lead students to see that Sentence 5 does not follow the sequence of events. Then have them identify where Sentence 5 could be placed so that the events are in time order.

Independent Practice Have students complete Item 3 independently. Have students share their answers with a partner and describe how they chose their answers.

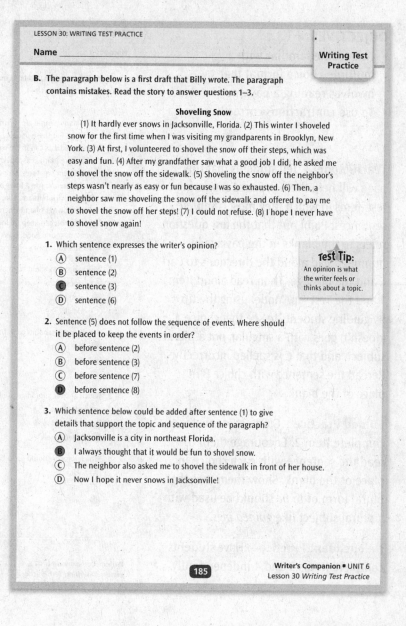

LESSON 30: WRITING TEST PRACTICE

Name _____

Writing Test Practice

B. The paragraph below is a first draft that Billy wrote. The paragraph contains mistakes. Read the story to answer questions 1–3.

Shoveling Snow
(1) It hardly ever snows in Jacksonville, Florida. (2) This winter I shoveled snow for the first time when I was visiting my grandparents in Brooklyn, New York. (3) At first, I volunteered to shovel the snow off their steps, which was easy and fun. (4) After my grandfather saw what a good job I did, he asked me to shovel the snow off the sidewalk. (5) Shoveling the snow off the neighbor's steps wasn't nearly as easy or fun because I was so exhausted. (6) Then, a neighbor saw me shoveling the snow off the sidewalk and offered to pay me to shovel the snow off her steps! (7) I could not refuse. (8) I hope I never have to shovel snow again!

1. Which sentence expresses the writer's opinion?
   - (A) sentence (1)
   - (B) sentence (2)
   - (C) sentence (3)
   - (D) sentence (6)

Test Tip: An opinion is what the writer feels or thinks about a topic.

2. Sentence (5) does not follow the sequence of events. Where should it be placed to keep the events in order?
   - (A) before sentence (2)
   - (B) before sentence (3)
   - (C) before sentence (7)
   - (D) before sentence (8)

3. Which sentence below could be added after sentence (1) to give details that support the topic and sequence of the paragraph?
   - (A) Jacksonville is a city in northeast Florida.
   - (B) I always thought that it would be fun to shovel snow.
   - (C) The neighbor also asked me to shovel the sidewalk in front of her house.
   - (D) Now I hope it never snows in Jacksonville!

185

Writer's Companion • UNIT 6
Lesson 30 *Writing Test Practice*

ASSESSING STUDENT RESPONSES

Have students who consistently answer test items incorrectly explain the process they use to answer questions. Make sure that students are rereading passages before answering questions. Also make sure that students understand how the sentences in the passage are numbered. Remind students that the sentence number appears at the beginning of the sentence, not at the end. Tell students that for the questions in Items 1 and 2, they should also reread each sentence that is an answer choice.

© Harcourt

Answering Multiple-Choice Questions (cont.)

OBJECTIVES
- To become familiar with a multiple-choice format that involves reading a passage
- To use contractions correctly

Teach/Model   Tell students that this page will help them practice answering test items in which they must complete sentences. Point out that the test question refers to the blanks in the passage by number. Read aloud the directions to Part C and the passage. Then read aloud Item 1 and the Test Tip. Model using the tip by guiding students to see that choice *A* (doesn't) goes with a singular, not a plural subject, and that *C* is spelled incorrectly. Reread the sentence with choice *B* in place of the blank.

Guided Practice   Guide students to complete Item 2. Encourage them to read the sentence with each choice in place of the blank. Show them that the plural form of *to be* should be used with a plural subject like *guinea pigs*.

Independent Practice   Have students complete Items 3 and 4 independently.

LESSON 30: WRITING TEST PRACTICE

Name _____

Writing Test Practice

C. Read the paragraph, "Rats!" Choose the word or words that correctly completes questions 1–4.

Rats!

Many people are terrified by rats and could never imagine keeping one as a pet. What these people ____(1)____ know is that rats are rodents and that some rodents can make wonderful pets. Guinea pigs are the best example, and there are many reasons why they make great pets. First of all, they are quite intelligent creatures. Guinea pigs ____(2)____ so smart that, like cats, you can train them to use a litter box. Secondly, guinea pigs are very social and love to play with humans. Like a dog or a cat, a guinea pig will even ____(3)____ lick its owner's hand when it is petted. Finally, guinea pigs don't need a lot of space. You can keep them comfortable in a medium-sized cage. If all these reasons sound good, then maybe ____(4)____ ready to let a rodent—or at least a guinea pig—into your home!

1. Which answer should go in blank (1)?
   - (A) doesn't
   - (B) don't
   - (C) do'nt

2. Which answer should go in blank (2)?
   - (A) are
   - (B) be
   - (C) is

3. Which answer should go in blank (3)?
   - (A) affection
   - (B) affectionate
   - (C) affectionately

4. Which answer should go in blank (4)?
   - (A) your
   - (B) your'e
   - (C) you're

Test Tip:
A contraction is two words combined into one with an apostrophe (').

The apostrophe fills in the place where there are missing letters.

have + not = haven't

Reaching All Learners

BELOW LEVEL
Help students restate what the questions ask them to do. For example: **Item 1 is asking me to choose a word for blank 1. Only one of the words is correct for the sentence. I need to choose the word that fits the sentence.**

ADVANCED
Challenge students to write their own tests. Have students write multiple-choice questions for sentences that they have written. Ask them to use the test on this page as a model. Have students trade tests with a partner.

ENGLISH-LANGUAGE LEARNERS
Read aloud each test item. For each answer choice, read the completed sentence from the passage. Point out the key differences in each choice. For example: **Note that the apostrophe in Item 4B is after the** *r*.

Answering Multiple-Choice Questions (cont.)

OBJECTIVES

- To become familiar with test items that require identifying the type of mistake in a sentence
- To use adjectives and adverbs correctly

Standard: LA.5.3.5.3 use agreement

Teach/Model Tell students that some multiple-choice questions will ask them to identify the type of mistake that was made in a sentence. Read aloud the directions to Part D and then Item 1. Model completing the item by reading aloud the answer choices, then looking back at the underlined section. Guide students to see that the section does not contain a punctuation or capitalization error. Then point out that *brought,* not *brung,* is the correct past form of the verb *to bring,* so they should choose choice *C.*

Guided Practice Guide students to complete Item 2. Have students discuss whether the underlined phrase is punctuated correctly or if the word *Mississippi* is spelled correctly. Then remind students that if a proper noun has more than one word, each important word begins with a capital letter.

Independent Practice . Have students complete Items 3 and 4 independently.

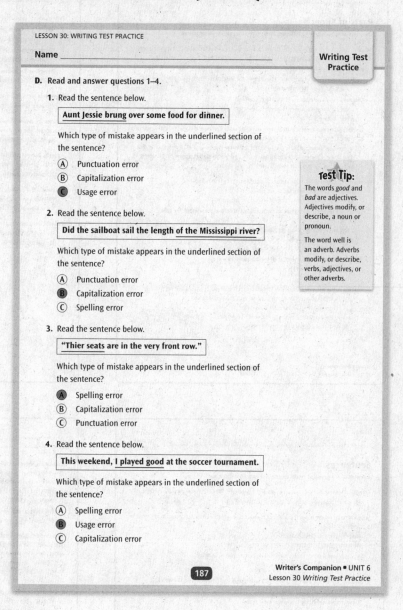

SHARING AND DISCUSSING

Direct students to work with a partner to share their answers to Items 3 and 4. Once students have identified the type of mistake, ask them to describe the particular error. For example, say: **The word *their* is spelled incorrectly.** Encourage students to discuss the strategies they used to answer the questions on this page. Then prompt them to discuss whether these strategies could be used to complete the other types of test questions in the lesson.

© Harcourt

Writer's Grammar Guide

Parts of Speech

The parts of speech are the different kinds of words you use in sentences.

Nouns are words that name people, places, and things. They can name things that can be seen or touched. They also can name things that cannot be seen or touched.

Proper nouns are nouns that name a special person, place, or thing.

Mr. Henderson (person) wants to sail down the **Mississippi River** (place) in the world-famous **Old Time Steamboat** (thing).

Common nouns name any person, place, or thing.

I just saw my **aunt** (person) walking to **town** (place) and holding her favorite **umbrella** (thing) in case it rains.

Compound nouns are made up of more than one word. Compound nouns may be separated by hyphens, combined to make a new word, or separated by a space.

When I was young, I always got my sisters' **hand-me-downs** instead of new clothes. But I didn't care. I knew when I was an adult, I'd just drive my **station wagon** to the store and pick out new clothes that I bought with my own money.

Verbs are words that show an action or tell what something is or is like.

Matt and Lauren **flew** to San Francisco. (action)
Liz **was** delighted to see them. (tells what the subject is)

Verbs have **tenses**. Tenses show *when* an action takes place–the present, the past, or the future.

I **sing** in the school chorus. (present tense)
I **sang** in the school chorus last year. (past tense)
I **will sing** in the school chorus next year. (future tense)

Action verbs tell what someone is doing, has done, or will do.

Jack **grew** a wonderful beanstalk.
He **will climb** up it.

Linking verbs tell how someone or something feels or thinks or what a person, place, or thing is like. Linking verbs are often forms of *to be*, such as *am*, *is*, and *are*.

Jack **is** very happy about his giant beanstalk.
Jack **seemed** surprised by the height of the beanstalk.
It **looked** huge in front of his small house.

Pronouns are words that take the place of nouns. There are several types of pronouns.

Subject pronouns are pronouns that act as the subject of a sentence.

The Barrymore family moved last week. **They** put all of their furniture inside a huge truck.

Object pronouns are pronouns that receive the action of a verb.

Where is that suitcase? I can't remember where I put **it**.

Possessive pronouns are pronouns that show ownership.

The bat found **its** new home in the attic.

Adjectives are words that describe, or **modify**, a noun or a pronoun.

You are a **funny** person because you tell **clever** jokes.

Articles are a special type of adjective. *A*, *an*, and *the* are articles. Articles come before nouns, and they answer the question *Which one*?

An island in a lake is **the** place where I would like to be.

Adverbs also are words that describe, or **modify**. Most adverbs describe verbs. Sometimes adverbs describe adjectives or other adverbs.

The students **quickly** headed to the cafeteria. They were **very** hungry for lunch.

Prepositions are words that link a noun or pronoun to another word in the sentence.

Will you have lunch **with** me this afternoon?
We will eat **at** the table **in** the corner **of** the lunchroom.

Conjunctions are words that join words or groups of words. **And**, **but**, and **or** are conjunctions.

We could eat at noon, **or** we could eat at one o'clock.
Jana **or** Maria will join us.

Sentences

A sentence is a group of words that tells a complete thought.

Complete sentences have both a subject and a predicate. They express a complete thought.

Kara and I went to visit the Statue of Liberty last week.

Subjects name whom or what a sentence is about. The subject of a sentence usually is a noun or a pronoun.

Barney joined in the applause.
He enjoys going to concerts.

A **compound subject** names two or more people, places, or things.

Ina and Maria are sisters.

Predicates tell what action the subject of a sentence does. The predicate has a verb in it.

The audience **gave the band an ovation**.

A **compound predicate** has two or more verbs.

The sisters **dance and sing**.

Simple sentences are made up of a single independent clause. Simple sentences can be short or long. They can have compound subjects or compound predicates. Below, the subjects are underlined once. The verbs are underlined twice.

One subject and verb: The sun rose.
Compound subject: The sun and clouds were in the sky.
Compound verb: The moon rose and shone last night.
Compound subject and compound verb: The boy and girl thought it over and decided to bring raincoats.

Compound sentences are made up of two or more independent clauses. The independent clauses are usually joined by a comma and a conjunction such as *and, but, for, nor, so,* or *yet.*

Flags were displayed all over the arena, **but** the Olympic athletes had not yet appeared.

Fragments are incomplete sentences. You correct them and make them complete by adding a subject or a predicate.

FRAGMENT: Finding a place to sit.
COMPLETE: Finding a place to sit **is part of the game of "Musical Chairs."**

FRAGMENT: Bought a red car.
COMPLETE: **The Jackson family** bought a red car.

Combining sentences makes a single sentence out of two or more sentences. It makes writing flow and keeps it interesting. Use a conjunction to join the subject and predicate parts of the sentence or to join parts of the subject or predicate.

Two short sentences: I like riding on roller coasters. I enjoy Ferris wheels.
Combined sentence: I like riding on roller coasters, and I enjoy Ferris wheels.

Two short sentences: Robin enjoys jogging. Fern enjoys jogging.
Combined sentence: Robin and Fern enjoy jogging.

Run-On Sentences A run-on sentence puts two ideas together incorrectly. Run-on sentences sometimes have a comma in them, and sometimes they have no punctuation. The two ideas should be either joined or separated by correct punctuation.

RUN-ON: The girls ran into the gym, they had to do fifty sit-ups on the mats.
CORRECTED: The girls ran into the gym. **They** had to do fifty sit-ups on the mats.
(separated by an end mark, such as a period, question mark, or exclamation point)

RUN-ON: I prefer to climb the rope I'm always the first one in line.
CORRECTED: I prefer to climb the rope, **and** I'm always the first one in line. (joined with a comma and a conjunction)

© Harcourt

Writer's Grammar Guide

Capitalization and Punctuation

Capitalization is used to emphasize the important words in a sentence. It helps make sentences easier for the reader to understand.

First Word in a Sentence The first word in a sentence is always capitalized.

Can you help me find my house key?

Proper nouns, as well as the pronoun *I*, are always capitalized.

My aunt **Harriet** in **Detroit** and **I** talked on the phone last night.

Punctuation refers to symbols, or marks, that help a reader know how to read a sentence.

End Marks are used at the end of a complete sentence.

Periods are used to end declarative sentences, which make a statement. They also are used to end imperative sentences that make a polite request.

There is a meeting of the track club after school today**.**

Please come, if you are interested in the club**.**

Question marks are used to end interrogative sentences, which ask a question.

Will you come to the meeting**?**

Exclamation points are used to end sentences and short statements that show strong emotion.

Give that back**!**

No**!** Stop that**!**

Commas are used to show a brief pause. Here are a few rules to remember about commas.

Commas are used with **compound sentences**.

Jana and Dot wrote stories, and then they decided to publish them.

Commas are used to separate **items in a series** of three or more items.

The colors of the American flag are red, white, and blue.

Commas are used to **separate adjectives that are equal in their importance**. You can test this rule by changing the order of the adjectives. If the meaning of the sentence is unchanged, the adjectives are equal in importance.

Yuri chose a long, blue jacket to wear to the dance.

(You can also write *Yuri chose a blue, long jacket to wear to the dance* without changing the meaning of the sentence.)

Commas are *not* used to separate adjectives that must stay in a specific order.

Jane wore a bright yellow shirt.

(You cannot write *Jane wore a yellow bright shirt.*)

Commas are used sometimes **to introduce ideas in a sentence**.

First, we will need to beat two eggs.

Colons are used in several situations.

To introduce a list--The following visitors attended the modern art exhibit today: school children, foreign travelers, and senior citizens.

To give the time--It is 4:08 P.M.

To begin a business letter--To Whom it May Concern:

Quotation Marks are used to show when people are speaking. Periods and commas are always placed inside final quotation marks.

Tamara said, **"**I have had enough hiking for today.**"**

"We had a good time, though,**"** she admitted.

Italics give special emphasis to words. They are also used for certain kinds of titles, such as the titles of books.

The word *illuminate* comes from a Latin root that means "to light."

Oliver Twist is just one of Charles Dickens's books that has been made into a film.

Apostrophes are used to show ownership. Apostrophes are also used in contractions.

Add an apostrophe and an *s* to show the possessive of most singular nouns, even when the noun ends in an *s*.

The mitt of the baseball player = The baseball player**'s** mitt

The view from the lens = The lens**'s** view

Add only an apostrophe to show the possessive of plural nouns that end in *-s* or *-es*.

The color of the blueberries = The blueberries**'** color

Add an apostrophe and an *s* to show the possessive of plural nouns that do not end in *s* or *es*.

The project of the children = The children**'s** project

Apostrophes can take the place of a missing letter or letters. (See **Contractions**)

are not = aren**'**t

I am = I**'**m

he would = he**'**d

Abbreviations are shortened versions of words or phrases. They are used for titles, the names of states, and measurements. Most, but not all, abbreviations end in periods.

Mister = **Mr.**

New Jersey = **NJ** (no period)

Avenue = **Ave.**

teaspoons = **tsp.**

millimeters = **mm** (no period)

Usage

Usage refers to how words and sentences are used in speaking or writing.

Plural Nouns The plural form refers to more than one person, place or thing. There are two kinds of plural nouns—**regular** and **irregular**.

To form the plural of a regular noun, you add *–s* or *–es*. Some nouns change their spelling when you create the plural form.

I have three different **rings** I like to wear.

Usually, I keep them inside their **boxes**.

I only take them out to wear them to **parties**.

Irregular plurals have their own unique spellings. It is best to memorize them or to use a dictionary to check their spelling.

There were four **children** in the kitchen.

The **women** of the early 1900s fought for the right to vote.

Do you know the song "Three Blind **Mice**"?

Possessive Nouns are used to show ownership.

Add an apostrophe and an *s* to show the possessive of most singular nouns, even when the noun ends in an *s*.

The music of the singer = The singer**'s** music

The desk of the boss = The boss**'s** desk

Add only an apostrophe to show the possessive of plural nouns that end in *s* or *es*.

The meeting of the coaches = The coaches**'** meeting

Add an apostrophe and an *s* in order to show the possessive of plural nouns that do not end in *s* or *es*.

The whiteness of the teeth = The teeth**'s** whiteness

Contractions are shortened versions of words and phrases. Contractions are used more often in speech than in writing. They are formed by using apostrophes to show where the missing letters are located.

You can use a verb plus the word *not* to form a contraction.

Ted and Mary **aren't** going to the soccer game today.

They **couldn't** get a ride to the stadium.

You can use a pronoun plus the word *will* to form a contraction.

We'll meet you outside the ticket booth.

Do you think **you'll** be able to find us?

Writer's Grammar Guide

You can use a pronoun or noun plus the verb *be* to form a contraction.

Arlene's saving seats for us.

She's also going to get some popcorn for everyone.

You can use a pronoun or noun plus the verb *would* to form a contraction.

I'd like to get there early to get a good seat.

Who'd like to come with me?

Subject-Verb Agreement means that a verb must agree with its subject in number. You should make sure that both the subject and the verb are either singular or plural.

INCORRECT: My sister run to the playground in the park.

CORRECT: My sister **runs** to the playground in the park.

INCORRECT: We moves back and forth in time to the music.

CORRECT: We **move** back and forth in time to the music.

Pronoun Agreement Pronouns must agree with their *antecedents*, or the words they refer back to.

A personal pronoun must agree with its antecedent in person, number, and gender. *Person* means the person speaking, the person spoken to, or the person spoken about. *Number* means singular or plural. *Gender* means masculine or feminine.

INCORRECT: Jonah told Daphne to bring a backpack with them.

CORRECT: Jonah told Daphne to bring a backpack with **her**.

INCORRECT: Travelers know that you can choose from many destinations.

CORRECT: Travelers know that they can choose from many destinations.

Double Negatives A double negative is the use of two negative words in a sentence. Avoid double negatives. They change the meaning of the sentence.

DOUBLE NEGATIVE: I don't have no more money.

CORRECTION: I have no more money.

DOUBLE NEGATIVE: No one did nothing about cleaning up.

CORRECTION: No one did anything about cleaning up.

Irregular Verbs Many common verbs have unusual, or *irregular*, forms in the past tense. These verbs are irregular because they do not add *–ed* or *–d* to form the past tense.

Sometimes, irregular verbs have the same past and past participle forms.

PRESENT FORM: bring; pay; lose

PAST FORM: brought; paid; lost

PAST PARTICIPLE: (have) brought; (have) paid; (have) lost

Sometimes, irregular verbs have the same present, past, and past participle forms.

PRESENT FORM: cost; hurt; put

PAST FORM: cost; hurt; put

PAST PARTICIPLE: (have) cost; (have) hurt; (have) put

Sometimes, irregular verbs have present, past, and past participle forms that change in other ways.

PRESENT FORM: run; sing; wear

PAST FORM: ran; sang; wore

PAST PARTICIPLE: (have) run; (have) sung; (have) worn

Tricky Words

The meanings, sounds, and spelling of some words have to be memorized.

Homographs and Homophones

Homographs are words that are spelled the same way but have different meanings.

Homophones are words that sound the same, but they are spelled differently and have different meanings.

The italicized words in these sentences are spelled the same but have different meanings.

HOMOGRAPHS: I felt *fine* today after I paid the overdue *fine* for my library book.

HOMOGRAPHS: I can't *bear* to see another *bear* in this zoo.

The italicized words in these sentences sound the same but have different meanings and spellings.

HOMOPHONES: I can't *bear* to feel too much sun on my *bare* arms.

HOMOPHONES: Look over *there*. Ingrid and Maude are cooking *their* breakfast over a campfire. *They're* making scrambled eggs.

Spelling Tips

Some spelling words have to be memorized. Others follow patterns that can be applied to several different words.

Memorize words that are easily misspelled by keeping a list in a notebook. Learn their meanings to help you memorize how they are spelled.

EASILY MISSPELLED WORDS: absence; aisle; calendar; curious; eighth; foreign; interfere; knowledge; nuisance; receipt; succeed; tomorrow

Plurals The plural form of most nouns is formed by adding *–s* or *–es* to the singular form.

My new friend John brought his **friends** to my house.

For words that end in *–s, -ss, -x, -z, -sh,* or *–ch,* add *–es* to create the plural form.

atlas; atlases
compass; compasses
fox; foxes
waltz; waltzes
match; matches

For words that end in *–o* preceded by a consonant, add either *–es* or *–s* to create the plural form.

tomato; tomatoes
piano; pianos

For words that end in *–o* preceded by a vowel, add *–s* to create the plural form.

ratio; ratios

For words that end in *–y* preceded by a consonant, change the *–y* to an *–i* and add *–es* to create the plural form.

party; parties

For words that end in *–y* preceded by a vowel, add *–s* to create the plural form.

monkey; monkeys

For words that end in *–f* or *–ff,* add *–s* to create the plural form or change *–f* to *–v* and add *–es* to create the plural form.

cliff; cliffs
leaf; leaves

For words that end in *–fe,* change *–f* to *–v* and add *–es* to create the plural form.

knife; knives

Prefixes The spelling of a word usually does not change when a prefix is added.

dis- + appoint = disappoint

re- + appear = reappear

Suffixes The spelling of some words changes when a suffix is added.

For words that end in *–y* preceded by a consonant, change the *–y* to an *–i* and add the suffix.

happy changes to **happiness**

For words that end in *–y* preceded by a vowel, simply add the suffix.

enjoy becomes **enjoyment**

When a suffix beginning with a vowel is added to a word that ends in *–e,* the *–e* is usually dropped when the suffix is added.

believe becomes **believable**

When a suffix beginning with a consonant is added to a word that ends in *–e,* simply add the suffix.

price becomes **priceless**

Spelling Rules help you learn a pattern that you can apply to several words.

The most famous spelling rule is "*i* before *e* except after *c,* or when sounded like *a,* as in *neighbor* and *weigh.*"

ie words: believe; siege

ei words: deceive; receipt

There are some exceptions to this rule that must be memorized.

leisure; foreign; their; weird

Writer's Companion
Writer's Grammar Guide

Student Edition Appendices

Proofreading Strategies

Written English follows certain **conventions,** or rules, that make it clear for readers. As you proofread, look for errors in your use of conventions. Once you have revised your writing to improve organization, tone, and word use, you can polish it in the proofreading stage.

Wait before proofreading. If you can, avoid proofreading your writing immediately. Set your draft aside, and return to it with a fresh eye.

Proofread in stages. You might want to follow these steps:

1. Read your composition for meaning. Notice whether you have indented paragraphs and whether your sentences make sense. Correct any fragments and run-ons.
2. Next, look at grammar, usage, capitalization, and punctuation. Think about the rules you have learned, and apply them to your own writing.
3. Last, focus on spelling. Take the time to look up any words that might be misspelled in a dictionary.

Proofread with a partner. A classmate may see problems that you have overlooked.

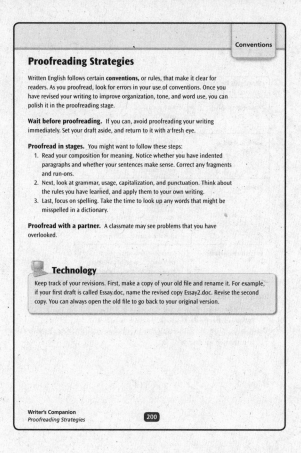

Technology

Keep track of your revisions. First, make a copy of your old file and rename it. For example, if your first draft is called Essay.doc, name the revised copy Essay2.doc. Revise the second copy. You can always open the old file to go back to your original version.

Writer's Companion
Proofreading Strategies

200

Proofreading Checklist

This checklist will help you as you proofread your work.

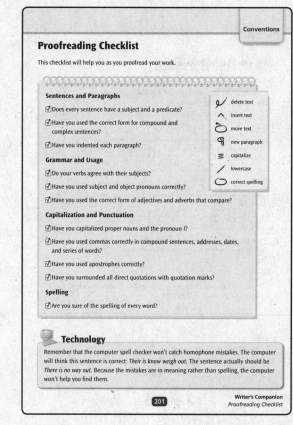

Sentences and Paragraphs

☑ Does every sentence have a subject and a predicate?

☑ Have you used the correct form for compound and complex sentences?

☑ Have you indented each paragraph?

Grammar and Usage

☑ Do your verbs agree with their subjects?

☑ Have you used subject and object pronouns correctly?

☑ Have you used the correct form of adjectives and adverbs that compare?

Capitalization and Punctuation

☑ Have you capitalized proper nouns and the pronoun *I*?

☑ Have you used commas correctly in compound sentences, addresses, dates, and series of words?

☑ Have you used apostrophes correctly?

☑ Have you surrounded all direct quotations with quotation marks?

Spelling

☑ Are you sure of the spelling of every word?

delete text
insert text
move text
new paragraph
capitalize
lowercase
correct spelling

Technology

Remember that the computer spell checker won't catch homophone mistakes. The computer will think this sentence is correct: *Their is know weigh out.* The sentence actually should be *There is no way out.* Because the mistakes are in meaning rather than spelling, the computer won't help you find them.

201

Writer's Companion
Proofreading Checklist

Presenting Your Work

Most writing is meant to reach an audience. The final writing stage is to publish your work, or present it to your readers. Here are some ideas that can help you connect your writing with your audience.

Publishing Ideas for Any Type of Writing

- Read it aloud.
- Place it in a class reading library or post it on a bulletin board.
- Have a partner read it silently.
- Send it to a friend as an e-mail attachment.

Publishing Ideas for Descriptive Writing

- Use music to enhance your writing. Record yourself reading to music.
- Take or find photographs to create an illustrated essay or magazine article.
- Use art materials to make a pictorial brochure.
- Make your writing the centerpiece of a collage, poster, or other artwork.

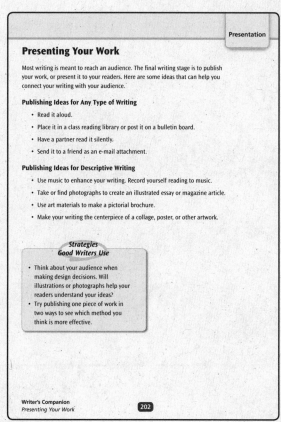

Strategies
Good Writers Use

- Think about your audience when making design decisions. Will illustrations or photographs help your readers understand your ideas?
- Try publishing one piece of work in two ways to see which method you think is more effective.

Writer's Companion
Presenting Your Work

202

Publishing Ideas for Narrative Writing

- Create an illustrated book for the classroom library.
- Direct a play or video based on your story.
- Share your story with students in another region by sending it as an e-mail attachment.
- Submit your writing to your school literary magazine.
- Enter your story in a writing contest.
- Include your story in a classroom anthology.

Publishing Ideas for Persuasive Writing

- Send your work as a letter to the editor of your school or local paper.
- Hold a classroom debate on the topic.
- Create a newsletter or pamphlet to distribute in your school or community.
- Give a speech to your class or to a school assembly.
- Post your work on your school's website.

Publishing Ideas for Expository Writing

- Collect class essays in an anthology with a broad topic, such as American history or biology.
- Make a poster for the school hallway.
- Use specialized software to create a multimedia report.
- Create a table display for the classroom or for a school fair.
- Take over as "teacher," and instruct your classmates.

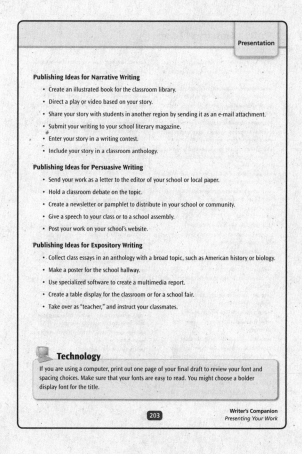

Technology

If you are using a computer, print out one page of your final draft to review your font and spacing choices. Make sure that your fonts are easy to read. You might choose a bolder display font for the title.

203

Writer's Companion
Presenting Your Work

Writer's Companion
Student Edition Appendices

Student Edition Appendices

Giving a Multimedia Presentation

Step 1
Reread your report. Choose information to show through photographs, a map, a poster, or other visual aids.

Step 2
Look in the library for audio or video recordings to accompany your report. Download from the Internet any images or sounds that you can use. Prepare any charts or graphs.

Step 3
Organize the equipment you need, such as a VCR, an audio player, or a computer.

Step 4
Plan and practice your presentation. Decide when to stop and what to show or play. Ask a classmate to assist you with equipment.

Step 5
Present your report with confidence. Speak loudly and clearly, looking at your audience. Answer questions at the end.

Strategies Good Writers Use

- Write legibly, or choose legible fonts.
- Leave adequate margins.
- Indent paragraphs.
- Put your name on your work.

Writer's Companion
Presenting Your Work
204

Strategies for Making an Oral Presentation	Applying the Strategies
Make note cards.	• Write each main idea with major details on a note card. Put your cards in order, and number them.
Use visual aids.	• Identify ideas to illustrate. Create pictures, charts, diagrams, music, video, or PowerPoint™ slides to add visual interest.
Practice.	• Practice in front of a mirror, a friend, or a family member, or tape your rehearsal. • Practice looking at your audience as you speak. Listeners will be more alert if you connect with them.
Present competently.	• Share your ideas with a firm and clear voice. Be prepared to answer questions from your audience.

Strategies for Listeners

- Identify the speaker's purpose, main idea, and point of view.
- Evaluate whether the speaker effectively supports the main idea.
- Determine if you agree with the speaker. What parts of the presentation do you like best? Which parts are less effective?

Writer's Companion
Presenting Your Work
205

Writer's Glossary of Terms

adjective: a word that describes a noun

adverb: a word that describes a verb, an adjective, or another adverb

autobiographical composition: a composition that tells about an event or events in the writer's life

autobiographical narrative: the writer describes an event that happened in his or her life

biography: a factual account about a real person's life

cause-and-effect paragraph: a paragraph that tells about something that happens and why it happens

character description paragraph: a paragraph that gives a clear picture of what someone is like, usually using sensory details

compare-and-contrast essay: an essay that tells how things are alike and different

descriptive paragraph: a paragraph that tells what something or someone is like

detail: a fact, event, or statement; details usually tell abut a main idea

draft: a first attempt at a piece of writing

essay: a piece of writing that is not a story, usually with a clear purpose for writing

essay of explanation: an essay that tells how something is done, what something is like, or how to do something

fact: something that is true

how-to paragraph: a paragraph that tells how to do something

journal entry: a daily record of the writer's observations written in the first person

letter: a written message to someone

letter of request: a letter asking someone to do something

main idea: what something is mostly about

narrative composition: a story; some stories are fictional, with made-up characters, setting, and plot

narrative paragraph: a paragraph that tells a story

news article: a story about current events that appears or might appear in a newspaper

notes: writing that records facts or ideas from a source of information

outline: a system of organizing information and notes

paragraph: a group of sentences with a single main idea or topic

paragraph of explanation: a paragraph that tells how something works or how or why something is done

paragraph of historical information: a paragraph that presents facts and data

personal response paragraph: a paragraph in which the writer gives an opinion on a topic, supporting that opinion with facts and examples

persuasive letter: a letter that tries to convince someone to do something or to think a certain way

persuasive paragraph: a paragraph that tries to convince someone to do something or to think a certain way

poem: a piece of writing, often with rhyme

predicate: what the subject of a sentence does or is like

purpose for writing: the reason why someone writes something

reason: why something happens or is true

rhyme: a system of writing in which the sounds of words are alike, usually in a poem

rubric: a guide for scoring or evaluating something

sensory detail: a detail that "speaks" to one of the senses—sight, sound, touch, smell, or taste

sequence: the order in which things happen

skit: a short play using characters and dialogue to tell a story

story: a made-up tale

subject: what a sentence is about

summary: a short piece of writing that wraps up the main points of a longer piece of writing

suspense story: a mystery in which readers are not sure what will happen

topic: what something is about

verb: a word that names an action

Writer's Companion
Writer's Glossary of Terms
206

Writer's Companion
Student Edition Appendices

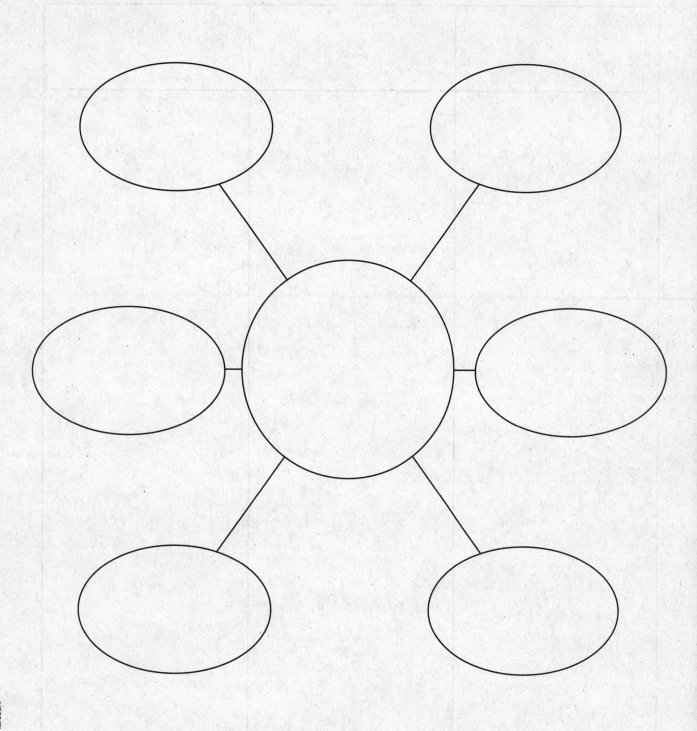

Three-Column Chart

Main Idea

Detail

Detail

Detail

Flow Chart

Venn Diagram

Cause-and-Effect Chart

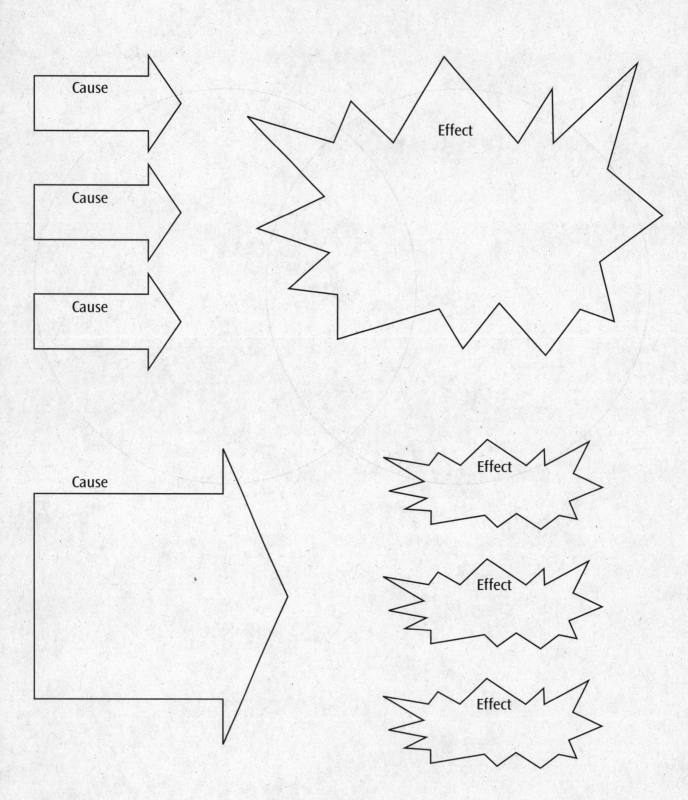

Cause

Cause

Cause

Effect

Cause

Effect

Effect

Effect

© Harcourt

Using Student Rubrics

A rubric is a tool a teacher can use to score a student's work. A rubric lists the criteria for evaluating the work, and it describes different levels of success in meeting those criteria. Rubrics are useful assessment tools for teachers, but they can be just as useful for students. In fact, rubrics can be powerful teaching tools.

Before Writing

- When you introduce students to a **new kind of writing** through a Student Writing Model, discuss the criteria used on the rubric, and ask students to decide how well the Student Writing Model meets each criterion. Have students add to the rubric other criteria they think are important.
- Before students attempt a new kind of writing, have them focus on the **criteria** listed on the rubric so that they have specific goals to aim for.

During Writing and Editing

- As students are **prewriting** and **drafting,** have them refer to the rubric for important writing traits that they need to include in their writing.
- When students are ready to **revise,** have them check their writing against the rubric to determine if there are any writing traits that they can improve.

After Writing

- The rubric can be used by individuals to **score their own writing** or by peers or small groups for peer assessment. Students can highlight the parts of the rubric that they believe apply to a piece of writing.
- Students can keep the marked rubric in their portfolios with the piece of writing it refers to. The marked rubrics will help students **see their progress** through the school year. In conferences with students and family members, you can refer to the rubrics to point out both strengths and weaknesses.

Guidelines for Interpreting Holistic Scores

Holistic scoring has been used for many years to evaluate writing samples. Many state writing assessments, for example, employ some form of holistic scoring. In holistic scoring, the reader takes several features into consideration—weighing and balancing strengths in one feature against weaknesses in another—to arrive at a single, overall score.

A 4-point Scoring Rubric for Writing can be found in this section and in the back matter of the Student Edition. The rubric defines the characteristics of performance for each of the four possible scores. This rubric is similar to those used in many state writing assessments. Unfortunately, the numbers—1, 2, 3, and 4—carry no intrinsic meaning. To help interpret holistic scores to parents, other teachers, or administrators, use the following guidelines.

© Harcourt

Score	Qualitative Label	Characteristics
4	Advanced	Students at this level exhibit superior performance. Their writing is thoughtful, organized, well developed, and fluent. They also exhibit consistent control of written language.
3	Proficient	Students at this level display solid performance. Their writing is mostly thoughtful and organized, moderately developed, and reasonably fluent. They may display a general control of written language.
2	Basic	Students at this level show uneven performance. Their writing is sometimes thoughtful and organized, mostly undeveloped, and lacking in fluency. They may display a lack of control of written language.
1	Limited	Students at this level exhibit very limited performance. Their writing is not thoughtful, often disorganized, usually undeveloped, and lacking in fluency. They may display great difficulty in controlling the conventions of written language.

What if your state or district uses a different rubric, say a 6-point rubric? Included in this section is a 6-point rubric for those teachers who may want to use a 6-point scale.

Regardless of which system your state or district uses, keep the following point in mind. The writing features being evaluated are more important than the numbers or scale used on the rubric (i.e., 4-point, 6-point). Ideally, the rubric used for classroom assessment should be aligned with the rubric used for the state assessment. For example, if the state rubric evaluates "development of ideas," then the classroom rubric should also evaluate this feature. The scoring rubrics used in the *Writer's Companion* have been designed to match the rubrics used in most state assessments.

© Harcourt

Scoring Rubric for Writing

		Score of 4	Score of 3	Score of 2	Score of 1
		☆☆☆☆	☆☆☆	☆☆	☆
FOCUS/IDEAS		The paper is completely focused on the task and has a clear purpose.	The paper is generally focused on the task and the purpose.	The paper is somewhat focused on the task and purpose.	The paper does not have a clear focus or a purpose.
ORGANIZATION/PARAGRAPHS		The paper has a clear beginning, middle, and ending. The ideas and details are presented in logical order. The writer uses transitions, such as *Finally, The next day,* or *However,* to show the relationships among ideas.	The ideas and details are mostly presented in logical order. The writer uses some transitions to show the relationships among ideas.	The organization is not clear in some places.	The paper has little or no organization.
DEVELOPMENT		The paper has a clear central idea that is supported by strong specific details.	The paper has a central idea and is supported by details.	The paper does not have a clear central idea and has few supporting details.	The central idea is not clear and there are few or no supporting details.
VOICE		The writer's viewpoint is clear. The writer uses creative and original phrases and expressions where appropriate.	The writer's viewpoint is somewhat clear. The writer uses some original phrases and expressions.	The writer's viewpoint is unclear.	The writer seems uninterested in what he or she is writing about.
WORD CHOICE		The writer uses clear, exact words and phrases. The writing is interesting to read.	The word choices are clear. The writer uses some interesting words and phrases.	The writer does not use words or phrases that make the writing clear to the reader.	The writer uses word choices that are unclear or inappropriate.
SENTENCES		The writer uses a variety of sentences. The writing flows smoothly.	The writer uses some variety in sentences.	The writer does not use much variety in his or her sentences.	There is little or no variety in sentences. Some of the sentences are unclear.
CONVENTIONS		There are few or no errors in grammar, punctuation, capitalization, and spelling.	There are a few errors in grammar, punctuation, capitalization, and spelling.	There are some errors in grammar, punctuation, capitalization, and spelling.	There are many errors in grammar, punctuation, capitalization, and spelling.

© Harcourt

Writer's Companion
4-Point Scoring Rubric for Writing

Scoring Rubric for Writing

	FOCUS	ORGANIZATION	SUPPORT	CONVENTIONS
Score of 6 ☆☆☆☆☆	The writing is completely focused on the topic and has a clear purpose.	The ideas in the paper are well-organized and presented in logical order. The paper seems complete to the reader.	The writing has strong, specific details. The word choices are clear and fresh.	The writer uses a variety of sentences. There are few or no errors in grammar, spelling, punctuation, and capitalization.
Score of 5 ☆☆☆☆	The writing is focused on the topic and purpose.	The organization of the paper is mostly clear. The paper seems complete.	The writing has strong, specific details and clear word choices.	The writer uses a variety of sentences. There are few errors in grammar, spelling, punctuation, and capitalization.
Score of 4 ☆☆☆	The writing is generally focused on the topic and purpose.	The organization is mostly clear, but the paper may seem unfinished.	The writing has supporting details and some variety in word choice.	The writer uses some variety in sentences. There are a few errors in grammar, spelling, punctuation, and capitalization.
Score of 3 ☆☆☆	The writing is somewhat focused on the topic and purpose.	The paper is somewhat organized, but seems unfinished.	The writing has few supporting details. It needs more variety in word choice.	The writer uses simple sentences. There are some errors in grammar, spelling, punctuation, and capitalization.
Score of 2 ☆☆	The writing is related to the topic but does not have a clear focus.	There is little organization to the paper.	The writing has few supporting details and very little variety in word choice.	The writer uses simple sentences. There are many errors in grammar, spelling, punctuation, and capitalization.
Score of 1 ☆	The writing is not focused on the topic and purpose.	There is no organization to the paper.	There are few or no supporting details. The word choices are unclear.	The writer uses unclear sentences. There are many errors in grammar, spelling, punctuation, and capitalization.

Writer's Companion
6-Point Scoring Rubric for Writing